AF761405

Non-exhaust Particulate Emissions from Road Transport

AN IGNORED ENVIRONMENTAL POLICY CHALLENGE

OECD

BETTER POLICIES FOR BETTER LIVES

This document, as well as any data and map included herein, are without prejudice to the status of or sovereignty over any territory, to the delimitation of international frontiers and boundaries and to the name of any territory, city or area.

Please cite this publication as:
OECD (2020), *Non-exhaust Particulate Emissions from Road Transport: An Ignored Environmental Policy Challenge*, OECD Publishing, Paris, *https://doi.org/10.1787/4a4dc6ca-en*.

ISBN 978-92-64-45244-2 (print)
ISBN 978-92-64-88885-2 (pdf)
ISBN 978-92-64-90102-5 (HTML)
ISBN 978-92-64-50119-5 (epub)

Revised version, December 2020
Details of revisions available at: *https://www.oecd.org/about/publishing/Corrigendum-notice.pdf*

Photo credits: Cover © schank/Shutterstock.com.

Corrigenda to publications may be found on line at: *www.oecd.org/about/publishing/corrigenda.htm*.

Foreword

Despite technological advances to reduce energy and materials use and growing political will to pursue green development, population growth in cities is putting ever-greater pressure on the pursuit of sustainability in urban areas. As cities grapple with ongoing environmental challenges, they also face interactions between environmental pollution and public health risks. A notable example is local air pollution, which has been associated with greater susceptibility to respiratory infections. Growing populations increase the exposure to particulate matter in urban areas, and rising incomes increase the total amount of emissions produced as more people are able to own vehicles.

While the overall amount of particulate matter from road traffic has decreased in past decades thanks to increasingly stringent standards regulating exhaust emissions, emerging evidence shows that particulate matter is also emitted from the wearing down of tyres, brakes, and road surfaces, and from the resuspension of road dust. Particulate matter from these "non-exhaust" sources is less well-understood than particulate matter from exhaust emissions, and the policy options to address them are consequently less well-explored. Importantly, non-exhaust particulate matter emissions will not be addressed by increasing the stringency of existing emissions standards. As a result, almost all particulate matter from road traffic is expected to come from non-exhaust emission sources in future years. Given the significant negative impacts of particulate matter on public health, is incumbent on policymakers to consider how to manage these emissions.

This report synthesizes the state of knowledge on the nature, causes and consequences of non-exhaust particulate emissions from tyre, brake, and road wear as well as road dust resuspension. It also simulates how particulate matter emissions from non-exhaust sources will evolve in future years and identifies existing technological and policy measures to mitigate these emissions. Finally, the report proposes a policy framework for internalising the social costs associated with these emissions.

The evidence presented herein is intended to bring attention to this important but overlooked environmental policy issue and provide preliminary insights regarding how to address them. First, it emphasizes that even electric vehicles produce non-exhaust emissions. While this observation may not alter the appeal of electric vehicles relative to conventional vehicles in terms of overall environmental performance, it nevertheless invites a reappraisal of the net social benefits that can be expected from the use of electric vehicles. Addressing non-exhaust emissions can notably have implications for the design of electric vehicles moving forward. Finally, the findings of the report lend additional rationale for minimising private vehicle travel in favour of less polluting modes of transportation in urban areas, such as efficient mass public transit and walking and cycling. Assessing the public health burden of non-exhaust emissions and addressing them accordingly is also likely to involve a number of co-benefits, including reduced congestion, improved quality of life as well as enhanced societal resilience to potential public health risks.

Acknowledgements

This report is an output of the OECD Environmental Policy Committee and its Working Party on Integrating Environmental and Economic Policies (WPIEEP). The report was carried out under the overall responsibility of Shardul Agrawala, Head of the Environment and Economy Integration Division in the OECD Environment Directorate.

All chapters of the report were authored by Fulvio Amato of the Institute of Environmental Assessment and Water Research (IDÆA) and the Spanish National Research Council (CSIC), Alexandros Dimitropoulos of PBL Netherlands Environmental Assessment Agency, and Katherine Farrow and Walid Oueslati of the OECD Environment Directorate. The individual inputs of the key contributors are as follows:

Fulvio Amato	Conceptualisation, data collection and visualisation, scenario development, calculation of emission factors and projected emissions, drafting, and communication with stakeholders.
Alexandros Dimitropoulos	Conceptualisation, drafting, data visualisation, scenario development, and communication with stakeholders.
Katherine Farrow	Conceptualisation, drafting, data visualisation, scenario development, and communication with stakeholders.
Walid Oueslati	Project co-ordination and supervision, conceptualisation, drafting and communication with stakeholders.

The authors would like to thank delegates to the OECD Working Party on Integrating Environmental and Economic Policies (WPIEEP) for useful comments and suggestions on earlier versions of the report. Feedback and comments from Nils Axel Braathen and Shardul Agrawala of the OECD Environment Directorate are gratefully acknowledged. The authors also greatly appreciate input and comments from: Theodoros Grigoratos and Giorgio Martini (Joint Research Centre, European Commission), Marina Kousoulidou (Innovations and Networks Executive Agency, European Commission), Maurizio Maggiore (DG Research and Innovation, European Commission), Richard Kranenburg and Martijn Schaap (TNO, Utrecht), Philip K. Hopke (University of Rochester School of Medicine and Dentistry), Jorge Pachón (La Salle University of Bogotá), Marco Bedogni (AMAT, Milan), Xavier Querol and Andrés Alastuey (CSIC, Spain), Marc Guevara (Barcelona Supercomputing Center), Marc Houyoux (United States Environmental Protection Agency) and Vicken Etyemezian (Desert Research Institute).

This report is part of the stream of work on Greening Transport and Mobility.

Table of contents

FIGURES

TABLES

List of acronyms

BEV: battery electric vehicle

CMB: Chemical Mass Balance receptor model

CTM: Chemistry Transport model

DAS: Driver assistance systems

EF: Emission factor

EFTA: European Free Trade Association

EMEP/EEA: European Monitoring and Evaluation Programme/ European Environment Agency

HDV: heavy duty vehicle

LDV: light duty vehicle

LM: Low metallic brake pad

NAO: Non-Asbesto Organics brake pad

NFR: Nomenclature for Reporting

OC: organic carbon

PAH: polycyclic aromatic hydrocarbon

PHEVs: plug-in hybrid electric vehicles

PM: Atmospheric particulate matter; atmospheric particles; aerosol

PM10: atmospheric particles with aerodynamic diameter below 10 µm

PM2.5: atmospheric particles with aerodynamic diameter below 2.5 µm

PMF: Positive Matrix Factorization receptor model

RBS: Regenerative braking system

SM: Semi metallic brake pad

SMA: stone mastic asphalt

SUV: sport utility vehicles

TSP: total suspended particles

UFP: ultrafine particles

UNECE: United Nations Economic Commission for Europe

WHO: World Health Organisation

Executive Summary

Non-exhaust particle emissions from road traffic consist of airborne particulate matter (PM) generated by the wearing down of brakes, clutches, tyres and road surfaces, as well as by the suspension of road dust. A growing body of evidence shows that PM emissions have significant implications for human health. Furthermore, the damages to human health caused by PM emissions from road traffic can be disproportionately large relative to other sources of PM emissions, as the highest emission levels tend to be localised in areas with the greatest population density, leading to high levels of exposure. Despite the significant burden of non-exhaust emissions on public health, few public policies target them explicitly.

While emission standards for exhaust particles from motor vehicles are becoming more stringent worldwide, non-exhaust PM emissions are largely unregulated. As a result, the proportion of PM emissions from non-exhaust sources has increased in recent years due to the significant reductions in PM from exhaust emissions over this period. Non-exhaust emissions are expected to be responsible for the vast majority of PM emissions from road traffic in future years.

This report analyses the nature, drivers and health consequences of non-exhaust emissions and reports estimates of total PM emission factors for electric and conventional vehicles, including primary and secondary PM from exhaust sources as well as primary PM from non-exhaust sources. Based on these estimates, the report explores the implications of anticipated electric vehicle uptake for non-exhaust PM emission levels. It then provides an overview of existing policies that contribute to the reduction of non-exhaust PM emissions and proposes a framework for the design of targeted policy action to address the negative externalities associated with these emissions. The report emphasises that the development and implementation of such targeted policy action depends on a robust understanding of the processes that generate non-exhaust emissions, the relationship between exposure to these emissions and health impacts, and the effectiveness of various mitigation measures in reducing emission rates and exposure.

What are the causes and impacts of non-exhaust emissions?

Four main processes are responsible for the bulk of non-exhaust emissions: the wearing down of brakes, tyres, and road surfaces, and the resuspension of road dust. The amount of PM emissions that a vehicle emits is determined by many factors, including vehicle weight, the material composition of brakes, tyres, and roads, the amount of dust on road surfaces, and driving styles. Although uncertainty remains with respect to the amount of PM emitted from non-exhaust sources under real-world driving conditions, non-exhaust emissions will increase in the coming years along with increases in the demand for urban passenger travel, which is projected to more than double by 2050.

In the context of growing travel demand, electric vehicles are widely regarded as a solution to mitigating greenhouse gas emissions and other air pollutants from road transport. While they stand to eliminate exhaust emissions, this report shows that electric vehicles are not likely to provide substantial benefits in terms of non-exhaust emissions reductions. Regenerative braking systems can reduce brake wear, but tyre wear, road wear, and road dust resuspension remain significant sources of non-exhaust emissions from electric vehicles. Non-exhaust emissions from these sources can in fact be higher for electric vehicles than for their conventional counterparts, as the heavy batteries in electric vehicles imply that they typically weigh more than similar conventional vehicles. This is particularly the case for electric vehicles with greater autonomy (driving range) that require larger battery packs.

Epidemiological studies have established that exposure to non-exhaust PM emissions, and to PM2.5 in particular, is associated with a variety of adverse health outcomes in the short and long term, such as increased risks of cardiovascular, respiratory, and developmental conditions, as well as an increased risk of overall mortality. The oxidative stress induced by the metals and organic compounds found in PM emissions is considered to be a main biological mechanism responsible for these negative health impacts. Recent research has also suggested that air pollution exacerbates coronavirus epidemics such as SARS and Covid-19. Impacts are greatest in urban areas, where emission levels – due *inter alia* to congestion – and population exposure are highest.

What is the current situation and how will it evolve with the uptake of electric vehicles?

Globally, road traffic is responsible for an estimated quarter of ambient PM in urban areas. Given increasingly stringent standards regarding the PM content of exhaust emissions, non-exhaust emissions are quickly becoming the dominant source of PM emissions from road traffic, and are expected to comprise the vast majority of all PM from road traffic as early as 2035. While the uptake of electric vehicles (EVs) will contribute to reducing exhaust PM in future years, non-exhaust PM will not noticeably fall unless targeted policies are undertaken.

Electric vehicles are estimated to emit 5-19% less PM10 from non-exhaust sources per kilometre than internal combustion engine vehicles (ICEVs) across vehicle classes. However, EVs do not necessarily emit less PM2.5 than ICEVs. Although lightweight EVs emit an estimated 11-13% less PM2.5 than ICEV equivalents, heavier weight EVs emit an estimated 3-8% more PM2.5 than ICEVs. In the absence of targeted policies to reduce non-exhaust emissions, consumer preferences for greater autonomy and larger vehicle size could therefore drive an increase in PM2.5 emissions in future years with the uptake of heavier EVs.

Projection exercises presented in this report show that the total amount of non-exhaust PM (PM2.5 and PM10) emitted by passenger vehicles worldwide will rise by 53.5% along with transport demand, from approximately 0.85 Mtonnes today to 1.3 Mtonnes in 2030 in a business-as-usual scenario with low uptake of heavier weight EVs. The reduction in PM emissions made possible by a scenario assuming greater overall EV uptake is very slight: a doubling of EV uptake leads to an estimated 1.29 tonnes in non-exhaust PM in 2030, or a 52.4% increase.

How should policymakers address non-exhaust emissions?

The evidence presented in this report reveals a need for policy action to reduce non-exhaust emissions and mitigate their consequences for public health. The majority of public policies addressing PM from road traffic target exhaust emissions. Given the lack of robust understanding of many aspects of non-exhaust emissions, addressing them effectively and efficiently will hinge on advancing the state of knowledge in critical areas, including regarding their magnitude, their impacts and the effectiveness of measures designed to mitigate them. To the extent that the development and implementation of public policies targeting non-exhaust emissions will rely on the use of standardized measurement methodologies, establishing standardized approaches to measuring non-exhaust PM and developing an understanding of how various factors (e.g. vehicle characteristics) influence the amount of PM generated, should be a first priority. Some progress has been made in this regard for brake wear, but similar work remains to be done with respect to tyre wear, road wear and road dust resuspension.

PM from non-exhaust sources can be mitigated by reducing the amount of PM emitted per vehicle-kilometre travelled and by reducing the number of vehicle-kilometres travelled. A distance-based charge designed to internalise the social costs of non-exhaust emissions is a theoretically effective mitigation instrument insofar as it incentivises both a reduction in emission factors as well as in vehicle-kilometres travelled. No precedent currently exists for such a charge, in part because non-exhaust emissions have largely been overlooked in policymaking to date, but also due to the uncertainty surrounding the amount of PM emitted, the factors that influence this amount, and the social costs of the attendant impacts.

While the quantitative evidence basis regarding the magnitude, causes and consequences of non-exhaust emissions continues to be developed, other measures should be implemented to reduce these emissions in the near term. Policy options for reducing non-exhaust emission factors (i.e. the amount of non-exhaust PM emitted per vehicle-kilometre travelled) include vehicle lightweighting and regulations on tyre composition. Insofar as lighter vehicles emit less brake and tyre wear, vehicle lightweighting measures constitute a particularly useful technological measure for reducing emission factors.

Vehicle-kilometres travelled in urban areas can be reduced using a variety of policies that disincentivise the use of private vehicles and incentivise the use of alternative modes such as public transport, cycling, and walking. As population exposure to PM from non-exhaust emissions is greatest in urban areas, urban vehicle access regulations (UVARs) such as low-emission zones and congestion pricing schemes can also be an effective means of reducing the social costs of non-exhaust emissions.

The insights that issue from the findings of this report stand at odds with prevailing policy stances regarding electric vehicles. In the context of most climate and air pollution mitigation policies, increasing electric vehicle uptake is generally considered desirable insofar as it reduces exhaust emissions and their associated social costs. In practice, this means that electric vehicles are often exempt from policies to discourage conventional vehicle use, such as congestion charges and tolls. However, given that electric vehicles emit similar levels of non-exhaust emissions as conventional vehicles, and potentially more PM2.5, this analysis suggests that electric vehicles should not be exempt from such policies. Policymakers seeking to reduce non-exhaust PM emissions from road transport should therefore reconsider policy approaches that provide blanket support for electric vehicles. Instead, they should pursue the implementation of more sophisticated instruments that are designed based on the determinants of a vehicle's non-exhaust emissions rather than on its drivetrain only.

1. Introduction

1.1. The relevance of non-exhaust emissions for public policy

Emissions of particulate matter (PM) from motor vehicles originate from two main sources: the combustion of fossil fuel, which is emitted via tailpipe exhaust, and from non-exhaust processes including the degradation of vehicle parts and road surfaces and the resuspension of road dust. The airborne particulate emissions generated by these processes are defined as non-exhaust PM emissions.

Consensus exists in the scientific literature that non-exhaust emissions are an increasingly important source of PM from road traffic and that exposure to PM can have significant adverse effects on human health. A large fraction of the world's population is exposed to levels of fine particulate matter in excess of limit values set for the protection of human health. In Europe, an average of 8.6 months of YPLL (years of potential life lost) are attributed to excessive PM2.5 exposure. Globally, exposure to ambient PM has been ranked as the seventh most important risk factor for mortality, causing an estimated 4.2 million premature deaths in 2015 (Cohen et al., 2017[1]).[1] The welfare costs of premature deaths due to PM exposure amounted to approximately 4.15% of global GDP in 2017 (OECD, 2019[2]).

Despite these demonstrated negative effects, non-exhaust emissions have been only tangentially addressed by public policies to date. Given the magnitude of the social costs they entail and the fact that the transition to electric vehicles will not generate significant reductions in non-exhaust emissions, policymakers should invest resources in determining how best to reduce them via targeted policy instruments.

1.2. The objectives of this report

The report relies on a multidisciplinary review of the current knowledge on non-exhaust emissions as well as on a quantitative analysis that estimates non-exhaust emission factors for three vehicle categories of conventional internal combustion engine vehicles and of battery electric vehicles. The main objectives of the report are the following:

- Describe the sources and processes involved in the generation of non-exhaust emissions;
- Review the main vehicle, road, and driving features determining the magnitude of non-exhaust emissions;
- Review the current knowledge on the health impacts of non-exhaust emissions;
- Estimate the non-exhaust PM emission factors from electric vehicles and compare these factors with those of internal combustion engine vehicles;
- Identify existing technological and policy measures to mitigate non-exhaust emissions;

- Propose a framework for the design of a pricing instrument to address non-exhaust emissions.

Identify next steps regarding research and policy needs to better understand the causes and consequences of non-exhaust emissions and to reduce their external social costs.

Overall, the report urges action in developing a commonly accepted methodology to measure non-exhaust emissions and in carrying out further research to better understand the drivers of non-exhaust emissions and the causal relationships between these emissions and environmental and health effects. Although existing evidence is not mature enough to make specific policy recommendations, the report aims to provide some initial considerations regarding policy instrument mixes that could be used to internalise the social costs of non-exhaust emissions.

1.3. Key findings on the drivers, impacts, and policy responses to non-exhaust emissions

The drivers and impacts of non-exhaust emissions

Non-exhaust emissions are comprised of brake wear, tyre wear, road wear, and road dust resuspension. Brake wear emissions can be influenced by a vehicle's weight, rate of deceleration, the composition of brake discs and pads, rotor temperatures, sliding speed, and contact pressure. Tyre and road wear are also affected by the composition of tyres and road surfaces. Emissions from road dust resuspension depend on a vehicle's speed, size and shape, the porosity and amount of dust on road surfaces, as well as weather conditions. Considerable uncertainty remains regarding the amount of PM that is emitted by non-exhaust sources in real world driving conditions and how this amount varies with changes in the factors identified above.

Exposure to PM emissions is associated with a variety of adverse health impacts in the short and long term, including an increased risk of cardiovascular, respiratory, and developmental conditions, as well as an increased risk of overall mortality. Numerous epidemiological studies have demonstrated, for example, that PM exposure is associated with acute respiratory infections, lung cancer, and chronic respiratory and cardiovascular diseases (de Kok et al., 2006[3]; Heinrich and Slama, 2007[4]), and the effects of PM2.5 are considered to be particularly damaging. The mechanisms underlying the health effects of inhaled PM have been well studied in the laboratory and there is general agreement regarding the key roles played by oxidative stress and inflammation in the physiopathology of the documented health impacts. Research has also found significant correlations between exposure to PM2.5 and fatality rates in previous coronavirus epidemics (Cui et al., 2003[5]; Wu et al., 2020[6])), further increasing the relevance of air quality for public health and the resilience of social systems more generally.

How non-exhaust emissions will develop in future years

Globally, road traffic is responsible for an average of 25% of ambient PM2.5 in urban areas (Karagulian et al., 2015[7]). Although it is difficult to be precise about the overall contribution of non-exhaust emissions to ambient PM, the current body of evidence shows that PM from non-exhaust sources comprise a rising share of PM emissions from road transport (Timmers and Achten, 2016[8]; CEIP, 2019[9]). As the global fleet of vehicles becomes newer and the amount of PM from exhaust emissions continues to fall, the vast majority of PM from road transport is expected to come from non-exhaust emissions in future years (Rexeis and Hausberger, 2009[10]).

In light of the ongoing electrification of passenger road transport, the report provides estimates of the expected changes of non-exhaust emissions due to shifts from internal combustion engine vehicles (ICEVs) to electric ones. To this end, it compares non-exhaust emission factors of new EVs with those of new ICEVs. Assuming lightweight EVs (i.e. with battery packs enabling a driving range of about 100 miles), the report finds that EVs emit an estimated 11-13% less non-exhaust PM2.5 and 18-19% less PM10 than ICEVs. Assuming that EV models are heavier (with battery packs enabling a driving range of 300 miles or higher), however, the report finds that they reduce PM10 by only 4-7% and increase PM2.5 by 3-8% relative to conventional vehicles.

When applied to current vehicle stocks in two sample cities, simulations show that these reductions will lead to very marginal decreases in total PM emissions from road traffic in future years. In scenarios where electric vehicles comprise 4% and 8% of the vehicle stock in 2030, their penetration reduces PM emissions by 0.3%-0.8% relative to current levels. On a global level, non-exhaust PM (PM2.5 and PM10 combined) are expected to rise significantly along with travel demand, increasing by 53.5% in 2030 relative to 2017 assuming an electric vehicle uptake of 4%. A doubling of electric vehicle uptake has a very marginal impact, leading to a growth in non-exhaust emissions of 52.4% by 2030.

Policy responses to non-exhaust emissions

A robust understanding of emission factors, their drivers, and the effectiveness of measures to reduce them will be necessary before being able to comprehensively assess the costs and benefits of various policy options. PM from non-exhaust sources can be mitigated by reducing the amount of PM emitted per vehicle-kilometre travelled (PM emission factor) and by reducing the number of vehicle-kilometres travelled. Given that vehicle travel entails a range of other negative externalities (e.g. congestion and greenhouse gas emissions), reducing the number of vehicle-kilometres travelled, especially in urban areas, should be a key component of policy portfolios to mitigate non-exhaust emissions.

A distance-based charge designed to internalise the social costs of non-exhaust emissions would be effective insofar as it would incentivise both a reduction in vehicle-kilometres travelled as well as a reduction in emission factors. No precedent currently exists for such a charge, in part because non-exhaust emissions have largely been overlooked in policymaking, but also due to the uncertainty surrounding their magnitude and its determinants, and the social costs of their health-related impacts. While a better understanding of the causes and effects of non-exhaust emissions continues to be developed, other measures will be necessary in order to address non-exhaust emissions in the near term.

Vehicle-kilometres travelled in urban areas can be reduced via a variety of policies that either disincentivise the ownership and use of private vehicles or incentivise the use of alternative modes such as public transport, cycling, and walking. Disincentives for private vehicle ownership and use include pecuniary measures, e.g. registration fees, fuel taxes, distance-based charges, and parking pricing, as well as regulatory measures, e.g. urban vehicle access regulations and other types of vehicle bans. Incentives to increase the uptake of alternative modes include improving the coverage, frequency, comfort, information provision, and payment systems of public transit services and improving the quality and coverage of infrastructure for non-motorised modes, such as protected bike lanes, sidewalks, and priority pedestrian crosswalks. In the long term, developing compact urban areas can also contribute to reducing demand for private vehicle use by shortening the distances required to access amenities.

Given the high proportion of non-exhaust emissions generated by tyre wear, priority should be placed on measures that seek to reduce PM emissions from this source in particular, namely vehicle lightweighting and regulations on tyre composition. To the extent that lighter vehicles also emit less PM emissions from brake wear, policies that more explicitly favour vehicle lightweighting can simultaneously address multiple sources of non-exhaust emissions,[2] though potential trade-offs (e.g. regarding safety and other environmental impacts) should be considered. Specific measures to incentivise vehicle lightweighting could include the expansion of weight-based charges. Investing in R&D to develop lighter materials (e.g. high-strength steel and aluminium alloy) will also advance this agenda.

Insofar as population exposure is greatest in urban areas and current congestion pricing schemes are an effective means of reducing motor vehicle traffic in these areas, another policy priority for addressing non-exhaust emissions is the more widespread use of congestion pricing in city centres. These pricing mechanisms could be further optimised to target non-exhaust emissions, for example, by finding ways to differentiate electronic congestion charges by vehicle weight and distance travelled.

Next steps to address non-exhaust emissions

A main finding of this work is that important gaps remain in the current state of knowledge about non-exhaust emissions, specifically with respect to their drivers, impacts, and the effectiveness of mitigation policies designed to address them. Although research on non-exhaust emissions has expanded rapidly in the last decade, more work is needed in this direction. As a result, immediate and continuing policy action should involve investing in research toward these aims.

Given that the development of regulations and policies regarding non-exhaust emissions rely on the use of a standardized measurement methodology, priority should be given to establishing this methodology for each of the processes that generate non-exhaust emissions. Some progress has been made in this regard for brake wear, but similar initiative remains to be taken for the measurement of tyre wear, road wear and road dust resuspension. Developing a commonly accepted methodology for emissions measurement and designing consequent regulations will take time. There is, however, an immediate need to reduce the public health burden associated with non-exhaust emissions in urban areas.

Navigating the report

The report is comprised of three subsequent sections. Section 2 reviews the scientific literature to identify the processes underpinning the generation of non-exhaust emissions including how vehicle, road and driving characteristics determine their magnitude, as well as the consequences of non-exhaust emissions for public health.

Section 3 compares PM10 and PM2.5 emission factors of battery electric vehicles with their internal combustion engine counterparts. Comparisons are carried out via a quantitative analysis that makes use of data from the literature, emission inventories and other sources. Three categories of light-duty vehicles are considered, namely passenger cars, sport utility vehicles and light commercial vehicles.

Section 4 surveys the scientific literature and industry reports to identify currently available technological solutions to reduce non-exhaust PM emissions from wear and road dust resuspension. Furthermore, it reviews policies that have an effect on non-exhaust emissions, even if that is not their primary aim. The report builds on this review by developing a framework for the design of an efficient public policy instrument to address non-exhaust emissions. Finally, Section 4 also provides an overview of the main uncertainties and data gaps on non-exhaust emissions, and proposes next steps for moving forward in better understanding and mitigating PM emissions from non-exhaust sources.

[1] See also http://www.who.int/gho/phe/outdoor_air_pollution/burden/en.

[2] Vehicle lightweighting, moreover, also reduces greenhouse gas emissions (ITF, 2017[11]).

References

CEIP (2019), *WebDab - EMEP database*, https://www.ceip.at/ms/ceip_home1/ceip_home/webdab_emepdatabase/ (accessed on 20 May 2019). [9]

Cohen, A. et al. (2017), "Estimates and 25-year trends of the global burden of disease attributable to ambient air pollution: an analysis of data from the Global Burden of Diseases Study 2015", *The Lancet*, Vol. 389/10082, pp. 1907-1918, http://dx.doi.org/10.1016/S0140-6736(17)30505-6. [1]

Cui, Y. et al. (2003), "Air pollution and case fatality of SARS in the People's Republic of China: an ecologic study", *Environmental Health*, Vol. 2/1, pp. 1-5, http://dx.doi.org/10.1186/1476-069x-2-15. [5]

de Kok, T. et al. (2006), *Toxicological assessment of ambient and traffic-related particulate matter: A review of recent studies*, http://dx.doi.org/10.1016/j.mrrev.2006.07.001. [3]

Heinrich, J. and R. Slama (2007), "Fine particles, a major threat to children", *International Journal of Hygiene and Environmental Health*, Vol. 210/5, pp. 617-622, http://dx.doi.org/10.1016/j.ijheh.2007.07.012. [4]

ITF (2017), *Lightening Up: How Less Heavy Vehicles Can Help Cut CO2 Emissions Case-Specific Policy Analysis*, https://www.itf-oecd.org/sites/default/files/docs/less-heavy-vehicles-cut-co2-emissions.pdf (accessed on 13 November 2019). [11]

Karagulian, F. et al. (2015), *Contributions to cities' ambient particulate matter (PM): A systematic review of local source contributions at global level*, Elsevier Ltd, http://dx.doi.org/10.1016/j.atmosenv.2015.08.087. [7]

OECD (2019), *Air quality and health: Mortality and welfare cost from exposure to air pollution*, OECD Environment Statistics (database). [2]

Rexeis, M. and S. Hausberger (2009), "Trend of vehicle emission levels until 2020 - Prognosis based on current vehicle measurements and future emission legislation", *Atmospheric Environment*, Vol. 43/31, pp. 4689-4698, http://dx.doi.org/10.1016/j.atmosenv.2008.09.034. [10]

Timmers, V. and P. Achten (2016), "Non-exhaust PM emissions from electric vehicles", *Atmospheric Environment*, Vol. 134, pp. 10-17, http://dx.doi.org/10.1016/j.atmosenv.2016.03.017. [8]

Wu, X. et al. (2020), "Exposure to air pollution and COVID-19 mortality in the United States", *medRxiv*, p. 2020.04.05.20054502, http://dx.doi.org/10.1101/2020.04.05.20054502. [6]

2. The causes and consequences of non-exhaust emissions from road transport

This chapter describes the sources and processes involved in the generation of non-exhaust emissions, reviews the main vehicle, road, and driving features determining the magnitude of non-exhaust emissions, and reviews the current knowledge on the health impacts of non-exhaust emissions. Non-exhaust emissions are comprised of brake wear, tyre wear, road wear, and road dust resuspension. Considerable uncertainty remains regarding the amount of PM that is emitted by non-exhaust sources in real world driving conditions and how this amount varies with changes in the factors identified above. PM from non-exhaust sources comprise a rising share of PM emissions from road transport. As the global fleet of vehicles becomes newer and the amount of PM from exhaust emissions continues to fall, the vast majority of PM from road transport is expected to come from non-exhaust emissions in future years. Exposure to PM emissions is associated with a variety of adverse health impacts in the short and long term, including an increased risk of cardiovascular, respiratory, and developmental conditions, as well as an increased risk of overall mortality.

2.1. Defining non-exhaust emissions

Emissions of particulate matter (PM) from motor vehicles originate from two main sources: the exhaust from combustion engines and the degradation of vehicle parts and road surfaces. The latter, comprising all airborne particulate emissions generated by vehicle and road wear and the resuspension of road dust, are defined as non-exhaust PM emissions. The proportion of PM emissions from non-exhaust sources has rapidly increased in recent years due to the significant reductions in exhaust emissions over this period, and are now responsible for about 90% of all PM emissions from road traffic (Timmers and Achten, 2016[1]; Rexeis and Hausberger, 2009[2]).

A further distinction can be made between primary and secondary emissions. Whereas primary emissions refer to particles that retain their chemical structure when airborne, secondary emissions refer to particles that, when emitted, react with other chemicals in the atmosphere to form new pollutants. Although most non-exhaust PM emissions are primary, recent findings indicate that they may also contribute to the generation of secondary aerosols due to the degradation of organic compounds found in brake and tyre materials (Kukutschová et al., 2011[3]; Plachá et al., 2017[4]). Particles originating from other sources that have been deposited on road surfaces can be also re-suspended by traffic-induced turbulence.

Following the terminology and hierarchy proposed by Padoan and Amato (2018[5]), non-exhaust PM emissions encompass:

- Direct wear emissions:

- Brake wear: particles abraded from brake pads and discs that are directly airborne. About half of total brake wear particles are not airborne (Grigoratos and Martini, 2015[6]).
- Tyre wear: the particles eroded from tyres that are directly airborne.
- Road wear: particles eroded from road surfaces that are directly airborne.

- Road dust suspension (or resuspension): the particles on (paved) road surfaces that are suspended in the air by vehicle traffic. Road dust can consist of brake, tyre and road wear particles that have been deposited on the road, as well as particles that have migrated to the road from other sources.

The relative proportion of non-exhaust emissions from each source can vary significantly across vehicle types.[1] The classification presented above is based on the emission process, not on the particle type, and is standard practice in emission inventories. The inclusion of PM from resuspension in emission inventorying is the subject of an ongoing debate. Double-counting is a commonly encountered issue in emission inventories and primarily results from using different methodologies to measure the particles emitted from different sources (Pulles and Heslinga, 2007[7]). Some authors claim that, insofar as the particles from direct brake, tyre, and road wear can be deposited on road surfaces and resuspended, the inclusion of these particles as road dust resuspension in emission inventorying implies double-counting.

This report argues that resuspension should be counted in emission inventorying for several reasons. First, the concept of double-counting should not be confounded with the concept of re-emissions. Re-emissions occur at a different time than initial emissions. A brake wear particle is, for example, considered an initial emission when generated and measured at hour t_1, this particle is considered a re-emission when it is deposited on the road surface at hour t_2, and later resuspended and measured again at hour t_3 (where $t_3 > t_2 > t_1$). Although re-emissions may be present in road dust, it also consists of particles that are not re-emissions, that is, that were not originally generated from brake, tyre, or road wear. Examples include particles that have migrated from road shoulders, gutters, or construction sites, and those created by the gradual fragmentation of much larger particles originating from road surfaces and vehicle components.

Double counting becomes problematic in emissions inventorying when the calculation of emission factors for resuspension do not deduct re-emissions. When, for example, an emission inventory combines EMEP/EEA emission factors for direct emissions (i.e. from brake, tyre and road wear) with an emission factor for resuspension that is calculated locally by inverse modelling, i.e. that is calculated without separating out direct wear emissions, this leads to double counting.

Second, recent evidence from PM source apportionment studies demonstrates that resuspension contributes significantly to PM levels even when direct wear emissions are excluded (Amato et al., 2014[8]; Gehrig et al., 2001[9]; Harrison et al., 2012[10]; Lawrence, Sokhi and Ravindra, 2016[11]; Wåhlin, Berkowicz and Palmgren, 2006[12]). Studies based on dispersion modelling demonstrate that including road dust resuspension in emission inventories significantly improves both mass closure and the correlation between simulated and observed PM data (Amato et al., 2016[13]; Denier van der Gon et al., 2010[14]; Schaap et al., 2009[15]).

Another critique of including resuspension emissions as a component of non-exhaust traffic emissions is the fact that ambient PM from resuspension exists even in the absence of vehicle traffic, as wind naturally suspends material on the roads. A variety of experimental evidence suggests, however, that although the wind does lift deposited dust, it is not responsible for all of the PM emissions from road dust that are measured on roadways. First, HDVs are associated with greater amounts of road dust than LDVs, indicating that vehicle characteristics (and thus vehicles) have some impact on the resuspension of road dust. Second, ambient road dust concentrations are significantly lower on the weekends (Amato et al., 2009[16]; Amato, 2010[17]). Another point of criticism is that resuspension does not depend on traffic itself but on pre-existing dust present on road surfaces (i.e. assuming that with no pollution, there would be no resuspension even with traffic). However, even in the absence of dust on road surfaces, vehicle traffic provokes the fragmentation of very large particles that had not previously been airborne, into smaller particles that can then be suspended.

Given these considerations, including resuspension as source of non-exhaust emissions in emission inventorying is therefore recommended, even if these emissions cannot be easily controlled via regulations regarding vehicle characteristics or via public policies regarding vehicle-kilometres travelled. Urban air quality plans can nevertheless address road dust resuspension through local management measures (see Section 4.1.1).

Emission standards for exhaust particles from motor vehicles are becoming more and more strict worldwide (e.g. EUROx and TIERx) and primary PM emission reduction technologies (e.g. diesel particle filters, continuously regenerating traps) have enabled these new standards to be met. In contrast, non-exhaust PM emissions go largely unregulated. Taken together, these two trends imply that the relative contribution of non-exhaust emissions to PM mass has considerably increased over the past two decades, not only in terms of primary emissions but also in terms of source contributions when secondary PM from vehicle exhaust are considered (Amato et al., 2014[18]; Denier van der Gon et al., 2013[19]; Denier van der Gon et al., 2018[20]).

Non-exhaust emissions have a direct impact on air quality and health not only through their contribution to PM mass, but also via a number of other pollutants, such as ultrafine particles (<0.1 μm in diameter) and heavy metals and metalloids, which are also widely unregulated (Box 2.1). The UN GRPE-PMP (Particle Measurement Program) and the Horizon 2020 EU-funded LOWBRASYS project[2] seek a better understanding of particle number emissions from brake wear, given that combustion-like processes resulting in the formation of ultrafine particles are very different from smaller nanometer-sized wear particles. The European Commission's DG Research unit has also launched a Horizon 2020 project that aims to pave the way for an accurate, reliable, and reproducible test methodology for measuring tyre abrasion rates and the correlation of abrasion rates with PM emissions.

Box 2.1. PM metrics: Mass and number

Atmospheric particles (PM) can be measured in terms of either mass (µg/m3) or number (number of particles/cm^3). Ambient air PM standards are mass-based: PM10 and PM2.5 are defined as the mass concentration of particles with diameters below 10 µm and 2.5 µm, respectively. PM mass concentration is dominated by primary coarse particles (with diameters larger than 1 µm). Particle number concentration is not regulated. It is dominated by particles smaller than 1 µm, and more specifically by ultrafine particles (with diameters smaller than 0.1 µm, UFP).

In contrast to the mass concentration, which is predominantly conservative, particles undergo several processes that modify their number and size, such as new particle formation (nucleation), evaporation, condensation, deposition, and coagulation. Epidemiological studies suggest that negative health effects may be exacerbated with decreasing particle size. Due to their small size, when inhaled, UFP can enter the alveoli and penetrate biological membranes, enabling them to pass into the circulatory system. Once in the circulatory system, these particles can enter all organ systems including the brain and nervous system, as well as traverse the placental barrier. Another recently discovered pathway allows nanoparticles to reach the brain directly from the nose through the olfactory nerve. Toxicological studies suggest that UFP have greater toxicity per mass unit than larger particles and may contribute to the development and progression of various diseases.

Epidemiological evidence for the health effects of UFP is still relatively scarce, mainly due to lack of data. In vitro studies, however, increasingly target these particles and the findings of these studies indicate that smaller particle size is associated with higher toxicity. The hypothesised health effects of UFP include cardiovascular and respiratory morbidity and mortality, local pulmonary and systemic inflammation and oxidative stress, carcinogenesis in several organs, and adverse impacts on the brain and on metabolic processes. A recent meta-analysis suggests short-term associations with inflammatory and cardiovascular changes, which may be at least partly independent of other pollutants. An increasing number of publications however point to hitherto unconsidered specific effects on carcinogenesis (liver, brain, mouth etc), and the onset of diabetes. For the other studied health outcomes, evidence on the independent health effects of UFP remains inconclusive or insufficient.

Source: (Harrison et al., 2018[21]; HEI Review Panel on Ultrafine Particles, 2013[22]; Kettunen et al., 2007[23]; Lanzinger et al., 2016[24]; Meng et al., 2013[25]; Ohlwein et al., 2019[26]; Samoli et al., 2016[27]; Sioutas, Delfino and Singh, 2005[28]; Stafoggia et al., 2017[29]; Tobías et al., 2018[30])

2.1.1. Brake wear

Brake wear PM are generated during the friction between brake pads (linings) and discs (shoes). Not all brake wear debris becomes airborne. It is estimated that approximately 50% of generated brake wear particles become airborne (Garg et al., 2000[31]; Sanders et al., 2003[32]; Barlow et al., 2007[33]; Kukutschová et al., 2011[3]).[3] Particles worn from brake pads and discs contribute almost equally to total PM from braking systems (Hulskotte, Roskam and Denier van der Gon, 2014[34]). While disc brakes typically consist of a rotating disc made of a pearlitic grey cast iron (in some cases made of steel, carbon-carbon, ceramic, or aluminium matrix composites), the composition of brake pads is very heterogeneous. A detailed presentation of the various compositions of brake pads is provided in Box 2.2.

The mass size distribution of brake wear particles (the distribution of particle mass over different categories of particle size) heavily depends on vehicle speed, deceleration and inertia, as well as on the composition of brake materials. Since mechanical wear is the main PM generation process, the mode of the distribution is generally observed to be above 1 µm (Iijima et al., 2007[35]; Iijima et al., 2008[36]; Kukutschová et al., 2011[3]; Sanders et al., 2003[37]). However, due to the high temperatures at the brake/rotor interface and consequent decomposition of brake lining materials, some studies find a mode in the submicrometric region: for example, Garg et al. (2000[38]) found that 33% of the mass of brake wear particles are smaller than 0.1 µm in diameter, varying the average mass median diameters from 0.62 to 2.49 µm depending on the brake pad and temperature. However, it is important to understand whether these conditions are met under typical real-world driving conditions. This is one of the major research topics addressed by the UNECE informal working group on the Particle Measurement Programme (PMP) (UNECE, 2019[39]). Recent PMP findings indicate that 60% of brake wear particles are PM10 and somewhat less than half are PM2.5.

2.1.2. Tyre wear

Tyre wear emissions are generated as a result of the tread abrasion caused by road surfaces. Consequently, it is difficult to measure tyre wear particles separately from road wear particles. As shown by scanning electron microscope (SEM) images and time-of-flight aerosol mass spectrometer studies, the particles formed from the interaction of tyres and pavement appear elongated, with a "sausage-like" shape, and consist of a complex mixture of tread rubber and encrusted mineral particles from pavement (Adachi and Tainosho, 2004[40]; Dall'Osto et al., 2014[41]; Kreider et al., 2010[42]). Tyre wear particles are composed of plasticisers and oils, polymers, carbon blacks and minerals (Kreider et al., 2010[42]), but special attention has been paid to their elemental content (mainly zinc and sulphur) and the abundance of polycyclic aromatic hydrocarbons (PAHs) due to their burden on public health and ecosystems. In Europe, PAHs have been eliminated from tyres since 2009 by the REACH regulation (Chapter 5).

Box 2.2. Chemical composition of brake pads

Brake pads are composed of several materials, including abrasives, binders, fillers, lubricants and reinforcing constituents. A number of chemical compounds are in turn used to produce each of these materials, which makes it difficult to characterise a generic chemical profile of brake pads. According to the combination of ingredients used, brake pads are generally classified as: non-asbestos organic (NAO), mainly composed of organic compounds, mineral fibres and graphite; low metallic (LM), composed of a mixture of metallic components and organic compounds; and semi-metallic (SM), with a metallic (mainly steel and iron) content typically between 30 and 60% by weight.

The chemical composition of pad-worn particles may be different from the bulk composition of the pad due to the physico-chemical transformations occurring during the friction process (e.g. size fractionation, oxidation and volatilisation). However, several components have been commonly identified as possible tracers in literature, mainly iron (Fe), barium (Ba), antimony (Sb), tin (Sn), and copper (Cu), although these elements can also be emitted from other sources, mostly from industrial processes.

The composition of brake pads has varied over time, but in recent years there has been a noticeable reduction in copper and antimony content motivated by the forthcoming implementation of regulations in a number of US states (California, New York, Rhode Island and Washington). There is also an increasing concern about the amount of phenolic resins used in brake pads, which may lead to similar regulations on the use of these constituents in the near future.

Source: (Amato et al., 2009[43]; Gietl et al., 2010[44]; Hulskotte, Roskam and Denier van der Gon, 2014[34]; Kukutschová et al., 2011[3]; Thorpe and Harrison, 2008[45]; Von Uexküll et al., 2005[46])

Concerning tyre wear particle size, less than 1% by volume (which is proportional to the mass) of the particles are less than 10 µm (Kreider et al., 2010[42]). Within PM10, studies conducted on a laboratory road simulator[4] show that more than 60% of tyre wear particles (by mass) are generally between 2.5 and 10 µm (McAtee et al., 2009[47]). However, a bimodal distribution is observed with peaks around 1 µm and between 5 and 8 µm. Several studies demonstrate that the use of studded tyres increases the emissions of tyre-road wear particles by orders of magnitude, and produces particles in the nanometre range from the interaction between the studs and the pavement (Gustafsson et al., 2009[48]).

2.1.3. Road wear

Road wear occurs due to the fragmentation and breakdown of road pavement surfaces as a result of vehicle traffic. Pavements are normally ballast bonded using bitumen, resulting in wear particles composed of minerals dominated by crustal elements but with a significant content of organic carbon (OC). In addition, furnace slag and mixed tyre rubber can be incorporated in road pavements in order to improve their durability and other technical properties.

Road wear is often merged with road dust resuspension in source apportionment studies. The reason for this is that the atmospheric deposition of other mineral particles originating from soil resuspension, traction sanding, building activities and desert dust hampers efforts to measure road wear and road dust separately.

A unique feature of road wear particles is their bitumen content.[5] Bitumen constitutes about 5% of roadside total suspended particles (TSP) mass and bitumen particles have a mean aerodynamic size of about 1 µm (Fauser et al., 2002[49]). Interest in road wear dust particles has been highest in countries where studded tyres are used during winter, as these tyres significantly increase road wear. Traction sand also increases road wear due to the "sandpaper effect" (Kupiainen, Tervahattu and Räisänen, 2003[50]), which results in a higher abrasion of road surfaces due to the interaction with quartz sand particles. In countries where studded tyres are not used, addressing road wear is less of a priority, which means that weaker rocks and less wear-resistant constructions are used. As a result, road wear can nevertheless be an important source of non-exhaust particle pollution in these countries (Gustafsson, 2018[51]).

Road wear emissions are mainly calculated and characterised by means of road simulators, where the contribution of emissions from road dust resuspension can be controlled for and measured separately (see Box 2.3). Gehrig et al. (2010[52]) found that road wear particles had a mass size distribution with a maximum of 6-7 µm in diameter and no particles below 0.5 µm. A number of laboratory tests have also shown that the maximum mass concentration is normally at 5-8 µm, and the total mass of particles below 1 µm is small.

Box 2.3. Road simulators

Three main road simulators have been used for air quality studies. The Model Mobile Load Simulator (MMLS) is a relatively small device simulating approximately one third of the load of the wheels of a light duty vehicle (LDV) at a low speed of 9 km/h.

The Mobile Load Simulator (MLS) is bigger than MMLS and simulates the abrasion processes of the wheels of a full-size heavy-duty vehicle (HDV) at a speed of 25 km/h.

The Swedish Road and Transport Research Institute (VTI) laboratory road simulator consists of an indoor circular track measuring 0.5 metres wide and 16 metres in diameter that can be surfaced with different types of pavement. The machine rotates around a central vertical axis on which six-wheel axles are mounted. The axels can accommodate different types of tyres and simulated speeds can reach up to 70 km/h.

Source: Gehrig et al. (2010[52])

2.1.4. Road dust resuspension

Road dust is a generic description for any form of solid particle deposited on the road surface that can be suspended in the air through traffic-induced turbulence. Road dust emissions contribute significantly to ambient PM10 and PM2.5 levels. Larger particles can also be of concern if they are crushed to generate smaller particles, but since no information is available on the crushing potential, frequency and duration of the fragmentation of larger particles, the first priority of research on road dust resuspension should be to better understand the thoracic fraction, or the fraction of particles the size of PM10 or less.

Road dust can come from a variety of sources, including traffic (exhaust and wear PM deposited on road surfaces), construction and other "dusty" sites, migration from neighbouring environments, deposition from the atmosphere, and the application of road salt and sand. The relative contribution of different sources and the overall chemical composition of road dust likely varies from one site to another, so individual findings in one environment may not be applicable to others (Amato et al., 2011[53]; Denby, Kupiainen and Gustafsson, 2018[54]).

Road dust emissions strongly depend also on the redistribution of particles, dry and wet losses, and processes affecting the distribution of particle sizes (Denby et al., 2013[55]). The physico-chemical properties of road dust have been studied using different approaches, and targeting different size ranges, yielding a wide variation in documented chemical compositions and size distributions. The chemical profile of road dust for the fraction below 10 µm heavily depends on the sources of these particles, but is typically comprised of minerals (silicon, aluminium, calcium, titanium, strontium among others) with enrichments in antimony, tin, barium, iron, copper and manganese (brake wear), zinc and carbon (elemental and organic), and polycyclic aromatic hydrocarbons, when compared to a general soil dust factor.[6]

In order to avoid double-counting, emission factors used for resuspension should not include the contribution of direct brake, tyre or road wear. However, road dust resuspension should definitively be included in emission inventories to enable a better understanding of the origins of real-world ambient PM concentrations currently observed in large cities and their streets (Denier van der Gon et al., 2018[20]).

The main characteristics of the chemical composition of each category of non-exhaust emissions, as well as the most common approaches used for their measurement are presented in Table 2.1.

2.2. Approaches to measuring non-exhaust emissions

The approaches used to estimate the magnitude of non-exhaust emissions can be grouped in two main categories: i) approaches based on estimates of emissions (e.g. mg/vehicle-km or tons/year); and ii) source apportionment studies based on exposure to air pollutant concentrations (µg/m^3). The most important difference between the two approaches is that source apportionment studies estimate the population exposure at a receptor site, whereas emission estimates analyse the amount of PM emitted at the source, such that the transport and transformation of pollutants are neglected.

This section briefly describes the different methods used in each category in order to provide insight into the reliability of estimates and measurements provided by different approaches, as well as into their limitations.

Table 2.1. Chemical composition of non-exhaust PM and emission measurement

Non-exhaust emissions category	PM10 (% of TSP)	PM2.5 (% of TSP)	Main component (> 1% in mass).*	Common methods/approaches for the estimation of emissions (mg/vehicle-km)
Brake wear	63-98%[1-4]	39-63%[1-4]	**Iron, Copper, Barium, Antimony,** Zinc Aluminium, Chromium, Potassium, Titanium, and Magnesium[9]	Brake dynamometer Pin on disc
Tyre wear	60%[4] 1% of total tread wear[5, 6]	42%[4] 0.4% of total tread wear[5, 6]	**Zinc**, Silicon, Sulfur[10]	Road simulator
Road wear	50%[4]	27%[4]	**Silicon, Calcium**, Potassium and Iron.[11]	Road simulator

Road dust resuspension	2-42%[7,8] of PM<250 µm	1-11%[7,8] of PM<250 µm	Silicon, Calcium, Aluminium, Iron, Potassium, Magnesium, Titanium, Copper, Zinc and Barium[12]	Road dust sampling Kerbside ambient air PM or deposition monitoring

* Most common tracers are in bold.

Note: Total suspended particles (TSP) are PM<50-100 µm.

Data sources: [1]Garg et al. (2000[38]); [2]Sanders et al. (2003[37]); [3]Iijima et al. (2007[35]); [4]Ntziachristos and Boulter (2016[56]); [5]Kreider et al. (2010[42])2; [6] McAtee et al. (2009[47]); [7]Ramirez et al. (2019[57]); [8]Escrig et al. (2011[58]); [9]Grigoratos and Martini (2015[6]); [10]Panko, Kreider and Unice (2018[59]); [11]Gustafsson (2018[51]); [12]Amato et al. (2009[43]).

2.2.1. Emission estimates

This family of approaches focuses on the direct measurement of vehicle emissions. The main advantage of this approach is that it provides highly accurate estimates of primary emissions. The main limitation of these approaches, however, is that they do not address population exposure. A second important limitation of emission estimates is that they do not consider secondary aerosols, which are generated in the atmosphere from gaseous precursors such as nitrogen and sulphur oxides (NOx and SOx), ammonia (NH_3) and volatile organic compounds (VOCs) (see Box 2.4). Although secondary aerosols might not be so relevant for non-exhaust processes, they are relevant for exhaust emissions. As such, they should be considered when non-exhaust emissions are evaluated *relative to* total traffic emissions or emissions from all sources. Secondary aerosols can represent an important share of PM. For example, Amato et al. (2016[60]) estimated that 37-82% of PM2.5 and 40-71% of PM10 were secondary particles in five European cities.

Within this category, there are two main types of studies, those focusing on the measurement of emission factors and those concentrating on the compilation pf emission inventories.

Box 2.4. Primary and secondary aerosols

Understanding pollution from motor vehicles requires a knowledge of both primary PM and gas emissions and of how these pollutants interact and age in the atmosphere. While primary non-exhaust PM is emitted directly in solid or liquid form, secondary PM are formed in the atmosphere by the physico-chemical reaction of gaseous precursors, emitted from vehicles and other sources. The main precursors are SOx, NOx, NH3 and volatile organic compounds. The gas-to-particle conversion is not linear: it depends on a complex set of interactions between gas concentrations, free radicals, air temperature and humidity.

Secondary PM from road traffic are mainly due to exhaust emissions, namely NOx, VOCs and SO2 in countries with high sulphur content in diesel fuel. NOx and SOx interact mainly with ammonia (from agriculture) – forming ammonium nitrate and sulphate – as well as with sea salt and mineral dust cations (mainly sodium and calcium) depending on the local conditions. Secondary nitrate and sulphate salts are named secondary inorganic aerosols (SIA), while secondary organic aerosols (SOA) denote particles formed from volatile organic compounds.

Source: Platt et al., (2017[61])

Emission factors

Emission factors (EFs) measure the mass of PM emitted per unit of activity, e.g. per vehicle-km, from different traffic sources. Studies in this category estimate emission factors for non-exhaust sources in different settings. The main limitation of this group of studies is the representativeness of the retrieved EFs for other environments. Two main approaches are followed within this group: inverse modelling and simulation methods.

Inverse modelling

Studies based on real-world PM measurements, such as experimental measurements next to roads (Amato et al., 2010[62]; Amato et al., 2012[63]; Amato et al., 2016[13]; Bukowiecki et al., 2009[64]; Bukowiecki et al., 2010[65]; Escrig et al., 2011[58]; Gillies et al., 2005[66]; Lawrence, Sokhi and Ravindra, 2016[67]), should be preferred for two reasons. First, they provide a robust average of the PM emitted by circulating traffic, which implies higher representativeness than simulator studies. Second, EFs from different traffic sources, i.e. exhaust, and each non-exhaust source, can be sometimes obtained simultaneously, thereby allowing the evaluation of the relative importance of each source. Measurements can be carried out for PM (together with NOx) at a given height, or for deposited dust across a vertical profile (several heights). Studies focusing on road dust EFs should take care to avoid double counting direct wear emissions.

Road dust emissions are often calculated based on the AP-42 model (U.S. Environmental Protection Agency, 2011[68]).[7] The mathematical formula proposed for the model entails a large variation (up to two-orders of magnitude) of possible observed EFs for a given predicted value. For example, when the predicted EF is 0.5 g/vehicle-km, the observed EF varies from 0.1 to 10 g/vehicle-km (Venkatram, 2000[69]). This variation has led to some criticism for the broader applicability of the model (Kantamaneni et al., 1996[70]; Venkatram, 2000[69]).

For a local emission inventory, it is generally recommendable to experimentally derive EFs by carrying out specific local studies, such as those based on inverse modelling.

Simulator studies

Measurements in these studies are based on a single vehicle or simulator, such as a dynamometer, pin-on-disc or road simulator. While such measurements are useful to investigate the impact of factors influencing the magnitude of emissions, including vehicle mass, speed, and type of tyre and brake, they lack generalisability and are not suitable for direct emission comparisons between different traffic sources.

Emission inventories

Emission inventories compile total emissions in a given geographical domain (e.g. country) using a bottom-up approach. To this end, total activity underpinning each emission source is multiplied by an emission factor (California Air Resources Board, 2019[71]; Centre on Emission Inventories and Projections, 2019[72]; Pachón et al., 2018[73]). Emission factors are generally extracted from the literature and their applicability to a given area of study is not always guaranteed. Emission inventories have the additional limitation that estimates of PM shares depend on the sources included in the inventory. In this context, it is important that emission inventories include resuspension. However, care should be taken to ensure that the EFs used for resuspension do not include direct wear emissions in order to avoid double counting.

Information from emission inventories is not necessarily indicative of population exposure, as e.g. power plants and industries are usually located far from most populated areas.

2.2.2. Source apportionment

This category is the most frequently used, as it reflects concentrations and takes into account secondary aerosols. The latter enables better estimates of relative contribution to PM10 and PM2.5. Within this category, three main measurement approaches can be distinguished:

Standard

The ISO/TS 20593:2017 standard specifies a method for the determination of the airborne concentration (μg/m3), mass concentration (μg/g) and mass fraction (%) of ambient PM from tyre and road wear. ISO/TS 20593:2017 establishes standard practices for the collection of air samples, the generation of pyrolysis fragments from the sample, and the measurement of the generated polymer fragments. The quantified polymer mass is used to calculate the fraction of tyre tread in PM and the concentration of tyre tread in the air. These quantities are expressed on a tyre and road wear particle (TRWP) basis, which encompasses the mass of tyre tread and mass of road wear encrustations, and can also be expressed on a tyre rubber polymer or tyre tread basis.

Receptor models

These models apportion the measured mass of PM at a given site to its emission sources by solving a mass balance equation between the observed PM species concentrations and the predicted ones, expressed as sum of contributions from different sources. Receptor models require a large number of observations (more than 100) of PM component concentrations (PM speciation data), including concentrations of major and trace components.

These models have the advantage of providing information derived from real-world measurements, including the estimation of uncertainty surrounding the model's output. However, it is difficult to separate the contribution of different non-exhaust sources using these models due to a lack of unique tracers. They are widely used for source apportionment at local and regional scales all over the world. In the past decade, the number of scientific publications and technical reports using this method has steadily increased and tools with improved capabilities are in constant development (Belis et al., 2014[74]).

Within receptor models, the most common tool is Positive Matrix Factorization (PMF). PMF offers the advantage of obtaining the chemical profiles of the sources as output, as opposed to Chemical Mass Balance (CMB) that requires them as input information, additional to the chemical composition of ambient air PM.

Dispersion or Chemistry Transport models (CTM)

Dispersion models combine emission inventories, information about weather conditions, and the characteristics of dispersion processes and chemical reactions to simulate PM concentrations at a given receptor site or within a given area. Although dispersion models have been used extensively for PM simulation, their application to source apportionment studies has been limited due to their high computational demand. As a result, only a few such studies are available.

The advantage of receptor models is that they allow apportioning the total (measured) PM concentrations, while dispersion models can only apportion the modelled fraction. This fraction can be significantly lower – likely by 50% in cities – due to the lack of specific sources in the emission inventory and/or physico-chemical reactions in the atmosphere. On the other hand, receptor models are more limited in the number of identifiable sources than dispersion models: the latter can quantify the contribution of all sources included in the inventory. Therefore, attention should be paid when labelling sources: for example, a "road dust" source should always be combined with a "direct wear emission" one; otherwise a generic "non-exhaust" label should be created. Another disadvantage of receptor models is that most secondary inorganic aerosols are identified as a single source, i.e. not apportioned to their precursors' sources.

Table 2.2. Main methods to estimate the magnitude of non-exhaust emissions

	Emission estimates			Source apportionment		
Model type (measurement unit)	Emission factors (mg/vehicle-km)		Emission inventories (tonnes/year)	Receptor models (µg/m³)		Dispersion models (µg/m³)
	Inverse modelling	Simulator studies		PMF	CMB	
Principle	EFs are estimated by fitting simplified models to observations (least squares fit).	EFs are estimated under specific conditions (e.g. single vehicle, brake/tyre system).	Total emissions are calculated by multiplying EF by activity data (e.g. traffic volume)	A mass balance equation is solved between the observed concentration of PM components at a given receptor and the sum of contributions from different sources.		A "labelling" technique is applied to estimated emissions, allowing to estimate contributions on a given receptor.
Usage	Medium	Medium	High	High	Medium	Low
Type of data used	PM and NOx data measured at kerbside; Vertical deposition profiles in case of resuspension.	Vehicle and driving characteristics (e.g. weight, speed)	EFs and activity data for a given geographical domain	PM speciation data with major and trace components. For PMF a large number of samples is needed (>100)		Emission inventory, meteo fields and a CTM model. "Labelling" tool; High computing demand.

Advantages	**Provides robust average of real-world conditions**; Allows for direct comparison among different traffic sources.	Allows for an investigation of the impact of vehicle/driving characteristics on different emission sources.	**Allows for the evaluation of a large number of sources**; Allows for projections.	**Apportions total measured PM mass**	**Secondary aerosols are apportioned** **Contributions of all inventoried sources can be quantified;** Allows for projections
				Reflects population exposure; Includes secondary particles	
Limitations	**Does not reflect population exposure; Neglects secondary particles**			**Reduced number of sources identified (collinearity), e.g. it merges road wear and road dust resuspension.**	**Only the modelled fraction of PM is apportioned**
	EFs for road dust should be calculated minimising double-counting of direct wear emissions.		**Estimated share of PM can be biased in the absence of important sources (e.g. resuspension)**	Importance of factor interpretation, in order to avoid double-counting in meta-analyses. / **Requires representative chemical source profiles**	
	Applicability to other environments may be limited	**Limited representativeness of real-world conditions**	Relies heavily on the quality and representativeness of EFs	Very limited apportionment of secondary aerosols	
		Do not allow simultaneous comparison with other non-exhaust sources.	Allows for time series analysis		

Note: Main advantages and limitations are highlighted in bold.

The following section provides a brief overview of the two most common types of studies described in Table 2.2, namely "Emission Inventories" and "Source Apportionment" with the aim of evaluating the importance of non-exhaust emissions, mostly when compared to exhaust emissions on a global perspective.

2.3. The growing importance of non-exhaust emissions for air pollution

2.3.1. Emission inventories

Emission inventories provide important evidence of the growing importance of non-exhaust sources for air pollution. However, this evidence should be considered in light of the limitations associated with emissions inventories discussed in the previous section. Specifically, emission inventories: i) do not reflect population exposure well, as inventories are summed over large areas and include sources located far away from populated areas; ii) do not consider secondary aerosols, which can be significantly increased by exhaust emissions; iii) often discard road dust resuspension, which is the dominant part of non-exhaust emissions; and iv) rely on the quality and representativeness of the emission factors used. The last limitation is also crucial when analysing time trends, since a change in the estimation method of an emission factor may create a break in the series and affect intertemporal analyses.

Keeping these considerations in mind, emission inventories at different administrative levels were explored, prioritising those that enabled a direct comparison of exhaust with non-exhaust emissions from road transport. Inventories providing future projections of different emission categories were of particular interest for the study. Only a few emission inventories met these criteria.

Europe

Under the UNECE Convention on Long-range Transboundary Air Pollution (CLRTAP) and the EU National Emission Ceilings Directive (2016/2284/EU), European Union Member States, EFTA countries and Turkey report their national emissions according to the following categories: passenger cars, light duty vehicles (LDVs), heavy duty vehicles (HDVs) and busses, mopeds and motorcycles, gasoline evaporation, automobile tyre and brake wear, automobile road abrasion (i.e. road wear).

Traffic-induced resuspension of deposited road dust is not included in the European emission inventory, at least not as a mandatory category. Ntziachristos and Boulter (2016, pp. 3,10[56]) justify the exclusion of resuspension from the European emission inventory guidebook as follows: "The focus is on (…) particles emitted directly as a result of the wear of surfaces —and not those resulting from the resuspension of previously deposited matter. (….). Due to the open discussion with regard to the definition of resuspension as a primary source, and the uncertainty in the methods used for the estimation of its effect, no methodology to estimate PM concentrations from resuspension is provided". However, some countries already consider resuspension in their national inventories, such as the United Kingdom, which includes it in a "natural sources" category.8

The growing importance of wear sources relative to exhaust emissions in the EU-28 is illustrated in Figure 2.1, which draws on PM10 data for the period 2000-2014. While a clear downward trend is observed for exhaust emissions due to the implementation of EUROx directives, the sum of reported wear emissions is quite stable (see the dark grey and dark blue bars at the bottom of the columns). The same pattern is observed for PM2.5, although the percentage of wear emissions in total road transport is considerably lower than that for PM10.

Kousoulidou et al. (2008[75]) projected the evolution of non-exhaust PM emissions in European urban environments, finding that the share of non-exhaust emissions to total PM2.5 is on the order of 77% for gasoline PCs, 12% for HDVs and 8% for diesel PCs. The high share of non-exhaust PM2.5 for gasoline PCs in particular is an important finding, as these emissions are not always estimated in studies dealing with air-quality targets, as exhaust emissions have the primary focus.

To put it into perspective, gasoline PC non-exhaust PM2.5 emissions are roughly twice as high as the exhaust PM2.5 of diesel PC at the Euro 5 level. The increasing share of non-exhaust PM with respect to total PM has significant implications for the assessment of the effectiveness of emission control measures in the attainment of air-quality standards. Specific measures for PM control introduce the widespread application of diesel particle filters (DPFs) for Euro 5 and Euro 6 diesel PCs and Euro VI HDVs. According to the findings of Kousoulidou et al. there is clear evidence that non-exhaust sources become increasingly important and that vehicle categories previously not considered as key sources of PM emissions, such as gasoline passenger cars, now need to be taken into account in the total emissions.

The contribution of exhaust emissions may be somewhat underestimated in the inventory, as the emission factors underlying the estimation of exhaust emissions are based on measurements according to type-approval tests. Under real-world driving conditions, PM emissions from vehicle exhaust have been shown to be higher. As a result, the share of wear emissions as a part of total emissions reported is likely to be an upper bound.

However, keeping in mind these limitations, and also the fact that resuspension is not included in the analysis, Figure 2.2 shows a break point for PM10 in 2014, when PM from wear emissions were already larger (51%) than PM from primary exhaust emissions (49%) at the EU-28 level. For PM2.5 this point has not been reached yet; wear represented 34% of total emissions from road transport in EU-28 in 2014.

In terms of percentages to total *primary* emissions (secondary PM is not considered) from all sources, wear emissions showed a clear increase since 2000, reaching a 5% share of total PM10 and 4% of total PM2.5 in 2014 (Figure 2.2). Exhaust emissions represented a similar share of primary PM10, and a share of primary PM2.5 almost double that of wear (8%) in that year.

In the UK, vehicle exhaust emissions are already estimated to be a smaller source than non-exhaust PM and expected to be less than 10% of total road transport PM by 2030. As other emission sources of PM are addressed, it is estimated that the non-exhaust component will increase in importance, growing from less than 8% of national emissions in 2017 to 10% in 2030.

Figure 2.1. Annual PM emissions from road transport, EU-28, 2000-2014

PM10 (top) and PM2.5 (bottom)

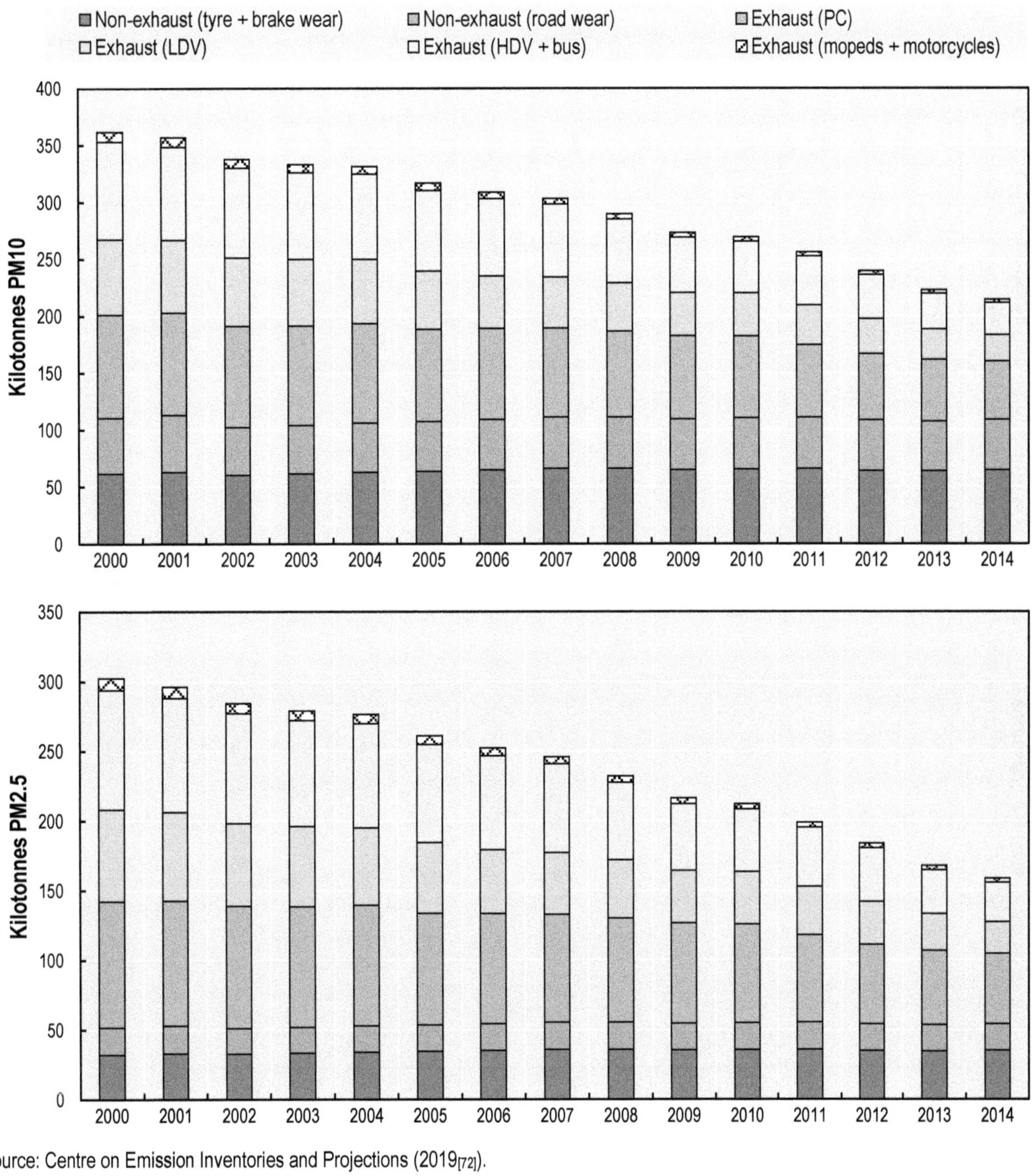

Source: Centre on Emission Inventories and Projections (2019[72]).

Figure 2.2. Exhaust vs. non-exhaust wear PM emissions

Percentage of total PM emissions from road transport (top) and total PM emissions (bottom)

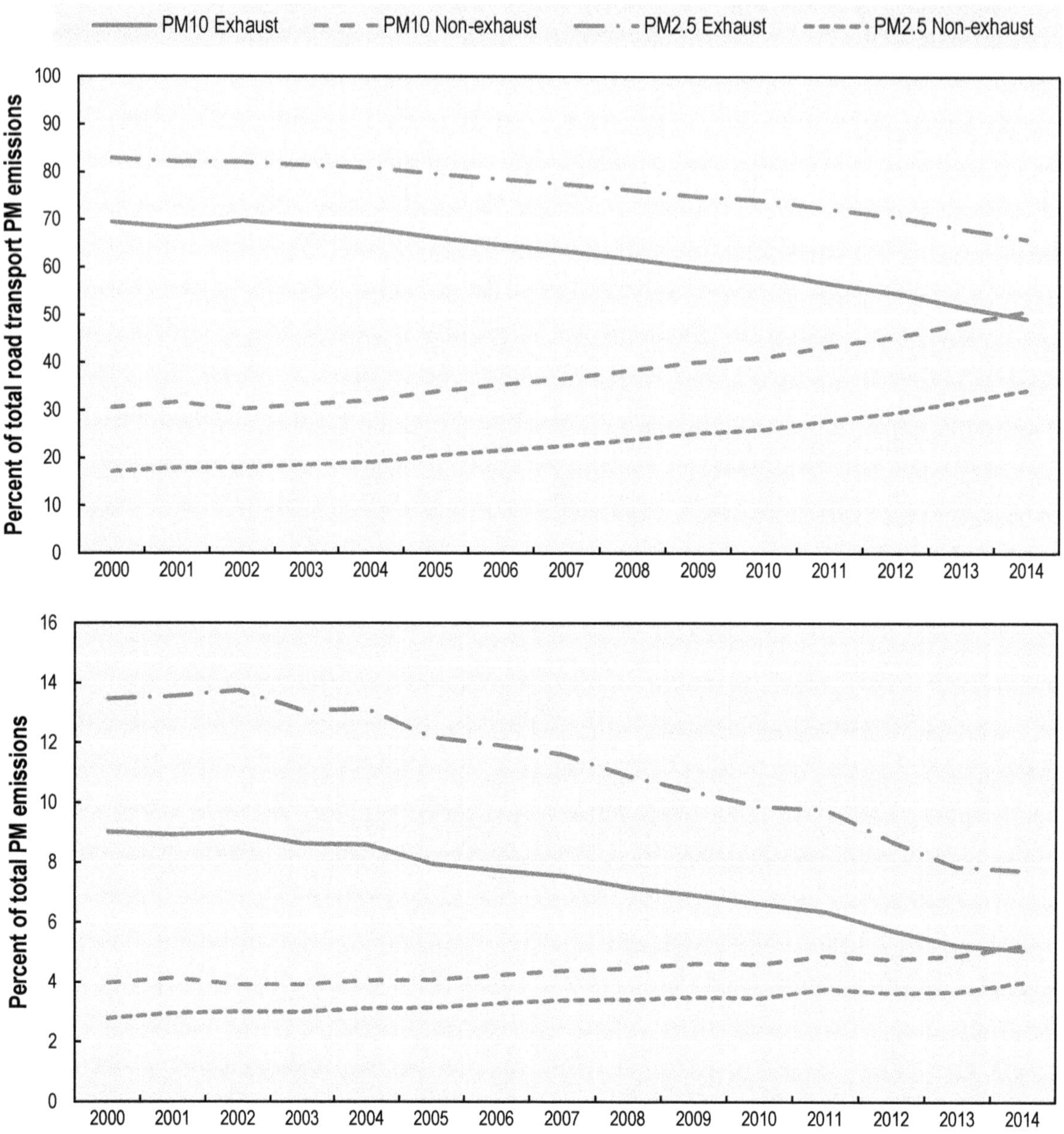

Source: Centre on Emissions Inventories and Projections (2019)

United States

In the United States, the National Emission Inventory (NEI) provides aggregate emission data for 3 years (2008, 2011 and 2014) (U.S. Environmental Protection Agency, 2019[76]).[9] While road dust emissions are clearly identified as "Paved road dust", brake wear and tyre wear emissions are merged in the "on-road mobile" category. Road dust emissions are calculated based on the AP-42 model (U.S. Environmental Protection Agency, 2011[68]), which, as mentioned before, has certain limitations. Taking into consideration these limitations, emissions from road dust represented at least 74-76% and 51-58% of PM10 and PM2.5 emissions from road traffic respectively in the period 2008-2014 (Table 2.3). In absolute levels, emissions show a slight decrease of around 10% in 6 years. With respect to total sources, road dust emissions represented at least 5% of PM10 and 4% of PM2.5, while mobile emissions (including brake and tyre wear) less than 2% and 3-4% respectively (Table 2.3).

The California Air Resources Board (CARB) website provides emission data on a 5-year basis from 2000 and includes projections until 2035 (California Air Resources Board, 2019[71]). A CARB project is ongoing to update the emission factors, as they are considered dated. However, with the information available today, brake wear and tyre wear are also included in the "on-road mobile" category, but they are specifically labelled and can be extracted; road dust resuspension is labelled as "paved roads". The sum of non-exhaust emissions can thus be calculated by subtracting brake and tyre wear from the total "on-road mobile" category and adding the resulting amount to that of the "paved road" category. It is important to note that road wear is not identified as a separate category in the inventory.

Table 2.3. US-wide estimates for road dust vs. on-road mobile emissions

		Kilotonnes		% of road traffic		% of total	
PM10		Road dust	Mobile[1]	Road dust	Mobile[1]	Road dust	Mobile[1]
	2008	1 037.320	331.899	76	24	5	2
	2011	1 047.690	370.825	74	26	5	2
	2014	944.948	304.269	76	24	5	2
PM2.5							
	2008	259.330	252.603	51	49	4	4
	2011	261.922	197.527	57	43	4	3
	2014	229.466	163.092	58	42	4	3

Note: [1] Includes brake and tyre wear emissions.
Data source: (U.S. Environmental Protection Agency, 2019[76]).

Figure 2.3. Exhaust vs. non-exhaust emissions of PM10 and PM2.5, California, 2000-2035

Non-exhaust PM10 and PM2.5 emissions from road transport in kilotonnes/year and percentage of non-exhaust PM emissions from road transport

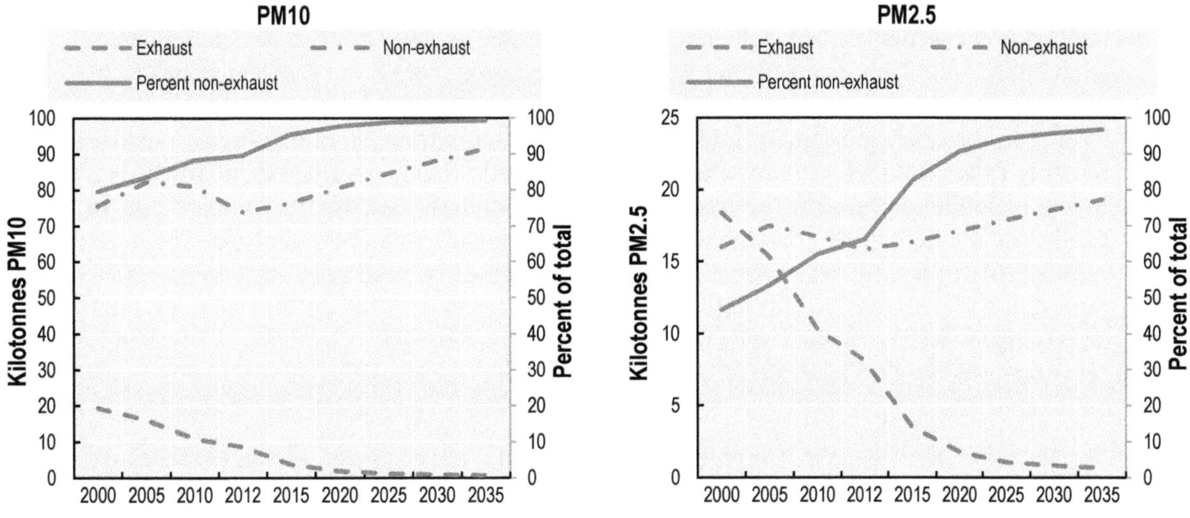

Source: California Air Resources Board (2019[71]).

In contrast with the European case, the sum of non-exhaust emissions represented in 2015 already 95% of total primary PM10 from road traffic. The large difference between the contribution of non-exhaust emissions to primary PM10 from traffic in Europe and California can be attributed to two reasons: first, the inclusion of resuspension in the Californian inventory leads to much higher estimates of non-exhaust emissions; second, the amount of exhaust emissions per vehicle kilometre is lower in California due to the very low penetration of diesel light duty vehicles (their share to the total stock of light duty vehicles is around 0.5%.

Besides a decrease in 2012 due to the change of the methodological approach,[10] a clearly increasing trend can be observed for non-exhaust emissions, due to an increase in vehicle kilometres travelled. In contrast, exhaust emissions keep decreasing until 2035. Emission projections show an increase of non-exhaust emissions to up to 98% of total primary PM10 emissions from road traffic and 15% of total primary PM10 emissions already from 2020. The share then remains quite stable until 2035.

With respect to PM2.5, non-exhaust emissions represented already from 2015 more than 80% of road traffic emissions. Their share is projected to increase to 97% in 2030 and then remain relatively stable until 2035. Their share to total PM2.5 emissions is projected to be around 13% in 2035. Exhaust emissions in 2035 are projected to represent about 3% and 1% of road traffic and total PM2.5 emissions respectively.

Latin America

In Latin America, non-exhaust emissions were found to be included only in three local (municipal or metropolitan level) emission inventories: Mexico D.F. (Metropolitan area), Bogotá (city) and Santiago de Chile (metropolitan region).

Mexico

The emission inventory of the metropolitan area of Mexico D.F. is reported every 2 years (Secretaria del Medio Ambiente de la Ciudad de Mexico, 2018[77]). Following the MOVES software, it distinguishes between mobile sources (including exhaust, brake and tyre wear) and road dust resuspension. Road wear is not considered. Similarly to the US National Emission Inventory, it does not distinguish the contribution of brake and tyre wear from the contribution of other mobile sources.

Intertemporal analysis of emissions does not point to a clear trend, probably due to methodological changes which are not always reported. Two periods can be distinguished: from 2002 to 2008, emissions from road dust resuspension were lower than emissions from mobile sources, but they were increasing over time. From 2010 to 2016, emissions from road dust resuspension remain quite stable, while those from mobile sources increase (sharply from 2014). The authors claim that these drastic changes are due to modifications in the methodology used to estimate emissions (Secretaria del Medio Ambiente de la Ciudad de Mexico, 2018[77]), which eventually hampers intertemporal analysis. The most recent (2016) scenario highlights the current importance of road dust emissions, which represent 35% of road traffic emissions of PM10 (21% of PM2.5) and 16% of total emissions of PM10 (9% for PM2.5).

Bogota

For the city of Bogota in Colombia, (Pachón et al., 2018[73]) and (Pérez-Peña et al., 2017[78]) have published PM10 and PM2.5 emission inventories using the AP-42 method

(U.S. Environmental Protection Agency, 2011[68]) for road dust, the COPERT IV model for brake and tyre wear, and the MOVES model for motor exhaust. They found road dust resuspension to be the dominant source of total emissions of PM10 (46%) and PM2.5 (56%), even after correcting emissions for mitigation due to precipitation. Brake and tyre wear represented 1.4% of total PM10 emissions and 0.8% of PM2.5 ones, while motor exhaust 3% and 11%, respectively. The authors concluded that road dust emissions were likely overestimated due to the low applicability of the AP-42 method. Further research is underway to estimate real-world emission factors for road dust and apply an adjustment factor that considers the effects of land use, for example.

Santiago

In Santiago de Chile, the Regional Government published an inventory with projections for 2010, using the MODEM model which separates road dust resuspension from mobile sources. The mobile category is separated between urban roads and highways. While urban mobile sources are further broken down to engine exhaust, brake and tyre wear, this breakdown does not exist for highway sources. Brake and tyre wear are not considered in PM2.5 emissions. Road wear is not considered at all. Similarly to the case of Bogota, the inventory revealed a dominant role of non-exhaust emissions, in the area of 54% of PM10 and 28% of PM2.5 total emissions. Mobile sources (including brake and tyre wear in highways) represented only 6% of total PM10 emissions and 21% of total PM2.5 emissions (DICTUC, 2007[79]).

Summarizing, emission inventories worldwide allow concluding that already in 2014 non-exhaust emissions represented at least 50% of total traffic emissions (primary PM) and 5% of total PM10 emissions, even excluding resuspension. Regarding PM2.5, the corresponding shares decrease to 34% and 4% respectively. In California, where resuspension is taken into account in emission inventories, non-exhaust emissions were found to represent 95% of primary traffic PM10 emissions and 15% of PM10 emissions from all sources (for 2015). Estimates are somewhat lower for PM2.5, but still very significant: non-exhaust emissions account for 82% of primary PM2.5 caused by road traffic and 12% of primary total PM2.5. However, the quality of such estimates is directly linked to the representativeness of emission factors used for resuspension, which may be questionable for the AP-42 model. The same problem applies to the local inventories in Latin America, where road dust contributions may be overestimated due to the lack of reliable emission factors.

2.3.2. Source apportionment studies

When compared to emission inventories, source apportionment studies have the advantage of reflecting population exposure, since they are based on measured (or simulated) concentrations at receptors. Another important advantage is that they consider secondary PM, so that estimates of the share of non-exhaust emissions in traffic PM, or total PM are much more comprehensive. However, caution should be taken when comparing results from different studies: a miss-interpretation of factors can lead to double counting. Padoan and Amato (2018[5]) reviewed about 100 peer-reviewed articles providing more than 250 estimates of non-exhaust sources contributions (µg/m3) worldwide. There is a clearly increasing trend in the number of articles per year from 2000 onwards.

The most common method used in the reviewed studies is receptor modelling (84%), dominated by Positive Matrix Factorization (PMF),[11] which offers multiple advantages but cannot easily separate road wear from road dust resuspension (Table 2.2), while only 10% of studies were performed by means of CTM modelling. The remaining studies used other techniques or measures different from PM mass.

Shares of the relative contribution of each non-exhaust emission source to PM10 and PM2.5 concentrations are listed in Table 2.4, distinguishing between urban background and traffic sites. Road dust was identified much more frequently than wear sources, which can be due to several reasons. If contributions from wear sources are merged under contributions from another source (e.g. road dust or exhaust), summing over cells in a row of Table 2.4 would lead to double-counting. If wear contributions are excluded because they are too small to be quantified by the receptor model, no such risk for double counting exists.

Considering this limitation, Table 2.4 shows that PM10 contribution ranges for road dust resuspension for urban background – places in urban areas where levels are representative of the exposure of the general urban population – are wide due to the important influence of local factors, such as microclimate and road conditions. The contribution of road dust is the highest among all traffic sources (median of 21%), followed by exhaust emissions (16%) and brake and tyre wear (4% each). For urban background PM2.5, exhaust emissions clearly dominate (median of 22%), followed by road dust resuspension (7%), and brake and tyre wear (5%).

Table 2.4. Percent of non-exhaust and exhaust emissions contributions to ambient PM10 and PM2.5: Estimates from source apportionment studies

	Brake wear	Tyre wear	Road dust resuspension /Road wear	Exhaust emissions
		Background sites		
PM10 (observations)	7*	5*	50	59
Range	3-6	2-6	6-59	2-64
Median	4	4	21	16
Mean	4	4	22	20
PM2.5 (observations)	3**	3**	59	60
Range	5-9	3-5	1-31	3-57
Median	5	5	7	22
Mean	7	5	9	24
		Traffic sites		
PM10 (observations)	4	7	11	13
Range	5-20	2-8	11-76	13-36
Median	7	6	23	20
Mean	8	5	29	21
PM2.5 (observations)	-	4***	6	9
Range	-	0-1	5-31	12-62
Median	-	0.1	18	26
Mean	-	0.4	17	30

Note: * A mixed brake/tyre wear component was found in 3 studies; ** A mixed brake/tyre wear component was found in 2 studies, *** A mixed brake/tyre wear component was found in 1 study. Ranges for PM10 and PM2.5 are not derived from the same number of observations. For exhaust emissions, only the studies identifying also non-exhaust emissions are considered.

The number of studies decreases significantly at traffic sites, but the overall picture does not change significantly except for the higher contributions, as expected. Road dust resuspension is still the most important source (median of 23%) followed by exhaust (20%), brake wear (7%) and tyre wear (6%). Regarding PM2.5, street level contributions mainly result from exhaust emissions (26%) and road dust resuspension (18%). Negligible contributions were found for tyre wear (0.1%), while no data on brake wear are available, possibly due to the specific local driving conditions at these sites. If brakes do not face severe stops, their temperature does not increase above 170 C, thus the emitted PM is mostly coarse (Alemani et al., 2015[80]).

The relatively wide ranges observed in Table 2.4 for the contribution of road dust resuspension suggests an important impact of weather conditions and other local features. In order to explore this hypothesis further, contributions are presented for selected countries with different climate conditions in Table 2.5. Road dust contributions are highest during spring months in Sweden, where the use of studded tyres is the main reason behind a median contribution of 74% of kerbside PM10. On an annual basis, mean contributions go down to 23%, which is also the maximum observed in Europe. The median contribution found by studies in Spain is 17% of PM10, and by studies in central European countries 11%. On an annual basis, emissions from road dust are highest in India and China, where median contributions reach 36% and 31% respectively. For the Unites States, only PM2.5 estimates are available and reach a 6% median contribution, which is lower than China, India and Spain.

Recent analyses of trends in atmospheric concentrations of pollutants reported additional evidence of the increasing importance of non-exhaust emissions. Masri, Kang and Koutrakis (2015[81]) found an increase of the share of coarse particles in PM10, as PM2.5 have decreased at higher rates than PM10. Likewise, PM2.5 have declined more rapidly than coarse PM over the past decade at various European sites (Barmpadimos et al., 2012[82]). A similar pattern has also been found by Font and Fuller (2016[83]) for the city of London. In Southern Spain, road dust contributions to PM10 levels measured at a number of sites did not decrease in the period 2004-2011, whereas vehicle exhaust contributions decreased by 0.4 (0.24-0.57) mg/m3 year (Amato et al., 2014[18]).

Table 2.5. Average share of urban PM explained by road dust and exhaust emissions

	Urban PM10		Urban PM2.5	
	Road dust	Vehicle exhaust	Road dust	Vehicle exhaust
United States, 28 studies	-	-	**2-25% (6%)**	3-40% (22%)
Sweden (kerbside in spring), 3 studies	**66-76% (74%)**	<20%*	-	-
Central EU (CZ and DE), 2 studies	**9-20% (11%)**	11-17% (15%)	-	-
Spain, 10 studies	**8-34% (17%)**	10-31% (16%)	**8-31% (11%)**	10-32% (22%)
China, 15 studies	**7-59% (30%)**	7-62% (13%)	**1-13% (9%)**	6-22% (17%)
India, 11 studies	**18-51% (36%)**	6-26% (31%)	**6-26% (17%)**	31-57% (38%)

Note: * not specified. Road dust contributions may contain also wear emissions in some cases.

2.4. The negative consequences of exposure to non-exhaust emissions

The evidence for adverse health effects of particulate matter has grown dramatically in the past 20 years, and PM2.5 is understood to be associated with particularly harmful health effects. The Global Burden of Disease study ranked exposure to ambient fine particulate matter as the seventh most important risk factor for mortality – causing 4.2 million premature deaths in 2016 globally (OECD, 2017[84]; Wang et al., 2016[85]).[12] A large fraction of urban populations are exposed to levels of fine particulate matter in excess of limit values set for the protection of human health. In Europe, 8.6 months of YPLL (Years of Potential Life Lost) have been blamed to excessive PM2.5 exposure. Numerous epidemiological studies have also demonstrated correlations between PM exposure and the occurrence of acute respiratory infections, lung cancer, and chronic respiratory and cardiovascular diseases (de Kok et al., 2006[86]; Heinrich and Slama, 2007[87]).

Although they note that no comprehensive studies have directly linked brake wear PM with adverse health outcomes, Grigoratos and Martini (2014[88]) review evidence demonstrating the negative health impacts of PM and of the chemical components of non-exhaust emissions. The mechanisms underlying the health effects of inhaled PM have been well-studied in the laboratory and there is general agreement regarding the key roles played by cellular injury and inflammation. In 2013, the WHO noted the possibility of the negative impacts of non-exhaust emissions, identifying them among the main sources of ambient PM and stating that the toxicological evidence increasingly shows that non-exhaust emissions could be responsible for some of the health effects of traffic-related pollution (WHO Regional Office for Europe, 2013[89]).

Particle mass, number, size and chemistry all affect PM toxicity. Regarding PM chemical composition, evidence continues to accumulate on the adverse effects that oxidative stress, which is often related to transition metals and redox active organics, such as quinone, has on human health (Ayres et al., 2008[90]; Borm et al., 2007[91]; Cassee et al., 2013[92]; Kelly, 2003[93]). Ambient PM derived from vehicles has a high oxidative potential (Kelly, 2003[93]) and it has been found that a clear increment in roadside particulate oxidative potential is associated with metals arising from non-exhaust emissions (Fedotov et al., 2014[94]; Thorpe and Harrison, 2008[45]; Schauer et al., 2006[95]). The roadside increments of particulate oxidative potential are significant and the metal components identified as determinants of this oxidative activity have associated with toxicity in human beings (Atkinson et al., 2009[96]). These results are important, as they highlight the contribution of currently non-regulated non-exhaust pollutants to negative health outcomes.

While it is unlikely that transition metals can explain all of the health effects observed in epidemiological studies at present ambient levels, measures to reduce them will most likely lead to improvements in the health status of the population. It is also unlikely that metals concentrations in ambient air are due exclusively to non-exhaust sources. Metal oxides are substances traditionally considered to be relatively inert chemically, but in very small size ranges, they have been linked with significant oxidative stress-mediated toxicity (Duffin, Mills and Donaldson, 2007[97]).

The presence of aluminium and silicon in particles has been associated with health problems, particularly respiratory ones (Batalha et al., 2002[98]; Rhoden et al., 2004[99]; Wellenius et al., 2003[100]). Other elements, including iron, copper, zinc and sulphur have also shown associations with health impacts, such as cardio-pulmonary oxidative stress, heart-rate variability and tissue damage in vivo (Gurgueira et al., 2002[101]; Kodavanti et al., 2005[102]; Rohr et al., 2011[103]). For example, in tests with laboratory animals, it has been shown that combined exposure to tyre wear dust and zinc and copper at high concentrations can lead to cardiac oxidative stress (Gottipolu et al., 2008[104]).

This part summarizes the work reported by Amato et al. (2019[105]), who performed a systematic review of epidemiological studies on non-exhaust source contributions and 15 possible tracers (Cu, Pb, Zn, Fe, Mn, Ca, Al, Si, Ti, K, Ni, Cr, Mg, Sb, and Ba). That report extracts results for Cu, Zn, Fe, Ca, Si, Sb, and Ba considering these elements are the most reliable tracers according to Table 2.1. Epidemiological studies have assessed the impact of non-exhaust emissions through two main exposure indicators: i) elements, also defined as tracers (even though there are no unique tracers of non-exhaust sources); and ii) source contributions obtained from modelling activities. The main study designs used by epidemiologists to investigate the short- and long-run health effects of air pollution are presented in Box 2.5.

2.4.1. Elements

Studies based on elements are more common (45 studies). The main advantage of this approach is that elements can be analysed separately and there is no need for a full chemical speciation of PM samples. The main limitation is that elements are less suitable exposure indicators than source contributions, since they are usually emitted by multiple sources. However, most of the variance can be due to a single non-exhaust source. Among elements, studies analysed always a discrete group of elements including one or some non-exhaust tracers (Table 2.1) but often including also other elements/components.

Based on Table 2.1, results are presented for copper, iron, antimony, barium, calcium, silicon and zinc, which are more often identified as suitable tracers, although not unique. Among them, silicon and calcium, are probably those which serve less, since their non-traffic share is generally higher. Although antimony and copper will be significantly reduced in the future manufacturing, they can still offer valid information for time-series and case-crossover studies using historical data. The remaining elements of Table 2.1 have been excluded since they are less suitable tracers: their variance in ambient air is more due to other sources rather than to non-exhaust emissions. It is also noteworthy that barium have rarely been analysed, while it potentially offers very useful information, since it is more unique tracer than others in the sense that fewer other sources of barium exist.

Results from element-based studies can be influenced by the method employed. For example, for some trace elements, X-Ray Fluorescence (XRF) has a much higher detection limit than Inductively Coupled Plasma-Mass Spectrometry (ICP-MS) and this may affect determination of trace elements at low concentrations.

2.4.2. Source contributions

Studies based on source apportionment are much fewer (8 studies), due to two main factors: i) a large number of elements/compounds is needed, increasing considerably the costs; ii) the difficulty of receptor modelling tools to identify clearly non-exhaust contributions. The main advantage is that a source contribution is interpreted as the total contribution from that source, including all contained toxics. The main limitation is that one can hardly separate all non-exhaust sources, implying that if the factor is identified as a mix, e.g. "non-exhaust" or "road dust/brake wear", the estimated health effects cannot be attributed to a specific non-exhaust source; and that if the factor is not correctly labelled, e.g. labelled as "road dust" while also including direct wear emissions, the estimated health effects are erroneously attributed only to a single source.

The review presented below shows only the 8 studies where the contribution of non-exhaust emissions was well separated from other mineral sources (Table 2.6). In fact, most of the source apportionment studies showed a generic "road dust/crustal" and "soil/road dust" or even a "soil" source with the road dust component simply mentioned in the text as a possible contributor of the mixture, and were therefore excluded from the analysis. A study using PM1-10 mass concentration is also included to draw on the health effects of road and tyre wear emissions due to the use of studded tyres.

Box 2.5. Study designs for air pollution epidemiology

Studies of short-term effects

The two main study designs for investigating the short-term effects of air pollution are time-series and case-crossover studies. In time series studies, exposure is measured or estimated for each time unit (e.g. day) homogeneously across the study area. Health outcomes, such as daily health indicators (e.g. mortality or morbidity) are also measured in the same area, so that temporal variability in exposure can be related to temporal variability in the health outcome. An important advantage of time-series studies is that the exposed population is compared with itself, hence time-invariant population characteristics are automatically controlled for. Confounders like population dynamics and weather conditions are controlled for in the regression models. Models also control for time trends and seasonality.

In case-crossover studies, the underlying principle is that when the effect of an exposure is immediate and reversible, the observed cases can be matched with themselves on past periods when the studied outcome had not occurred. Then the exposure on the case day and the exposures on case-free (control) days are contrasted to derive an estimate of the effect of interest. This approach has the advantage of preventing confounding by individual time-fixed characteristics, since comparisons are done within subjects. The "time-stratified" approach (Levy et al., 2001[106]), uses same weekdays of the case period within the same month and year as control periods.

In general, time series analyses are more flexible than case-crossover designs to model time trend, but case-crossover designs are better suited to analyse individual characteristics as effect modifiers, or are the only possible option when the daily exposure of interest is not an average of a domain, but is heterogeneous over space (Stafoggia and Faustini, 2018[107]).

Studies of long-term effects

Long-term effects are investigated through cohort studies and survival analysis. A cohort is a group of people who share a common exposure within a defined period and whose effect on health may occur much later in time. Then, a cohort study is a particular form of longitudinal study enrolling a cohort and following it over time usually until the occurrence of a specified outcome, or the end of the study. Exposure is usually assessed at the residential address of cohort participants by land-use regression, dispersion models or hybrid approaches. Exposure can be "fixed" (when attributed only once at baseline or as a long-term average), or time-dependent (when assessed repeatedly over the follow-up years for each individual). At any point in time, the "risk set" is made of all subjects at risk of incurring the study outcome at that time, while the cases are the events occurring at that time.

In the analysis of long-term effects of air pollution, it is assumed that the risk of mortality/morbidity is higher for increasing levels of long-term exposure at the residence. In order to test this hypothesis, conventional approaches of survival analysis (analysis of time-to-event data) are applied. The most used survival model is the "Cox proportional-hazards model" which assumes that the effect of a unit increase in the exposure is multiplicative with respect to the hazard rate, and it imposes no assumption on the shape of the hazard function. In the analysis of the association between long-term exposure to air pollution and mortality/morbidity outcomes, individual hazard rates are regressed against (baseline or time-dependent) exposure attributed at the residential address of each subject, while controlling for individual-level covariates (e.g. age, gender, lifestyle variables and comorbidities) and area-level indicators of socio-economic status (Stafoggia and Faustini, 2018[107])

Source: Levy et al. (2001[106]); Stafoggia and Faustini (2018[107]).

2.4.3. Impacts of non-exhaust emissions on mortality

Short-term effects

The countries under study were the United States (6 studies), Chile (2), Canada, Korea, China, Spain, UK and a group of 5 Southern European cities (one study each). Thirteen studies used elements as indicators of exposure,[13] while three studies applied source apportionment. However, only one study clearly disentangled a non-exhaust source contribution (Ostro et al., 2011[108]). Results show that:

Seven studies found significant association between exposure to Zinc and natural/all cause causes (2 studies), cardiovascular (5 studies), respiratory (2 studies) and ischaemic heart disease (1 study) mortality; other four studies investigating natural/all cause (4 studies), cardiovascular (3 studies) and respiratory (3 studies) mortality did not find significant associations.

Six studies found significant association between exposure to Iron and natural/all cause (3 studies), cardiovascular (3 studies), respiratory (1 study) and ischaemic heart disease (1 study) mortality; other four studies investigating natural/all cause (3 studies), cardiovascular (3 studies), respiratory (2 studies), COPD (1 study) and cerebrovascular (1 study) mortality did not find significant associations.

Five studies found significant association between exposure to Copper and natural/all cause (3 studies), respiratory (2 studies) and ischaemic heart disease (1 study) mortality; other four studies investigating natural/all cause (2 studies), , cardiovascular (3 studies), respiratory (3 studies), COPD (1 study) and cerebrovascular (1 study) mortality did not find significant associations.

Four studies found significant association between exposure to silicon and natural/all cause (2 studies), cardiovascular (2 studies) and respiratory (1 study) mortality; other four studies investigating natural/all cause (3 studies), cardiovascular (4 studies), respiratory (4 studies), COPD (1 study) and cerebrovascular (1 study) mortality did not find significant associations.

Two studies found significant association between exposure to Calcium and natural/all cause (2 studies), cardiovascular and respiratory mortality (1 study); other four studies investigating natural/all cause (4 studies), cardiovascular (5 studies), respiratory (4 studies), COPD (1 study) and cerebrovascular (1 study) mortality did not find significant associations. Antimony and Barium were both associated with cardiovascular and respiratory mortality (1 study), but not with natural mortality (1 study).

The only study on source apportionment clearly identifying a non-exhaust contribution was carried out in Barcelona (see also Table 2.6) (Ostro et al., 2011[108]) where authors disentangled the road dust contribution from other mineral sources. They applied a constrained Positive Matrix Factorization on PM10 and PM2.5 filters in Barcelona to estimate daily contributions from eight sources from 2003 to 2007, including road dust and motor exhaust. They applied the case-crossover design (see Box 2.5) to estimate the association between daily source contribution and all-cause and cardiovascular mortality. They found a significant association between road dust PM2.5 and all-cause deaths, with mortality increasing by 4.2% per 1.8 µg/m3 increase in a daily road dust load in PM2.5. The estimate was similar to that found for the vehicle exhaust: mortality rises by 3.7% per 5.2 µg/m3 increase. For PM10, only vehicle exhaust emissions had a statistically significant impact on all-cause mortality, amounting to a 3.6% increase per 5.2 µg/m3. For cardiovascular mortality, road dust showed an excess risk of 6.7% per 1.8 µg/m3 increase in PM2.5 while vehicle exhaust had no significant effect. In contrast, vehicle exhaust emissions were associated with a 6.4% increase in the risk of cardiovascular mortality per 5.2 µg/m3 increase of PM10, while the impact of road dust was statistically insignificant.

In summary, 13 out of 14 studies found at least one statistically significant association between one of our selected indicators for non-exhaust emissions (either elemental or source contribution) and all-cause mortality as well as for specific causes, such as cardiovascular, respiratory and ischaemic heart disease. The only study with no positive associations for the selected indicators did find however significant association for Mg which has also been used as a possible indicator of road dust (Amato et al., 2019[105]).

Long-term effects

Long-term mortality studies have been carried out in the United States (7 studies) and Europe (5 studies). Most studies are based on the elemental tracer approach,[14] while two studies have used source apportioned data (Desikan et al., 2016[109]; Tonne et al., 2016[110]). Four studies found significant association between exposure to Iron and natural/all cause (2 studies),, cardiovascular (2 studies) and ischaemic heart disease (3 studies) mortality; other six studies investigating natural/all cause (3 studies), cardiovascular (2 studies), IHD (2 studies) and respiratory, pulmonary and lung cancer (1 study each) mortality did not find significant associations.

Three studies found significant association between exposure to Copper and natural/all cause (1 study), cardiovascular (1 study) and ischaemic heart disease (2 studies) mortality; other five studies investigating natural/all cause (3 studies), cardiovascular (2 studies), and respiratory, IHD and lung cancer (1 study each) mortality did not find significant associations.

Three studies found significant association between exposure to Zinc and natural/all cause (2 studies), cardiovascular (2 studies), and ischaemic heart disease (3 studies) mortality; other six studies investigating natural/all cause (3 studies), cardiovascular (2 studies), and respiratory, IHD, pulmonary, CHF, MI, COPD, Diabetes and lung cancer (1 study each) mortality did not find significant associations.

Five studies found significant association between exposure to Silicon and natural/all cause (2 studies), respiratory (1 study), cardiovascular (1 study), ischemic heart disease (2 studies), cardio-pulmonary (1 study) and pulmonary (1 study) mortality; other four studies investigating natural/all-cause (3 studies), cardiovascular (2 studies), ischemic heart disease (2 studies) and lung cancer (1 study) mortality did not find significant associations.

Two studies found significant association between exposure to Calcium and respiratory, CHF, MI, COPD, and diabetes mortality; other four studies investigating natural/all-cause (2 studies), ischemic heart disease (2 studies), cardiovascular (1 study) and lung cancer (1 study) mortality did not find significant associations. Barium was not associated with all-cause or cardiovascular mortality, and antimony was not associated with cardiovascular mortality

With respect to source apportionment studies, long term mortality was investigated for all causes and stroke (Table 2.6). Tonne et al. (2016[110]) investigated both long-term all-cause mortality and myocardial infarction morbidity using a modelling approach for exhaust and non-exhaust PM in Greater London. They followed more than 18 000 patients from the myocardial infarction National Audit Project for both death and readmission for myocardial infarction for the years 2003–2010. They found that most air pollutants were positively associated with all-cause mortality alone and in combination with hospital readmission. The largest associations with all-cause mortality per interquartile range (IQR) increase of pollutant were observed for non-exhaust contributions to PM10 (Hazard ratio

= 1.05, IQR = 1.1 μg/m3). For the PM2.5 fraction, the hazard ratio was slightly lower (1.04), for an IQR equal to 0.3 μg/m3. For both PM fractions, exhaust emissions were not significantly associated with morbidity or mortality.

Desikan et al. (2016[109]) combined a high-resolution urban air quality dispersion model for South London with a population-based stroke register to explore associations between long-term exposure to modelled non-exhaust and exhaust PM and mortality risk in post-stroke patients (within 5 years). The authors acknowledge that one limitation of their study is that they did not quantify individual pollution exposure, but instead used pollution levels at residential postcode addresses as a proxy for individual exposure to pollutants. Neither non-exhaust emissions of PM2.5 nor of PM10 were associated with increased mortality in post-stroke patients.

Of 12 studies, 11 found a statistically significant association between some non-exhaust indicator and long-term mortality. Besides all-cause and natural mortality, non-exhaust PM were also significantly associated with ischemic heart disease, cardiovascular/cardiopulmonary, respiratory, CHF, MI, COPD, and diabetes mortality.

2.4.4. Impact of non-exhaust emissions on morbidity and cognitive development

Short-term effects

Thirteen studies in this review investigate the impact of several constituent elements of non-exhaust emissions on short-term morbidity.[15] Zanobetti et al. (2009[111]) (Suh et al., 2011[112]; Tiittanen et al., 1999[113]; Sun et al., 2016[114]; Samoli et al., 2016[115]; Zanobetti et al., 2009[116]) also used source contributions as exposure indicators. A number of studies were conducted in the United States, and one study was conducted each in Chile, China, the UK, and a group of five Southern European cities.

Five studies found a significant association between exposure to Copper and cardiovascular and respiratory hospitalisations (4 studies and 2 studies, respectively). Three other studies investigating cardiovascular, respiratory, and stroke morbidity (1 study each) did not find significant associations between these elements and short term morbidity. Four studies found a significant association between exposure to Zinc and natural/all cause, cardiovascular and respiratory hospitalisations (1 study, 3 studies, and 2 studies, respectively). Another five studies investigating cardiovascular and respiratory conditions (3 studies each), and myocardial infarction, congestive heart failure, diabetes, stroke and heart rate morbidity (1 study each) did not find significant associations.

Four studies found a significant association between exposure to Iron and natural/all cause, cardiovascular and respiratory hospitalisations (1 study, 3 studies, and 1 study, respectively). Another six studies investigating cardiovascular and respiratory morbidity (2 studies each), and diabetes, stroke, heart rate and cough morbidity (1 study each) did not find significant associations with exposure to Iron. Three studies found a significant association between exposure to Calcium and natural/all cause, cardiovascular and respiratory hospitalisations (1 study, 1 study, and 2 studies, respectively). Six other studies investigating cardiovascular and respiratory morbidity (3 studies each) and diabetes and stroke morbidity (1 study each) did not find significant associations.

Three studies found a significant association between exposure to Silicon and natural/all cause, cardiovascular and respiratory hospitalisations (1 study, 1 study, and 3 studies, respectively). Five studies investigating cardiovascular and respiratory morbidity (4 studies and 3 studies, respectively) and diabetes, stroke, congestive heart failure and myocardial infarction morbidity (1 study each) did not find significant associations.

Antimony and Barium have been associated with natural/all cause and respiratory hospitalisations (1 study).

Results from studies analysing biomarkers and clinically specific outcomes should be considered with some caution, since they generally report wide confidence intervals. This also extends to studies of long-term morbidity effects, presented in the next subsection.

The only study using source apportionment that separates a non-exhaust contribution on morbidity was conducted by Kioumourtzoglou et al. (2014[117]) (Table 2.6). In this study, the authors examined the effects of PM2.5 sources on emergency cardiovascular hospital admissions among Medicare enrolees in Boston, MA between 2003 and 2010. They also studied the effect of uncertainty in source contributions using a block bootstrap procedure. While inconsistent associations across different source apportionment methods were observed for exposure to road dust, exposure to exhaust PM2.5 was associated with increased admissions.

In summary, six of the 13 studies reviewed found at least one statistically significant association between an indicator of non-exhaust PM (either elemental, ionic or source contribution) and short-term morbidity. Respiratory and cardiovascular morbidity were the principle types of morbidity associated with exposure to indicators of non-exhaust PM. Of the seven remaining studies, five found a significant association between other elements (e.g. Ni, Al and Mg) that have been also used as possible indicators of non-exhaust PM (Amato et al., 2019[105]) and short term morbidities.

Long-term effects

Fifteen studies included in the review investigated the association between long-term exposure to non-exhaust PM and hospitalisations or other biomarkers. Thirteen studies were carried out in Europe, mostly as part of the ESCAPE and TRANSPHORM projects[16] and two studies were conducted in the United States (Basu et al., 2014[118]; Vedal et al., 2013[119]). Eleven studies examined exposure to specific elements and four used source apportionment. Results show that:

Six studies found a significant association between exposure to Iron and cardiovascular and lung cancer hospitalisations, impaired lung function, high blood pressure, low birthweight and markers of inflammatory (1 study each). Four studies investigated cardiovascular morbidity, impaired lung function, pneumonia and low birthweight (1 study each) and did not find significant associations.

Six studies found significant association between exposure to Zinc and pneumonia (1 study) and lung cancer (1 study) hospitalisations, lung function (1 study), low birthweight size (2 studies) and inflammatory marker (1 study); other four studies investigating cardiovascular (2 studies), lung function, and blood pressure (1 study each) morbidity did not find significant associations

Five studies found significant association between exposure to Copper and a marker of cardiovascular disease, lung cancer hospitalisations, low birthweight and inflammatory markers (1 study, 1 study, 2 studies, and 1 study, respectively). Another five studies investigated cardiovascular morbidity (2 studies) and lung function, pneumonia and blood pressure morbidity (1 study each) did not find significant associations with exposure to Copper.

Three studies found a significant association between exposure to Silicon and cardiovascular hospitalisations, blood pressure and low birthweight (1 study each). Six studies investigating indicators of cardiovascular disease, lung cancer, impaired lung function, pneumonia, low birthweight and inflammatory markers (1 study each) did not find significant associations with exposure to Silicon.

Calcium was investigated for low birthweight (1 study) and carotid intima-media thickness and coronary artery calcium (1 study), finding no significant associations. Antimony and Barium were not associate with coronary artery calcium nor with carotid intima-media thickness.

Long-term effects on morbidity were investigated by four source apportionment studies (Table 2.6) (including the one by Tonne et al. (2016[110]), while another study investigated the effect of traffic sources on cognitive development in children. Willers et al. (2013[120]) investigated the effects of exposure to particulate matter fractions (PM1 and PM1-10) on respiratory health in the Swedish adult population, using an integrated assessment of sources at different geographical scales. They assumed PM1-10 to be a proxy of road-tyre wear particles, which is a reasonable assumption in the case of Sweden due to the use of studded tyres, implying that the dominant source of coarse PM is wear and road dust resuspension. The study was based on a nationwide environmental health survey performed in 2007, including 25 851 adults aged 18–80 years. Individual exposure to PM at residential addresses was estimated by dispersion modelling of regional, urban and local sources. Associations between different size fractions or source categories and respiratory outcomes were analysed using multiple logistic regression, controlling for individual and contextual factors. Exposure to locally generated wear particles showed associations for blocked nose or hay fever, chest tightness or cough, and restricted activity days with odds ratios of 1.5–2 per 10 µg/m3 increase.

Crichton et al. (2016[121]) combined a high resolution urban air quality model for South London with a population-based stroke register to explore associations between long-term exposure to PM sources and stroke incidence (2005–2012). No associations were observed between non-exhaust sources and overall ischemic or haemorrhagic incidence, while a 20% increase of total anterior circulation infarct for an interquartile range (0.78–0.96 µg/m3) of exhaust PM was found.

Dadvand et al. (2014[122]) investigated a hospital cohort of pregnant women (N=3182) residing in Barcelona, Spain, during 2003–2005. Positive Matrix Factorization source apportionment (PMF) was used to identify sources of PM10 and PM2.5 samples obtained by an urban background monitor, resulting in the detection of eight sources. They separated brake wear and vehicle exhaust and generated a comprehensive indicator of combined traffic sources, including also a fraction of secondary nitrate/organics. For the exposure during the entire pregnancy, they found a 44% increase in the risk of preeclampsia associated with one IQR increase in exposure to PM10 brake dust (4.7 µg/m3), and an 80% increase from one IQR rise in exposure to PM10 from all traffic-related sources (15.7 µg/m3) combined. For vehicle exhaust alone, they did not find a significant association with preeclampsia.

Finally, Basagaña et al. (2016[123]) investigated associations between traffic-related air pollution exposure at schools and cognitive development. Using a cohort of 2 618 schoolchildren (average age of 8.5 years) belonging to 39 schools in Barcelona, they found that an interquartile range (3.8 µg/m3) increase in motor exhaust PM2.5 was associated with reductions in cognitive growth equivalent to 22% of the annual change in working memory, 30% of the annual change in superior working memory, and 11% of the annual change in the inattentiveness scale. Non-exhaust PM2.5 sources were not associated with adverse effects on cognitive development.

In summary, 12 of the 15 studies found at least one statistically significant association between an indicator of non-exhaust PM (either elemental or source contribution) and long-term morbidity or increase in biomarkers. Non-exhaust PM were associated with several causes of morbidity, mainly cardiovascular, lung cancer, lung function, pneumonia, myocardial infarction, respiratory markers and preeclampsia. Significant associations were also found with other endpoints, such as carotid intima-media thickness (CIMT), inflammatory markers, fibrinogen, birthweight and blood pressure in children.

Table 2.6 summarizes results from source apportionment studies, allowing a comparison between vehicle exhaust and non-exhaust emissions. Since epidemiological studies imply a linear dose-response function, the increased risk can be normalised by the IQR, so that estimates per µg/m3 are obtained. Following this approach, road emissions in Barcelona resulted in a higher risk (2.3% per µg/m3) than exhaust emissions (0.7%) of short-term all-cause and cardiovascular mortality (Ostro et al., 2011[108]), but with some overlap of their confidence intervals (0.8-3.9 and 0.1-1.3 respectively). Since the study did not separate any direct wear emission factor, the "road dust" source should be probably interpreted as a general "non-exhaust" source. Kioumourtzoglou et al. (2014[117]) found that cardiovascular emergency visits in Boston were instead significantly associated only with exhaust emissions, but not with road dust.

For long-term effects, Tonne et al. (2016[110]) found that all-cause long-term mortality in London was positively associated with non-exhaust emissions, for both PM2.5 and PM10. Other long-term studies concluded that respiratory symptoms and preeclampsia were only associated with non-exhaust PM, rather than with exhaust ones, while the opposite was found for stroke incidence and cognitive development in children.

Table 2.7 summarizes the qualitative associations between exposure to non-exhaust emission indicators and increased risk of short-term and long-term mortality and morbidity.

Table 2.6. Overview of findings of epidemiological studies using source apportionment analysis

Study	Country	Period	Health outcome	Non-exhaust source	Increased risk (95% confidence interval) per increase of non-exhaust PM	Increased risk (95% confidence interval) per increase of exhaust PM
Ostro et al. (2011[108])	Spain	2003-2007	Short-term total mortality	Road dust (PM2.5)	4.2% (1.5-7.0%) per 1.8 µg/m3	3.7% (0.7-6.7%) per 5.2 µg/m3
				Road dust (PM10)	No effect	3.6% (0.1-7.2%) per 5.2 µg/m3
			Short-term cardiovascular mortality	Road dust (PM2.5)	6.7% (2.4-11.3%) per 1.8 µg/m3	No effect
				Road dust (PM10)	No effect	6.4% (1.5-11.6%) per 5.2 µg/m3
Kioumourtzoglou et al. (2014[117])	MA, USA	2003-2010	Short-term cardiovascular emergency visits	Road dust (PM2.5)	No effect	1.44% (0.02- 3.11%) per 1.1 µg/m3
Tonne et al. (2016[110])	UK	2003-2010	Long-term all-cause mortality	Non-exhaust contribution (PM10)	5% (0-10%) per 1.1 µg/m3	No effect
				Non-exhaust contribution (PM2.5)	4% (0-9%) per 0.3 µg/m3	No effect

Desikan et al. (2016[109])	UK	2005-2013	Long-term all-cause mortality	Non-exhaust contribution (PM10 and PM2.5)	No effect	No effect
Willers et al. (2013[120])	Sweden	2007	Long-term respiratory symptoms	Road and tyre wear (PM1-10)	1.5–2 odds ratio* per 10 µg/m3	No effect
Dadvand et al. (2014[122])	Spain	2003-2005	Preeclampsia in pregnant women	Brake wear (PM10)	1.44 (1.07-1.94) odds ratio per 0.5 µg/m3	No effect
Crichton et al. (2016[121])	UK	2005-2012	Long-term stroke incidence	Non-exhaust contribution (PM10 and PM2.5)	No effect	20% (1-41%) per 0.78–0.96 µg/m3
Basagaña et al. (2016[123])	Spain	2012-2013	Cognitive development	Road dust (PM2.5)	No effect	22% (2-42%) per 3.8 µg/m3

Note: Only studies clearly identifying a non-exhaust source are presented in this table. Studies analysing biomarkers and/or clinical specific outcomes should be considered with caution, since they reported very wide confidence intervals. *Range of observed symptoms, confidence intervals reported in Willers et al. (2013).

Table 2.7. Health effects of non-exhaust tracers concentrations and source contributions

Exposure indicator	Mortality		Morbidity		Other symptoms/biomarkers
	Short-term	Long-term	Short-term	Long-term	Long-term
Copper	All-cause, respiratory and ischemic heart disease	All-cause, cardiovascular and ischemic heart disease	Cardiovascular and respiratory	Lung cancer, carotid intima-media thickness	Low birthweight and inflammatory marker
Zinc	All-cause, cardiovascular, respiratory and ischemic heart disease	All-cause, cardiovascular and ischemic heart disease	Non-accidental, cardiovascular and respiratory	Pneumonia and lung cancer	Lung function, low birthweight and inflammatory marker
Iron	All-cause, cardiovascular, respiratory and ischemic heart disease	All-cause, cardiovascular and ischemic heart disease	Cardiovascular and respiratory	Cardiovascular and lung cancer	Lung function, blood pressure, low birthweight and inflammatory marker
Silicon	All-cause, cardiovascular and respiratory	All-cause, cardiovascular, respiratory, pulmonary and ischemic heart disease		Cardiovascular	Blood pressure and low birthweight
Calcium	All-cause, cardiovascular and respiratory	Respiratory	Non-accidental, cardiovascular and respiratory		
Barium	Cardiovascular and respiratory		Non-accidental and respiratory		
Antimony	Cardiovascular and respiratory		Non-accidental and respiratory		
Source contributions	All-cause and cardiovascular	All-cause		Myocardial infarction and Preeclampsia	Respiratory

2.5. The causes of non-exhaust emissions

This section is aimed at describing the mechanisms, vehicle and road features underpinning the generation and dispersion of non-exhaust emissions and analysis of their role in determining the magnitude of emissions. The different methodological approaches used to quantify the impact of each of these drivers are also reviewed.

2.5.1. Brake wear

When drivers press the brake pedal, kinetic energy is transformed mostly into frictional heat between the brake lining (pad) and a rotor (disc or drum) and wear particles are generated. A friction process is always accompanied by the formation of friction products. Friction products include an external layer on the pad surface made of newly formed materials, brake wear PM emissions and emissions of gaseous pollutants.

The air quality burden depends mostly on the generation of airborne particles with a diameter below 10 µm. During the friction process, not all worn particles become airborne, Sanders et al. (2003[37]) report that only 50% of brake wear was emitted as airborne and the PM10 fraction accounted for 63%-85% of the airborne material. The wear of pads and rotors generate particles of various sizes and morphology, and each combination of speed, pressure, and temperature leads to a different amount of wear (Kukutschová et al., 2009[124]). In addition, the amount (measured as mass or number) of emitted particles likely depend also on braking frequency, vehicle weight, and the composition and age of pad and disc. In sum, the size and number of emitted particles depends on driving, vehicle and brake characteristics.

Quantifying the role of each factor is a very difficult task since the operation of brake systems is quite complex and often stochastic in nature, so it is not possible to simulate all braking scenarios. This hampers quantitative comparisons among different studies, since testing devices, testing procedures, sampling conditions and brake materials are different. This is mostly because no recommended approach for the generation, measurement, and expression of brake wear emissions exists yet (Panko, Kreider and Unice, 2018[59]). For example, braking tests can be performed with simplified laboratory tests (e.g., pin-on-disc), or by subscale and full-scale brake dynamometers and real field tests.[17] Nevertheless, these tests can hardly predict the wear behaviour of real brake systems (Grigoratos and Martini, 2015[6]; Kukutschová and Filip, 2018[125]; Lee and Filip, 2013[126]). Depending on the set-up, laboratory studies can differ in size of the tested pad samples, adopted sliding velocity and deceleration, particle generation rate, airflow regime and driving regime from real-world conditions. These differences further result in differences in energy generated per area and mass and per unit time to heat up the tested materials, which can also influence parameters of wear particles (Kukutschová and Filip, 2018[125]).

Rotor temperature

Rotor temperature is the most studied parameter. Typically, wear increases with increasing temperature (Filip, 2013[127]; Filip, Weiss and Rafaja, 2002[128]). Depending on the temperature reached, we can distinguish between "mechanical" and "oxidative" wear. At high temperatures (probably reached under extreme braking) wear of polymer matrix pads is accompanied with oxidative processes associated with considerable mass loss due to polymer degradation and formation of volatiles. This is characteristic for high-temperature braking scenarios, when numerous thermally less stable components (e.g., phenolic resin, rubber, graphite, coke) interact with available gases and oxygen from the ambient air (Kukutschová et al., 2009[124]) or undergo a pyrolysis (Plachá et al., 2017[4]). This degradation of organic components is associated with emissions of very fine amorphous carbon particles with negligible contribution to PM mass and volatile organic compounds (Kukutschová et al., 2011[3]; Plachá et al., 2017[4]). At lower temperatures, "mechanical" wear dominates. In general, the adhesive wear mechanism is combined with abrasive wear, fatigue wear mechanisms, and oxidative wear as well. Thus, the produced brake wear debris is a complex mixture containing particles with sizes ranging from several nanometres to millimetres and the chemistry of wear debris is significantly different compared with the original pad material constituents, but typically comparable with the chemistry of a friction layer (Kukutschová et al., 2009[124]; Roubicek et al., 2008[129]).

Oxidative wear can generate very fine (submicron-sized), typically round-shaped particles. These submicrometric particles are formed by condensation of volatile gaseous compounds generated by thermal degradation of organic binder in brake pads. Iron oxide particles, produced not only by oxidative mild wear of the cast iron disc but also from oxidation of iron-based ingredients of metallic pads, are typically present in friction layer and together with elemental carbon from resin and other organic pad constituents represent one of the main components of airborne wear debris.

Mechanical wear (abrasive and fatigue wear) typically leads to the release of larger particles, belonging mainly to PM10 or PM2.5 fractions. These particles usually have sharper edges and irregular morphology (Kukutschová et al., 2011[3]). Alemani et al. (2016[130]) found that with temperature increasing from 100 to 300°C, the ultrafine particle emissions intensifies, while the coarse particle emission decreases. Similarly, Kukutschová et al. (2011[3]) found that testing conditions of a relatively cold rotor (below and around 200°C) led to negligible emissions of submicron particles. After the rotor temperature reached 300°C, a gradual increase of the finest fractions, including the nanosized particles (<100 nm) reaching concentration up to 10^6 per cm^3, was detected. From the shape of the particle size distributions and their variation with time, it could be assumed that submicron particles are formed by the evaporation/ condensation process with a subsequent aggregation of the primary nanosized particles. In contrast, the detected concentrations of larger microsized particles were not so strongly affected by increasing rotor temperature.

Sliding speed, deceleration and contact pressure

Mosleh et al. (2004[131]) generated wear particles from commercial metallic truck brake pads but focused on settled particles only (not airborne). The study addressed effects of contact pressure, sliding speed, and continuity of sliding contact on particle size distribution and the chemistry of collected wear particles. The generated particles had a bimodal distribution, with a first peak at approximately 350 nm (composition corresponding to the cast iron disc), and a second peak between 2 and 15 µm, depending on the pressure and sliding speed. Importantly, when the motion was discontinuous at a repeated brake action, smaller wear particles were generated. Wahlstrom et al (2017[132]) found that the specific wear rate of the disc decreases with increasing contact pressure and sliding velocity. The particle mass and number rates seem to decrease with increasing contact pressure and sliding velocity until the disc temperature is about 200 °C; thereafter they increase.

Few studies have evaluated the impact of acceleration or deceleration rate on non-exhaust PM generation. In general, acceleration results in slightly increased brake emissions due to the drag effect (zum Hagen et al., 2019[133]). Hagino, Oyama and Sasaki (2015[134]) focused on the quantification of PM10 and PM2.5 emissions by mass and the evaluation of resuspended particles. Airborne wear particles were not only detected at deceleration as a direct brake wear but also occurred at acceleration (non-braking event), suggesting resuspension of wear particles. These particles had increasing concentration during acceleration with an increasing initial speed. Based on their findings, the resuspended particles should be included in emission measurements.

Riediker et al. (2008) tested pad materials of six different passenger cars under controlled environmental conditions and found a bimodal PN distribution with peaks at 80 nm (depending on the tested car and braking behaviour) and at 200-400 nm (0.2-0.4 µm). They found that complete stops result in higher nanoparticle production compared with normal deceleration. Sanders et al. (2003[37]) found that emission factors were increasing by a factor of 4 when comparing a deceleration rate of 0.6-1.6 m/s^2 (typical urban driving pattern) to an aggressive deceleration rate of 1.8 m/s^2. Lee et al. (2013[135]) found that when a vehicle decelerates rapidly (2.6 m/s^2), considerable brake wear particles and particles from tyre/road interface are generated. The maximum value of the mass size distribution was located at 1-5 µm, and, unlike constant speed driving conditions, the ratio of nano-particles measuring 50 nm or less was very high.

Vehicle weight

Garg et al. (2000[38]) claim that the inertia weight being stopped is one of the factors contributing to brake wear rate, but they did not perform any tests with varying weights to confirm this. Several individual studies have found higher non-exhaust emission factors for heavier vehicle categories, indicating a correlation with weight. Despite varying definitions for the weight of vehicle categories, the consensus is that light duty trucks (including vans, pick-up trucks and SUVs) emit more PM than passenger cars (Luekewille et al., 2001[136]). Garg et al. (2000[38]) found that the brakes of large cars emit 55% more total suspended particles (TSP), PM10 and PM2.5, than small cars. Large pick-up trucks were found to emit more than double the quantity of particulates compared with small cars. The EMEP/EEA inventory guidebook provides PM10 and PM2.5 emission factors for brake wear for light duty trucks which is 55% higher than passenger cars, and a linear increase with the percentage of HDV load.[18] The recent UK government Survey "Call for Evidence on non-exhaust emissions" acknowledged that emissions vary hugely as a function of weight.

Assuming a linear relationship between weight and brake wear emission factor, Simons (2016[137]) estimated that brake wear PM10 emissions per vehicle-km increase by 0.004 per kg of vehicle weight, using the ecoinvent v2 database. A slightly higher value of 0.0053 can be obtained by dividing the EMEP/EEA PM10 emission factor by 1400, which is the average weight of EU passenger cars (ICCT, 2018[138]; Ntziachristos and Boulter, 2016[56]). For PM2.5 emissions per vehicle-km, the estimates of Simons (2016[137]) and EMEP/EEA factors would be 0.0017 and 0.0021 mg per kg of vehicle weight, respectively.

Brake pad type

Brake lining materials underwent a distinct development in the past three decades. This is related to an effort to develop materials responding to the demand for higher transportation safety, fuel economy, comfort, and performance, as well as to increasing environmental concerns. As a rule, the brake lining material should have: (i) appropriate mechanical and thermal properties, (ii) adequate and stable coefficient of friction in a wide range of operating conditions (temperature, pressure, environment, e.g., dust, water, de-icing agents), and (iii) high resistance to wear and good compatibility with the rubbing counterpart. Ideally, they should operate reliably under hot, dry, wet, or cold conditions, and without pollution and noise, and should be easily manufactured at low costs.

Despite the replacement of asbestos and a gradual elimination of copper in brake pad materials, they have environmental consequences. Wahlström et al. (2010[139]) indicated that the low metallic (LM) pads showed higher friction performance and caused more wear to the rotor than the non-asbestos organic (NAO) pads, resulting in higher mass losses and more concentrations of airborne wear particles. Although there were variations in the measured particle concentrations, similar size distributions of airborne wear particles were obtained regardless of the pad material. Perricone et al. (2016[140]) produced a ranking of pad-rotor combinations. This ranking revealed that NAO pads have the lowest emission factors with respect to mass, but the highest emission factors with respect to particle numbers. LM pads had higher emission factors with respect to mass, and lower ones with respect to particle number.

Sanders et al. (2003[37]), estimated that 60% of the wear debris comes from the rotor and 40% from the pads, as confirmed also by (Hulskotte, Roskam and Denier van der Gon, 2014[34]). The EU-funded LOWBRASYS project aims at demonstrating a novel and low environmental impact brake system that will reduce micro and nanoparticles emissions by at least 50%. Both, particulate emissions in the micrometer range (important for PM mass reduction), as well as ultrafine particles (important for Particulate Number, PN reduction) are addressed.

2.5.2. Tyre and road wear

Vehicle weight

Few studies link tyre wear to vehicle weight, mostly using tyre wear simulator and computational methods (Chen and Prathaban, 2013[141]; Li et al., 2012[142]; Salminen, 2014[143]; Simons, 2016[137]; Wang et al., 2017[144]). Studies agree that tyre wear increases with vehicle weight, but they do not reach a consensus on the shape of this relationship. Wang et al. (2017[144]) and Li et al. (2012[142]) found that the tyre wear (mass loss) increased linearly with increasing vertical load (or sprung mass). Furthermore, the vertical load had a marked influence on the contact pressure distribution. Despite the longer contact length, the vertical contact pressure becomes higher with increasing vertical load, which leads to higher slip forces, and then to more severe wear. Plotting the average wear rates of vehicles with different ranges of maximum admissible vehicle weight, Pohrt (2019[145]) found that the central value in each vehicle category correlates almost linearly with the emission rate. Salminen (2014[143]) simulated numerically an exponential increase but the experimental data used for validation indicated a rather linear relationship between vehicle weight and tyre wear.

Assuming a linear relationship between vehicle weight and tyre wear emissions and using information from the ecoinvent v2 (emission factors and vehicle weight) database, Simons (2016[137]) calculated that tyre wear PM10 emissions per vehicle-km increase at a rate of 0.0041 mg per kg of vehicle weight. A similar value (0.0046) can be obtained for tyre wear by dividing the EMEP/EEA emission factor for passenger car by 1400 Kg which is the mean curb weight in the EU market (ICCT, 2018[138]).[19] For PM2.5 emissions per vehicle-km, the estimates of Simons (2016[137]) and EMEP/EEA factors would be 0.0029 and 0.0032 mg/kg respectively.

The relationship between road wear and vehicle weight has hardly been studies in the literature. While Simons (2016[137]) calculated a value of 0.0049 mg PM10 emissions per kg of vehicle weight per km – assuming a linear relationship – the EMEP/EEA provides the same emission factor for cars and vans, implying that road wear is assumed to be insensitive to weight changes. For PM2.5 emissions per vehicle-km, the estimate of Simons (2016[137]) is 0.0026 mg/kg.

For road wear induced by heavy duty vehicles, (Žnidarič, 2015[146]) estimates a power law of 4 between increased axle load and road wear, but the applicability of this relationship to light duty vehicles is questionable.

Speed and acceleration/deceleration

According got the recent response on UK Survey on non-exhaust emissions, In 30% of tyre wear could be attribute to driving style, so the promotion of better, smoother, more efficient driving styles by incorporating 'eco' driving into standard driver training and custom courses could be a good means of reducing non-exhaust and other emissions.

Speed determines the amount of mechanical stress in the tyre material and thus the wear and temperature of the tyre. Chen and Prathaban (2013[141]) estimated that truck speed has an influence on tyre wear which can vary exponentially from 0.0242 to 0.0244 mm/100km, when vehicle speed increases from 20 km/h to 120 km/h. Wang et al. (2017[144]) found that the normalized amount of tyre wear increases from 0.812 to 1.148 as the rolling velocity increases from -40% to 40% compared with its initial value. Li et al. (2012[142]) found a linear relationship between tyre wear and vehicle speed between 10 and 40 m/s. Foitzik et al. (2018[147]) found similar results for particle number emissions.

Gustafsson et al. (2008[148]) investigated the wear of road surface on a road simulator at different speed levels (30, 50 and 70 km/h) concluding that road wear increases linearly with speed (on a stone mastic asphalt pavement). Speed increased particle mass concentration in the simulator for both studded and friction tyres, but the magnitude of the increase is much higher for studded tyres. Decreased speed of the road simulator results also in a lower particle number concentration, but with the same distribution.

Salminen (2014[143]) found that the wear increases exponentially with speed. He also found that the wear rate increases significantly with longitudinal slip, which occurs when braking or accelerating[20]: tyre wear can vary up to a factor of 2 within a longitudinal slip range of [-0.3,0.3]. Foitzik et al. (2018[147]) found similar results for particle number emissions.

Tyre type and properties

Three types of tyres are available in the market: summer tyres, winter tyres and studded tyres. Winter tyres have a higher natural rubber content that keeps them supple in the cold. They also have a deep tread pattern. Summer tyres provide better all-round performance in the warmer months (temperatures above 7°C). They are composed of a relatively hard compound that softens in milder temperatures to be able to adapt to dry as well as wet roads. Studded tyres contain metal studs embedded within the tread that are designed to dig into ice, providing added traction. When the driving surface is not covered in ice, however, studded tyres can damage road suraces. Many countries limit their use during non-winter months and some states have outlawed them completely. Early tests have shown a marked difference in PM10 generation by different pavement constructions with different rock aggregates when compared to friction tyres resulting from studded tyres (Gustafsson et al., 2009[48]).

Chen and Prathaban (2013[141]) use mathematical models to simulate the effect of varying inflation pressure from 55 to 165 psi on tyre wear concluding that wear decreases exponentially with higher inflation pressure (which is related to the contact patch area) from 0.0265 to 0.0240 mm/100km. Similar findings were found by Li et al. (2012[142]), Salminen (2014[143]) and Wang et al. (2017[144]). Tyre wear is also inversely proportional to tyre diameter and width, whilst it is invariant to tyre groove depth (Chen and Prathaban, 2013[141]; Le Maître, Süssner and Zarak, 1998[149]).[21]

Low rolling resistance tyres are designed to reduce the energy loss as a tyre rolls, decreasing the required rolling effort and improving vehicle fuel efficiency. As more research is being done, wear rates will likely improve, but, at present, no sources suggest that low rolling resistance tyres will have significantly lower wear rates.

Different tyre brand/model can have up to fourfold different wear rate (Grigoratos et al., 2018[150]). Tyre age was found to be an influencing parameter on tyre wear. New tyre can have 10% higher wear rate than used ones (Sakai, 1996[151]).

Road pavement properties

In Finland and Sweden, research has been conducted in similar laboratories to assess the influence of pavement properties on particle emissions, with a strong focus on PM10 and wear resistant pavement constructions, such as stone mastic asphalt (SMA). The Los Angeles abrasion test, measuring the fragmentation capacity of the road pavement material, has been proposed as a proxy measure of PM10 emission potential, since road simulator studies have found a correlation between different Los Angeles test value pavements and emission rates (Gustafsson and Johansson, 2012[152]).

In Finland, Räisänen, Kupiainen and Tervahattu (2005[153]) tested different road pavement using traction sand to increase wear, and concluded that a pavement made with a granitic aggregate composition with higher resistance to abrasive wear resulted in lower PM10 emissions than a pavement made with a mafic volcanic rock. However, it is not self-evident that a material of high abrasion resistance also generates lower PM10. Döse and Åkesson (2011[154]) (cited in Gustafsson and Johansson (2012[152])) studied the amount of PM10 produced in the Nordic ball mill test (with studded tyres) and showed that some materials have higher ball mill values (less resistant), but still do not produce higher PM10 amounts than far more resistant rock aggregates. For rocks with Nordic ball mill values below 10, the authors suggested that for each unit lower value, each ton of rock will produce 4 kg less PM10. However, the results shown are based on a single experimental design and on the specific studded tyre behaviour, so it is not relevant for soft materials like those used in normal tyres.

It is also believed that the diameter of aggregates in the pavements influences the total wear in as much as coarser material results in lesser wear (Jacobson and Wågberg, 2007[155]). Gustafsson and Johansson (2012[152]), China and James (2012[156]) and Amato et al. (2013[157]) found a -1.5 power relationship between mean size of pavement aggregates and road dust loading (R^2=0.52). Padoan et al. (2018[158]) found a -0.2 power relationship with the corrected aggregate mode (correcting the aggregate size mode by the textural depth). Gustafsson and Johansson (2012[152]) concluded that the lower the maximum size of coarse aggregate and the lower the Nordic abrasion value of the aggregate material, the lower the particle formation.

Most of European and American road surfaces consist of open asphalt. According to manufacturers, it is around 90% share of the EU market. Open asphalt has 15-25% hollow space which can retain wear particles (Kole et al., 2017[159]), but it has been found that lower-density asphalt had a higher wear rate (Do et al., 2003[160]; Gothie and Do, 2003[161]). Asphalt roads are also found to have higher rolling resistance (Ejsmont et al., 2014[162]) and higher wear rate than concrete roads. Because asphalt is an aggregate of particles with a bitumen binder, a distinction between the macro texture (size, distribution and geometrical configuration of particles) and the micro texture (of the individual particles) can be made (Pohrt, 2019[145]). With the wearing away of the bitumen binder and the resulting increase of surface voids, the macro texture tends to increase over time (Pohrt, 2019[145]). In contrast, the micro texture tends to diminish due to polishing (Veirh, 1992[163]).

The state of the pavement is also a relevant parameter. Gehrig et al (2010[52]) found that damaged asphalt concrete was emitting 10 times more road wear particles than the same pavement in good conditions, by means of a road simulator for HDV. Furthermore, alternative designs and materials, such as rubber mixed asphalt, furnace slag asphalt, porous asphalt, and cement concrete, have been tested for their PM10 emissions. Alternative materials for use in asphalt pavements as well as alternative constructions are often considered not only to improve pavement duration and properties but also to find ways to use or reuse residual or waste materials. Rubber asphalt with a gap grading was shown to slightly reduce wear PM10 production, whereas open-graded rubber asphalt did not differ from a reference SMA pavement. Furnace slag pavements were tested in (Viman and Gustafsson, 2015[164]). PM10 production from SMA8 and SMA11 slag asphalts were at similar levels to most asphalt wearing courses made from natural aggregates.

In cement concrete, cement replaces bitumen as a binder, while aggregate may be the same as the asphalt pavement Cement concrete pavements are more durable and wear resistant, but also more expensive to build than asphalt pavements (Wiman et al., 2009[165]). As they have advantages from a fire perspective, they are often considered for use in road tunnels (Bonati et al., 2012[166]). Cement concrete has been tested for PM10 emissions, and the results show that they emit more PM10 than the reference asphalt with the same rock used for the conglomerate stones (aggregates), even if the total wear is lower (Gustafsson et al., 2015[167]).

2.5.3. Road dust resuspension

The three main factors determining road dust emissions are vehicle speed and size, and road dust loading. The importance of each parameter on the magnitude of emission potential has been the object of research since several decades and empirical models have been developed to infer emission factors.

Speed and acceleration

Few studies have been undertaken on the effect of vehicle speed on road dust suspension. Lee et al. (2013[135]) used a mobile laboratory to track emissions in order to evaluate the concentration of roadway particles at different speeds of the vehicle. They found an increase in the mean concentrations only from 80 to 110 km/h, but with high standard deviations. Pirjola et al. (2009[168]; 2010[169]) found a linear increase in dust concentrations, measured behind the rear tyre of two testing vehicles, exploring the range 50-80 km/h, but no emission factors were calculated. Hussein et al. (2008[170]) found an important dependence of road dust emissions on vehicle speed when studded tyres are used: the particle mass concentrations behind the tyre at 100 km/h were about 10 times higher than that at 20 km/h. Although these studies were not able to attribute the speed dependence to direct wear and/or resuspension emissions, it is likely that results of Pirjola et al. (2009[168]; 2010[169]) and Hussein et al. (2008[170]) are to a large extent due to road/wear and resuspended dust, given the importance of these sources in Scandinavian countries. However, the speed dependence could also be attributed to the use of studded tyres. Interestingly, they eliminated from their studies the high PM concentrations observed during braking and hard acceleration (>0.5 m/s^2), which suggests that acceleration may also play also a role in road dust emissions.

Etyemezian et al. (2003[171]) and Zhu et al. (2009[172]) found that on the same road (i.e. same dust loading) emissions increase with vehicle speed to the power of approximately 3. More recently, Amato et al. (2017[173]) investigated the impact of traffic speed on road dust emissions in Milan. They used vertical deposition fluxes and calculated the emission factors at three sites along the same road with different instantaneous traffic speeds. Emission factor values were 24.6, 40.9 and 48.4 mg/VKT for instantaneous traffic speeds of 36, 47 and 57 km/h, respectively, which suggests that road dust resuspension increased with a power of 1.5 of vehicle speed. The 1.5 exponent is lower than that reported by Sehmel (1973[174]), who found that resuspension increased with the square of the car speed using fluorescent silica as tracer, but higher than the estimates of Nicholson and Branson (1990[175]), who suggested that only around 20% increase of emissions from 36 km/h to 57 km/h, using zinc sulphide as tracer. The difference between these estimates can be due to several factors, such as the amount, type and age of road dust, type of road dust (tracers were used by the aforementioned studies), road pavement and type of vehicles.[22]

Vehicle size/type

The fact that larger vehicles provoke higher road dust resuspension belongs to our everyday experience: on an unpaved road it can be readily observed that more dust is uplifted by a truck than a car.[23] Assuming higher resuspension for larger vehicles also on paved roads seems logical. Emission factors for HDVs are about 10 times higher than for LDVs. A similar estimate, namely a ratio of HDV over LDV of 9, was adopted by Schaap et al. (2009[176]) for modelling road dust emissions over Europe.

Whether such difference is only due to the larger size of the vehicle or also to the heavier load, is an open question, which needs further research. From an aerodynamic perspective only size matters, but heavier loads may enhance the tyre-induced lifting forces on deposited dust, which would enable more particles to be re-entrained in the air. In fact, the U.S. Environmental Protection Agency (2011[68]) AP-42 model for estimating road dust emissions, uses vehicle weight as predictor variable, adopting a nearly linear relationship with the emission factor (power of 1.02). Düring et al. (2002[177]), used instead a 2.14 power law relationship. A linear approach was followed by Timmers and Achten (2016[178]) to estimate the increase of road dust emissions due to the extra weight of electric vehicles.

Road dust loading

Road dust emissions also depend on the amount of material deposited on the road. Several empirical formulas were obtained relating emission factors with the amount of dust as silt loading (<75 μm) or thoracic dust loading (<10 μm) following generally a power law relationship (Amato et al., 2011[53]; Cowherd and Englehart, 1984[179]; Düring et al., 2002[177]; U.S. Environmental Protection Agency, 2011[68]) alone or in combination with vehicle weight. The variance of emission factors explained solely by the road dust loading is generally low, indicating that other factors, such as vehicle weight and speed are influencing emission rates. The power law relationships found generally have exponents lower than 1, indicating that changes in road dust loading are less influential than equivalent changes in vehicle weight (linear relationship) and speed (exponent varying between 1.5 and 2).

Road dust loading is a road property which in general corresponds to a steady-state condition between a complex combination of production, loss and redistribution processes. Production processes are mainly due to traffic intensity (i.e. wear and exhaust particle generation), atmospheric deposition, dust sources on the roadside, road shoulder, sanding/salting in countries with a lot of snowfall, the presence of additional fugitive sources (building and maintenance activities), and the deposition of pollen and other organic materials. Loss processes are mainly the resuspension itself – traffic or wind-induced – drainage, and road cleaning. Redistribution processes are particle crushing, aggregating and migration. Most of the aforementioned processes are heavily affected by road surface conditions, such as age, state, composition, texture, porosity and moisture.

Given the wide range of influencing factors, a wide spatial variation of road dust loadings has been observed at various scales. Important differences were found comparing Southern and Central European cities pointing at the presence of uncontrolled fugitive sources, lower vegetative cover and lower moisture as main responsible factors. Important variations were also found at the urban scale, with lower loadings generally found in high-speed roads, average values at urban roads and higher loadings at sites affected by construction activities, or next to unpaved areas (Amato et al., 2009[43]; 2011[53]; 2016[13]; 2017[173]).

Amato et al. (2011[53]; 2012[180]; 2014[18]; 2016[13]) investigated the source apportionment of the thoracic fraction (less than 10 μm) of road dust in several European cities, separating from 3 to 4 sources depending on the city. In the 2011-2012 studies (Northern Spain,

Netherlands and Switzerland), the main sources were related to tyre wear (16-38%), brake wear (27-44%), motor exhaust (5-20%), and mineral dust (13-37%) which likely involved road wear, soil and building dust, but could not be disentangled due to the chemical affinity of these sources. In Southern Spain, a carbonaceous factor (associated with tyre wear, motor exhaust and worn bitumen from asphalt) was found to dominate the mass (50% as average), while lower contributions were found for worn mineral particles from asphalt (20%) and brake wear (12%) on average (Amato et al., 2014[18]). In Paris, the carbonaceous factor was responsible for only one third of road dust mass, and the rest was equally apportioned between brake wear and road wear (Amato et al., 2016[13]).

Conversely, very little is known in terms of the time variability and seasonality of effects. Kantamaneni et al. (1996[70]) found that the addition of traction sand material on the road increased the PM10 emission factor from 1.04 to 1.45 g per vehicle-kilometre. Moreover, when roads were sanded, the correlation found between emission factors and relative humidity was not observed. On the other hand, Amato et al. (2013[181]) found that the 1-month variability of PM10 fraction of road dust was determined solely by rain, confirming that road dust loading can be seen as a constant feature of the road, which deviates from the equilibrium value only when there is precipitation or extraordinary dust intrusion (construction or desert dust).[24]

Porous pavements

Porous pavements are mainly used to reduce tyre-pavement noise and to increase water drainage from the surface. These pavements have been reported to decrease resuspension of road dust (Costabile et al., 2017[182]; Gehrig et al., 2010[52]) through reducing the amount of dust on the road surface. Direct wear emissions do not seem to be affected by porous pavements. Stationary and mobile measurements in Stockholm showed that the difference in PM10 emissions between the pavements (porous and reference), with studded tyres in use, was around 15% (Gustafsson and Johansson, 2012[152]). In a more recent study, no effect on PM coarse emission factors was observed after two years of implementation of porous asphalt on a Swedish highway (Norman et al., 2016[183]). One of the possible reasons was the higher wear rate of porous asphalt under studded tyre conditions, which makes it difficult to extrapolate their result to other regions.

Vehicle underside

It has been argued that a flatter undercarriage should improve the aerodynamics of the car and reduce resuspension. The only reference found on this matter is relative to emissions from unpaved roads (Gillies et al., 2005[66]), where it was concluded that the vehicle undercarriage area and the number of wheels have weak and no discernible relationships with emission factors. However, today' cars, and especially electric ones, have likely flatter undercarriage, thus more research is needed in order to evaluate the impact of this on the emission factor.

Weather conditions

Ambient air humidity and wind speed have the potential to influence emission factors from resuspension. Ambient air humidity directly affects road moisture, which is probably the most important determinant of the temporal variability of emissions (at least in countries where no studded tyres are used and no road sanding/salting is deployed). On urban paved roads, a negative correlation between road humidity and dust emission factors has been found. Kantamaneni et al. (1996[70]) estimated that a change of relative humidity from 10 to 70% was associated with a reduction of the road dust emission factors from 2.5 to 0.5 g/km, with relative humidity explaining 41% of the PM10 emission factors variance.

Wind speed increases emissions, but it has been difficult to isolate its impact. Amato et al. (2012[180]) identified a negative correlation between wind speed and road dust loadings by means of Principal Component Analysis (PCA). Thorpe et al. (2007[184]) investigated the effect of wind speed on road dust emissions at two sites in London. At the Bloomsbury background site, they found evidence of an increase in resuspension emission factors with wind speed, with the gradient appearing to diminish at higher wind speeds (above 5 m/s). The Bexley site suggested instead a different dependency, with emission factors appearing to decrease initially with increasing wind speed (below 3 m/s) before increasing during periods of high wind speed. Charron and Harrison (2005[185]) also suggested that PM2.5–10 concentrations were elevated as wind speed increased, based on the data collected at Marylebone Road, suggesting that road dust entrainment due to wind is apparent when a speed threshold (around 7 m/s) is reached.

Once airborne, the dispersion of non-exhaust particles in the atmosphere will depend mostly on atmospheric conditions (wind speed, direction and turbulence). The main removal mechanisms are dry and mostly wet deposition. Both removal mechanisms depend on the physico-chemical properties of the particles including size, shape, hygroscopicity and chemical composition.

Table 2.8 summarizes qualitatively the current knowledge on the impact of different vehicle, road and weather features, as well as driver choices, on each component of non-exhaust emissions. A preliminary attempt of estimating the share of emissions due to road or vehicle/driver features is presented at the bottom of the table based on the weight that each factor likely has in the literature.

Table 2.8. Overview of the influence of vehicle, driving and road features and weather conditions on non-exhaust emissions

	Brake wear	Tyre wear	Road wear	Resuspension
Vehicle features				
Rotor temperature	↑			
Vehicle size	↑	↑	↑	↑
Vehicle weight	↑	↑	?	?
Metal content in brake pads	↑			
Studded tyres		↑	↑	↑
Tyre diameter		↓		
Tyre width		↓		
Tyre tread depth		-		
Vehicle undercarriage				?
Tyre rolling resistance		?	?	
Tyre tread wear rating		–		
Mileage	?	↓		
Road features				
Allowed max speed	↑	↑	↑	↑
Allowed max weight	↑	↑	↑	↑
Pavement age/state		?	↑	↑
Resistant ballast rocks		↑	↓	?
Size of stones for road pavement conglomerate			↓	↓
Asphalt porosity		?	?	↓
Rubber asphalt		?	?	?

Cement concrete pavement		?	↑	?
Road dust loading			↑	↑
Road moisture		?	↓	↓
Side-slip angle	?	↑	?	?
Driving features				
Aggressive driving style	↑	↑	↑	↑
Speed	↑	↑	↑	↑
Acceleration/Deceleration	↑	↑	?	?
Tyre pressure		↓		
Wheels imbalance		↑		
Weather conditions				
Temperature	?	↑	?	↑
Humidity	?	?	?	↓
Precipitation	?	↓	?	↓
Wind speed				↑
	Brake wear	Tyre wear	Road wear	Resuspension
Estimated share due to road features	10%	30%	60%	70%
Estimated share due to vehicle/driving features	90%	70%	40%	30%

Note: ↑ indicates a positive effect (increases emissions); ↓ indicates a negative effect (decreases emissions); – indicates an insignificant effect; ? indicates that while there is likely an effect, it is unknown due to lack of evidence or mixed findings; empty cells indicate a hypothesis of no effect.

2.6. Implications for policy

More than 100 source apportionment studies reveal that, on a global level, non-exhaust emissions contribute similarly to exhaust emissions to ambient air PM2.5 and more than exhaust emissions to ambient air PM10. Road dust resuspension is the most polluting source of PM10 from road traffic, and the second most polluting source of PM2.5 (behind exhaust emissions). Moreover, emission trends and projections reveal that non-exhaust emissions may have already surpassed primary exhaust emissions of both PM2.5 and PM10, and their relative contribution to total emissions from road traffic is likely to continue increasing.

The impact of non-exhaust emissions is particularly severe in countries where studded tyres (and traction sand) are used to improve friction under snow/ice conditions. Beside these extreme conditions, maximum contributions to PM10 are found in India and China, while lower, but still significant, concentrations are recorded in European cities, with Mediterranean countries seemingly more affected than Central Europe. In the United States, non-exhaust sources' contributions to PM2.5 have been found to be lower than China, India and Spain.

More than 50 epidemiological studies have investigated the health outcomes associated with non-exhaust PM exposure indicators. Most of the studies used elemental tracers while a few applied source apportionment methods. Results indicate that exposure to PM emissions, and PM2.5 in particular, is associated with a variety of short- and long-term health effects. These impacts come in the form of increased risk of cardiovascular, respiratory, and developmental conditions, as well as overall mortality (Amato et al., 2019[105]).

Such evidence implies a need for immediate policy action to mitigate non-exhaust emissions and prevent their consequences for air quality and public health. In order to identify the most important drivers of non-exhaust emissions, a comprehensive literature review on the impact of different road, vehicle, driver and weather features has been carried out. Among the first three categories, vehicle weight, speed and acceleration, brake, tyre and pavement type, road moisture and road dust loading have been identified as the most important determinants of non-exhaust emissions.

---

[1] For a review of the literature, see Table 2.1, and for the estimations reported in this analysis see Tables 3.4 and 3.5.

[2] The LOWBRASYS has received funding from the European Union's Horizon 2020 research and innovation programme under grant agreement No 636592. The project is managed by the Innovations and Networks Executive Agency (INEA) of the European Commission.

[3] According to a JARI study published at the 48th PMP Meeting, the share of PM10 in brake wear emissions may be lower than the values mentioned above.

[4] A laboratory road simulator is a piece of equipment, which can be used to generate and study abrasion particles that are formed by the interaction between the tyre and pavement.

[5] Fauser et al. (2000[189]) suggested and used a method to identify bitumen in aerosols. They found that asphalt is the only source contributing to organic molecules with a molecular weight more than 2000 g/mol.

[6] The size distribution of road dust particles is also affected by existing sources, but is generally characterised by a coarse size distribution with size mode well above 10 µm, typical of any crustal material (Bi, Liang and Li, 2013[195]; Escrig et al., 2011[58]; Fedotov et al., 2014[196]; Janhäll et al., 2016[197]; Padoan, Romè and Ajmone-Marsan, 2017[198]; Ramírez et al., 2019[199]).

[7] The AP-42 model for estimating PM10 emissions from paved roads was developed by Midwest Research Institute under contract with the U.S. Environmental Protection Agency (Cowherd and Englehart, 1984[179]; U.S. Environmental Protection Agency, 2011[68]). The latest version of the model expresses the emission factor (EF), from a paved road in terms of the silt loading (sL), mean vehicle weight (W), days of precipitation (P) and total days (N) as follows:

$$\mathrm{EF} = k\,(sL)^{0.91} \times (W)^{1.02} \times (1 - P/4N)$$

where k is a particle size multiplier for particle size range and units of interest. This formula was obtained by a least squares regression between observed and predicted EFs using a dataset consisting of about 60 observations for a variety of roads ranging from public paved ones to unregulated industrial ones.

[8] Finland likely also includes resuspension within the "road wear" category in their inventory, as the emission factor used for road wear in the Finnish inventory is significantly higher than that in neighbouring countries that do not include resuspension.

[9] See also the U.S. Environmental Protection Agency website: https://www.epa.gov/air-emissions-inventories/national-emissions-inventory-nei. Additional years before 2014 are available but need to be calculated with the Motor Vehicle Emission Simulator (MOVES) model. While road dust emissions are clearly labelled as "Paved road dust", brake wear and tyre wear emissions are included in the "on-road mobile" categories and can be retrieved only by running the MOVES software, which uses emission factors in combination with activity (mileage) data.

[10] Since 2012, the road dust emission factor is corrected for precipitation, and brake and tyre wear have been subtracted from road dust to avoid double counting with mobile emissions (California Air Resources Board, 2019[71]).

[11] PMF offers multiple advantages, but cannot easily separate road wear from road dust resuspension.

[12] See also http://www.who.int/gho/phe/outdoor_air_pollution/burden/en.

[13] (Atkinson et al., 2016[191]; Basagaña et al., 2015[192]; Burnett et al., 2000[193]; Cahill et al., 2011[194]; Cakmak et al., 2009[200]; Franklin, Koutrakis and Schwartz, 2008[201]; Li et al., 2014[202]; Lippmann et al., 2013[203]; Ostro et al., 2007[204]; Ostro et al., 2008[205]; Son et al., 2012[206]; Valdés et al., 2012[207]; Zhou et al., 2011[208])

[14] Badaloni et al., 2017[209]; Beelen et al., 2015[210]; Lipfert et al., 2006[211]; Lippmann et al., 2013[203]; Ostro et al., 2010[212]; Ostro et al., 2015[213]; Thurston et al., 2016[214]; Vedal et al., 2013[215]; Wang et al., 2014[216]; Wang et al., 2017[217].

[15] Suh et al., 2011[113]; Tiittanen et al., 1999[114]; Sun et al., 2016[115]; Samoli et al., 2016[116]; Zanobetti et al., 2009[117]

[16] Basagaña et al., 2016[218]; Bilenko et al., 2015[219]; Crichton et al., 2016[220]; Dadvand et al., 2014[221]; Eeftens et al., 2014[222]; Fuertes et al., 2014[223]; Hampel et al., 2015[224]; Lagorio et al., 2006[225]; Pedersen et al., 2016[226]; Raaschou-Nielsen et al., 2016[227]; Tonne et al., 2016[228]; Willers et al., 2013[229]; Wolf et al., 2015[230].

[17] The advantage of small-size testers is typically related not only to cost but also to a considerably higher accuracy of detected physical variables compared to large-scale and field tests and often allows for a better understanding of wear mechanisms.

[18] See https://www.eng.auth.gr/mech0/lat/PM10.

[19] For tyre wear, the EMEP/EEA inventory guidebook attributes an approximately 60% higher emission factor to light duty trucks than passenger cars, and a linear increase of tyre wear emissions with the percentage of HDV load.

[20] In the extreme braking condition, locked wheels yet still moving forward, the value of the longitudinal slip reaches $\lambda = -1$. In the extreme acceleration condition, standing still while the tyre is spinning, the value of the longitudinal slip reaches $\lambda = 1$. In normal conditions, only the range $-0.3 \leq \lambda \leq 0.3$ is of interest.

[21] It has been argued that the tread wear rating (TWR) provided on the sidewall of the tyre and marking the expected durability of the tyre, could be a measure of tyre wear potential. Grigoratos et al. (2018[150]) discovered that, in general, the tyre tread mass loss shows no obvious statistical relation to PM10, PM2.5 or particle number concentration. A higher tread mass loss does not imply higher PM or PN emissions, since the size distribution of tread wear is very coarse and PM10 fraction is only 1%. Particle number is poorly correlated to mass, as it depends mostly from ultrafine particles which have negligible mass. Tires of the same tread wear rate but of different brands showed different behaviour in terms of material loss, PM, and PN emissions under the selected testing conditions. This means that it is not feasible to categorise tyres of different brands in terms of their emissions based on their TWR.

[22] Denby et al. (2013[55]) specified a quadratic dependence on speed for spray (water, dust and salt) emissions in the NORTRIP emission model but did not specify it for road dust suspension, stating that the model remains uncertain and requires further refinement based on experimental studies.

[23] Gillies et al. (2005[66]) estimated a linear relationship of 3 mg per kg of weight (using it as a proxy of size) and vehicle-km on an unpaved road, using vertical profile measurements of mass concentration at three instrumented towers. This is several orders of magnitude higher than Simons' (2016[137]) estimates for wear emissions. The reason for this is that Gillies et al.'s (2005[66]) study draws on measurements on unpaved roads, where the road dust reservoir is the road itself.

[24] For example, Amato et al. (2012[180]) calculated that a Saharan dust intrusion event in Barcelona, increasing ambient air PM10 concentrations by 6 µg/m3 on the daily average, provoked a 35% increase of dry deposition flux and a 30% increase in the instantaneous mobile road dust load.

References

Adachi, K. and Y. Tainosho (2004), "Characterization of heavy metal particles embedded in tire dust", *Environment International*, Vol. 30/8, pp. 1009-1017, http://dx.doi.org/10.1016/j.envint.2004.04.004. [40]

Alemani, M. et al. (2016), "A Study on Emission of Airborne Wear Particles from Car Brake Friction Pairs", *SAE International Journal of Materials and Manufacturing*, Vol. 9/1, http://dx.doi.org/10.4271/2015-01-2665. [130]

Alemani, M. et al. (2015), "A Study on Emission of Airborne Wear Particles from Car Brake Friction Pairs", *SAE International Journal of Materials and Manufacturing*, Vol. 9/1, http://dx.doi.org/10.4271/2015-01-2665. [80]

Amato, F. (2010), *Particulate Matter resuspension from urban paved roads: Impact on air quality and abatement strategies*, Polytechnic University of Catalonia. [17]

Amato, F. et al. (2014), "Trends of road dust emissions contributions on ambient air particulate levels at rural, urban and industrial sites in southern Spain", *Atmospheric Chemistry and Physics*, Vol. 14/7, pp. 3533-3544, http://dx.doi.org/10.5194/acp-14-3533-2014. [8]

Amato, F. et al. (2014), "Trends of road dust emissions contributions on ambient air particulate levels at rural, urban and industrial sites in southern Spain", *Atmospheric Chemistry and Physics*, Vol. 14/7, pp. 3533-3544, http://dx.doi.org/10.5194/acp-14-3533-2014. [18]

Amato, F. et al. (2016), "AIRUSE-LIFE+: a harmonized PM speciation and source apportionment in five southern European cities", *Atmospheric Chemistry and Physics*, Vol. 16/5, pp. 3289-3309, http://dx.doi.org/10.5194/acp-16-3289-2016. [60]

Amato, F. et al. (2017), "Characterization of road dust emissions in Milan: Impact of vehicle fleet speed", *Aerosol and Air Quality Research*, Vol. 17/10, http://dx.doi.org/10.4209/aaqr.2017.01.0017. [173]

Amato, F. et al. (2016), "Traffic induced particle resuspension in Paris: Emission factors and source contributions", *Atmospheric Environment*, Vol. 129, pp. 114-124, http://dx.doi.org/10.1016/j.atmosenv.2016.01.022. [13]

Amato, F. et al. (2012), "Emission factors from road dust resuspension in a Mediterranean freeway", *Atmospheric Environment*, Vol. 61, http://dx.doi.org/10.1016/j.atmosenv.2012.07.065. [63]

Amato, F. et al. (2010), "A comprehensive assessment of PM emissions from paved roads: Real-world Emission Factors and intense street cleaning trials", *Science of the Total Environment*, Vol. 408/20, pp. 4309-4318, http://dx.doi.org/10.1016/j.scitotenv.2010.06.008. [62]

Amato, F. et al. (2013), "Impact of traffic intensity and pavement aggregate size on road dust particles loading", *Atmospheric Environment*, Vol. 77, pp. 711-717, http://dx.doi.org/10.1016/j.atmosenv.2013.05.020. [157]

Amato, F. et al. (2009), "Quantifying road dust resuspension in urban environment by Multilinear Engine: A comparison with PMF2", *Atmospheric Environment*, Vol. 43/17, pp. 2770-2780, http://dx.doi.org/10.1016/j.atmosenv.2009.02.039. [16]

Amato, F. et al. (2011), "Sources and variability of inhalable road dust particles in three European cities", *Atmospheric Environment*, Vol. 45/37, pp. 6777-6787, http://dx.doi.org/10.1016/j.atmosenv.2011.06.003. [53]

Amato, F. et al. (2009), "Spatial and chemical patterns of PM10 in road dust deposited in urban environment", *Atmospheric Environment*, Vol. 43/9, pp. 1650-1659, http://dx.doi.org/10.1016/j.atmosenv.2008.12.009. [43]

Amato, F. et al. (2013), "Short-term variability of mineral dust, metals and carbon emission from road dust resuspension", *Atmospheric Environment*, Vol. 74, pp. 134-140, http://dx.doi.org/10.1016/j.atmosenv.2013.03.037. [181]

Amato, F. et al. (2012), "Effect of rain events on the mobility of road dust load in two Dutch and Spanish roads", *Atmospheric Environment*, Vol. 62, pp. 352-358, http://dx.doi.org/10.1016/j.atmosenv.2012.08.042. [180]

Amato, F. et al. (2019), "Non-exhaust emissions: sources and health effects.", *International Seminar on: RESPIRAMI 3 Air pollution and our health, Milan, 24-26 January..* [105]

Atkinson, R. et al. (2016), "Short-term exposure to traffic-related air pollution and daily mortality in London, UK", *Journal of Exposure Science and Environmental Epidemiology*, Vol. 26/2, pp. 125-132, http://dx.doi.org/10.1038/jes.2015.65. [190]

Atkinson, R. et al. (2009), "The impact of the congestion charging scheme on ambient air pollution concentrations in London", *Atmospheric Environment*, Vol. 43/34, pp. 5493-5500, http://dx.doi.org/10.1016/j.atmosenv.2009.07.023. [96]

Augsburg, K. and D. Hesse (2018), *Influence of regenerative braking on the emission behavior of friction brakes*. [187]

Ayres, J. et al. (2008), "Evaluating the Toxicity of Airborne Particulate Matter and Nanoparticles by Measuring Oxidative Stress Potential—A Workshop Report and Consensus Statement", *Inhalation Toxicology*, Vol. 20/1, pp. 75-99, http://dx.doi.org/10.1080/08958370701665517. [90]

Badaloni, C. et al. (2017), "Effects of long-term exposure to particulate matter and metal components on mortality in the Rome longitudinal study", *Environment International*, Vol. 109/September, pp. 146-154, http://dx.doi.org/10.1016/j.envint.2017.09.005. [208]

Barlow, T. et al. (2007), "NON-EXHAUST PARTICULATE MATTER EMISSIONS FROM ROAD TRAFFIC : SUMMARY REPORT Prepared for : Project Record :". [33]

Barmpadimos, I. et al. (2012), "One decade of parallel fine (PM 2.5) and coarse (PM 10-PM 2.5) particulate matter measurements in Europe: Trends and variability", *Atmospheric Chemistry and Physics*, Vol. 12/7, pp. 3189-3203, http://dx.doi.org/10.5194/acp-12-3189-2012. [82]

Basagaña, X. et al. (2016), "Neurodevelopmental deceleration by urban fine particles from different emission sources: A longitudinal observational study", *Environmental Health Perspectives*, Vol. 124/10, pp. 1630-1636, http://dx.doi.org/10.1289/EHP209. [123]

Basagaña, X. et al. (2016), "Neurodevelopmental deceleration by urban fine particles from different emission sources: A longitudinal observational study", *Environmental Health Perspectives*, Vol. 124/10, pp. 1630-1636, http://dx.doi.org/10.1289/EHP209. [217]

Basagaña, X. et al. (2015), "Short-term effects of particulate matter constituents on daily hospitalizations and mortality in five South-European cities: Results from the MED-PARTICLES project", *Environment International*, Vol. 75, pp. 151-158, http://dx.doi.org/10.1016/j.envint.2014.11.011. [191]

Basu, R. et al. (2014), "Effects of fine particulate matter and its constituents on low birth weight among full-term infants in California", *Environmental Research*, Vol. 128/2, pp. 42-51, http://dx.doi.org/10.1016/j.envres.2013.10.008. [118]

Batalha, J. et al. (2002), *Concentrated ambient air particles induce vasoconstriction of small pulmonary arteries in rats*, http://dx.doi.org/10.1289/ehp.021101191. [98]

Beelen, R. et al. (2015), "Natural-cause mortality and long-term exposure to particle components: An Analysis of 19 European cohorts within the multi-center ESCAPE project", *Environmental Health Perspectives*, Vol. 123/6, pp. 525-533, http://dx.doi.org/10.1289/ehp.1408095. [209]

Belis, C. et al. (2014), *European Guide on Air Pollution Source Apportionment with Receptor Models*, http://dx.doi.org/10.2788/9307. [74]

Bilenko, N. et al. (2015), "Associations between particulate matter composition and childhood blood pressure - The PIAMA study", *Environment International*, Vol. 84/2, pp. 1-6, http://dx.doi.org/10.1016/j.envint.2015.07.010. [218]

Bi, X., S. Liang and X. Li (2013), "A novel in situ method for sampling urban soil dust: Particle size distribution, trace metal concentrations, and stable lead isotopes", *Environmental Pollution*, Vol. 177, pp. 48-57, http://dx.doi.org/10.1016/j.envpol.2013.01.045. [194]

Bonati, A. et al. (2012), "Ignitability and thermal stability of asphalt binders and mastics for flexible pavements in highway tunnels", *Construction and Building Materials*, Vol. 37, pp. 660-668, http://dx.doi.org/10.1016/j.conbuildmat.2012.07.096. [166]

Borm, P. et al. (2007), "Oxidant generation by particulate matter: from biologically effective dose to a promising, novel metric.", *Occupational and Environmental Medicine*, Vol. 64/2, pp. 73-4, http://dx.doi.org/10.1136/oem.2006.029090. [91]

Bukowiecki, N. et al. (2009), *PM10 emission factors of abrasion particles from road traffic*, Federal Office of Roads, Swiss Federal Department of the Environment, Transport, Energy and Communications. [64]

Bukowiecki, N. et al. (2010), "PM10 emission factors for non-exhaust particles generated by road traffic in an urban street canyon and along a freeway in Switzerland", *Atmospheric Environment*, Vol. 44/19, pp. 2330-2340, http://dx.doi.org/10.1016/j.atmosenv.2010.03.039. [65]

Burnett, R. et al. (2000), "ASSOCIATION BETWEEN PARTICULATE- AND GAS-PHASE COMPONENTS OF URBAN AIR POLLUTION AND DAILY MORTALITY IN EIGHT CANADIAN CITIES Environmental Health Directorate , Health Canada , Ottawa , and Historically , extreme air pollution events , such as those exper", Vol. 12/February, pp. 15-39. [192]

Cahill, T. et al. (2011), "Very fine and ultrafine metals and ischemic heart disease in the California Central Valley 2: 1974-1991", *Aerosol Science and Technology*, Vol. 45/9, pp. 1135-1142, http://dx.doi.org/10.1080/02786826.2011.582196. [193]

Cakmak, S. et al. (2009), "Components of particulate air pollution and emergency department visits in Chile", *Archives of Environmental and Occupational Health*, Vol. 64/3, pp. 148-155, http://dx.doi.org/10.1080/19338240903240228. [199]

California Air Resources Board (2019), *EMFAC Web Database*, https://www.arb.ca.gov/emfac/ (accessed on 19 May 2019). [71]

Cassee, F. et al. (2013), *Particulate matter beyond mass: Recent health evidence on the role of fractions, chemical constituents and sources of emission*, http://dx.doi.org/10.3109/08958378.2013.850127. [92]

CEIP (2019), *WebDab - EMEP database*, https://www.ceip.at/ms/ceip_home1/ceip_home/webdab_emepdatabase/ (accessed on 20 May 2019). [186]

Centre on Emission Inventories and Projections (2019), *WebDab - EMEP database*, https://www.ceip.at/ms/ceip_home1/ceip_home/webdab_emepdatabase/ (accessed on 20 May 2019). [72]

Charron, A. and R. Harrison (2005), "Fine (PM2.5) and coarse (PM2.5-10) particulate matter on a heavily trafficked London highway: Sources and processes", *Environmental Science and Technology*, Vol. 39/20, pp. 7768-7776, http://dx.doi.org/10.1021/es050462i. [185]

Chen, Z. and S. Prathaban (2013), "Modeling of Tyre Parameters ' Influence on Transport Productivity for Heavy Trucks Master ' s Thesis in Automotive engineering". [141]

China, S. and D. James (2012), "Influence of pavement macrotexture on PM10 emissions from paved roads: A controlled study", *Atmospheric Environment*, Vol. 63, pp. 313-326, http://dx.doi.org/10.1016/j.atmosenv.2012.09.018. [156]

Costabile, F. et al. (2017), "First results of the "Carbonaceous Aerosol in Rome and Environs (CARE)" Experiment: Beyond current standards for PM 10", *Atmosphere*, Vol. 8/12, http://dx.doi.org/10.3390/atmos8120249. [182]

Cowherd, C. and P. Englehart (1984), *Paved Road Particulate Emissions*, Report prepared for the U.S. Environmental Protection Agency, https://nepis.epa.gov/Exe/ZyNET.exe/9100BWUQ.TXT?ZyActionD=ZyDocument&Client=EPA&Index=1981+Thru+1985&Docs=&Query=&Time=&EndTime=&SearchMethod=1&TocRestrict=n&Toc=&TocEntry=&QField=&QFieldYear=&QFieldMonth=&QFieldDay=&IntQFieldOp=0&ExtQFieldOp=0&XmlQuery= (accessed on 19 May 2019). [179]

Crichton, S. et al. (2016), "Associations between exhaust and non-exhaust particulate matter and stroke incidence by stroke subtype in South London", *Science of the Total Environment*, Vol. 568, pp. 278-284, http://dx.doi.org/10.1016/j.scitotenv.2016.06.009. [121]

Crichton, S. et al. (2016), "Associations between exhaust and non-exhaust particulate matter and stroke incidence by stroke subtype in South London", *Science of the Total Environment*, Vol. 568, pp. 278-284, http://dx.doi.org/10.1016/j.scitotenv.2016.06.009. [219]

Dadvand, P. et al. (2014), "Particulate air pollution and preeclampsia: a source-based analysis", *Occupational and Environmental Medicine*, Vol. 71/8, pp. 570-577, http://dx.doi.org/10.1136/oemed-2013-101693. [122]

Dadvand, P. et al. (2014), "Particulate air pollution and preeclampsia: a source-based analysis", *Occupational and Environmental Medicine*, Vol. 71/8, pp. 570-577, http://dx.doi.org/10.1136/oemed-2013-101693. [220]

Dall'Osto, M. et al. (2014), "Characteristics of tyre dust in polluted air: Studies by single particle mass spectrometry (ATOFMS)", *Atmospheric Environment*, Vol. 94, pp. 224-230, http://dx.doi.org/10.1016/j.atmosenv.2014.05.026. [41]

de Kok, T. et al. (2006), *Toxicological assessment of ambient and traffic-related particulate matter: A review of recent studies*, http://dx.doi.org/10.1016/j.mrrev.2006.07.001. [86]

Denby, B., K. Kupiainen and M. Gustafsson (2018), "Review of Road Dust Emissions", in *Non-Exhaust Emissions*, http://dx.doi.org/10.1016/b978-0-12-811770-5.00009-1. [54]

Denby, B. et al. (2013), "A coupled road dust and surface moisture model to predict non-exhaust road traffic induced particle emissions (NORTRIP). Part 1: Road dust loading and suspension modelling", *Atmospheric Environment*, Vol. 77, pp. 283-300, http://dx.doi.org/10.1016/j.atmosenv.2013.04.069. [55]

Denier van der Gon, H. et al. (2013), "The Policy Relevance of Wear Emissions from Road Transport, Now and in the Future - An International Workshop Report and Consensus Statement", *Journal of the Air and Waste Management Association*, Vol. 63/2, pp. 136-149, http://dx.doi.org/10.1080/10962247.2012.741055. [19]

Denier van der Gon, H. et al. (2018), "European Emission Inventories and Projections for Road Transport Non-Exhaust Emissions", in *Non-Exhaust Emissions*, http://dx.doi.org/10.1016/b978-0-12-811770-5.00005-4. [20]

Denier van der Gon, H. et al. (2010), "Mineral Dust as a component of Particulate Matters", p. 77. [14]

Desikan, A. et al. (2016), "Effect of Exhaust- and Nonexhaust-Related Components of Particulate Matter on Long-Term Survival after Stroke", *Stroke*, Vol. 47/12, pp. 2916-2922, http://dx.doi.org/10.1161/STROKEAHA.116.014242. [109]

DICTUC (2007), *Actualización del Inventario de Emisiones de Contaminantes Atmosféricos en la Región Metropolitana*, Report to the Comisión Nacional del Medio Ambiente Región Metropolitana, Santiago, Chile, https://www.cepal.org/ilpes/noticias/paginas/3/36023/DICTUC2007-Inventario2010.pdf (accessed on 20 May 2019). [79]

Do, M. et al. (2003), "Full Scale Tests for the Assessment of Wear of Pavement Surfaces", *Paper presented at the Transportation Research Board 82nd Annual Meeting*, https://hal.archives-ouvertes.fr/hal-00851295/ (accessed on 20 May 2019). [160]

Döse, M. and U. Åkesson (2011), *Förhållandet mellan nötning och polering samt deras förutsättningar att producera PM10 (Relationship between abrasion and polishing and the conditions for producing PM10)*, CBI. [154]

Duffin, R., N. Mills and K. Donaldson (2007), *Nanoparticles - A thoracic toxicology perspective*, http://dx.doi.org/10.3349/ymj.2007.48.4.561. [97]

Düring, I. et al. (2002), *Estimation of the "non exhaust pipe" PM10 emissions of streets for practical traffic air pollution modelling*, http://www.lohmeyer.de/de/system/files/content/download/publikationen/PM10EmissionsSymposiumGraz2002.pdf (accessed on 20 May 2019). [177]

Eeftens, M. et al. (2014), "Elemental composition of particulate matter and the association with lung function", *Epidemiology*, Vol. 25/5, pp. 648-657, http://dx.doi.org/10.1097/EDE.0000000000000136. [221]

Ejsmont, J. et al. (2014), *Rolling Resistance Measurements at the MnROAD Facility, Round 2*, Report to the Minnesota Department of Transportation, http://www.lrrb.org/pdf/201429.pdf (accessed on 20 May 2019). [162]

Escrig, A. et al. (2011), "Simple estimates of vehicle-induced resuspension rates", *Journal of Environmental Management*, Vol. 92/10, pp. 2855-2859, http://dx.doi.org/10.1016/j.jenvman.2011.06.042. [58]

Etyemezian, V. et al. (2003), "Vehicle-based road dust emission measurement (III): Effect of speed, traffic volume, location, and season on PM10 road dust emissions in the Treasure Valley, ID", *Atmospheric Environment*, Vol. 37/32, pp. 4583-4593, http://dx.doi.org/10.1016/S1352-2310(03)00530-2. [171]

Fauser, P. et al. (2002), "Tire-tread and bitumen particle concentrations in aerosol and soil samples", *Petroleum Science and Technology*, Vol. 20/1-2, pp. 127-141, http://dx.doi.org/10.1081/LFT-120002092. [49]

Fauser, P. et al. (2000), "Quantification of Bitumen Particles in Aerosol and Soil Samples Using HP-GPC", *Petroleum Science and Technology*, Vol. 18/9-10, pp. 991-1007, http://dx.doi.org/10.1080/10916460008949887. [189]

Fedotov, P. et al. (2014), "Characterization of size, morphology and elemental composition of nano-, submicron, and micron particles of street dust separated using field-flow fractionation in a rotating coiled column", *Talanta*, Vol. 130, pp. 1-7, http://dx.doi.org/10.1016/j.talanta.2014.06.040. [94]

Fedotov, P. et al. (2014), "Characterization of size, morphology and elemental composition of nano-, submicron, and micron particles of street dust separated using field-flow fractionation in a rotating coiled column", *Talanta*, Vol. 130, pp. 1-7, http://dx.doi.org/10.1016/j.talanta.2014.06.040. [195]

Filip, P. (2013), "Friction Brakes for Automotive and Aircraft", in *Encyclopedia of Tribology*, http://dx.doi.org/10.1007/978-0-387-92897-5_172. [127]

Filip, P., Z. Weiss and D. Rafaja (2002), "On friction layer formation in polymer matrix composite materials for brake applications", *Wear*, Vol. 252/3-4, pp. 189-198, http://dx.doi.org/10.1016/S0043-1648(01)00873-0. [128]

Foitzik, M. et al. (2018), "Investigation of ultra fine particulate matter emission of rubber tires", *Wear*, Vol. 394-395/October 2017, pp. 87-95, http://dx.doi.org/10.1016/j.wear.2017.09.023. [147]

Font, A. and G. Fuller (2016), "Did policies to abate atmospheric emissions from traffic have a positive effect in London?", *Environmental Pollution*, Vol. 218, pp. 463-474, http://dx.doi.org/10.1016/J.ENVPOL.2016.07.026. [83]

Franklin, M., P. Koutrakis and J. Schwartz (2008), "The role of particle composition on the association between PM2.5 and mortality", *Epidemiology*, Vol. 19/5, pp. 680-689, http://dx.doi.org/10.1097/EDE.0b013e3181812bb7. [200]

Fuertes, E. et al. (2014), "Associations between particulate matter elements and early-life pneumonia in seven birth cohorts: Results from the ESCAPE and TRANSPHORM projects", *International Journal of Hygiene and Environmental Health*, Vol. 217/8, pp. 819-829, http://dx.doi.org/10.1016/j.ijheh.2014.05.004. [222]

Garg, B. et al. (2000), "Brake wear particulate matter emissions", *Environmental Science and Technology*, Vol. 34/21, pp. 4463-4469, http://dx.doi.org/10.1021/es001108h. [31]

Garg, B. et al. (2000), "Brake wear particulate matter emissions", *Environmental Science and Technology*, Vol. 34/21, pp. 4463-4469, http://dx.doi.org/10.1021/es001108h. [38]

Gehrig, R. et al. (2001), *Contributions of Road Traffic to Ambient PM10 and PM2.5 Concentrations*. [9]

Gehrig, R. et al. (2010), "Mobile load simulators – A tool to distinguish between the emissions due to abrasion and resuspension of PM10 from road surfaces", *Atmospheric Environment*, Vol. 44/38, pp. 4937-4943, http://dx.doi.org/10.1016/j.atmosenv.2010.08.020. [52]

Gietl, J. et al. (2010), "Identification of brake wear particles and derivation of a quantitative tracer for brake dust at a major road", *Atmospheric Environment*, Vol. 44/2, pp. 141-146, http://dx.doi.org/10.1016/j.atmosenv.2009.10.016. [44]

Gillies, J. et al. (2005), "Effect of vehicle characteristics on unpaved road dust emissions", *Atmospheric Environment*, Vol. 39/13, pp. 2341-2347, http://dx.doi.org/10.1016/j.atmosenv.2004.05.064. [66]

Gothie, M. and M. Do (2003), "Road polishing assessment methodology 'TROWS'", *Paper presented ta the XXIIth PIARC World Road Congress*, https://hal.archives-ouvertes.fr/hal-00851423/ (accessed on 20 May 2019). [161]

Gottipolu, R. et al. (2008), "Cardiopulmonary responses of intratracheally instilled tire particles and constituent metal components", *Inhalation Toxicology*, Vol. 20/5, pp. 473-484, http://dx.doi.org/10.1080/08958370701858427. [104]

Grigoratos, T. et al. (2018), "Experimental investigation of tread wear and particle emission from tyres with different treadwear marking", *Atmospheric Environment*, Vol. 182, pp. 200-212, http://dx.doi.org/10.1016/j.atmosenv.2018.03.049. [150]

Grigoratos, T. and G. Martini (2015), "Brake wear particle emissions: a review.", *Environmental science and pollution research international*, Vol. 22/4, pp. 2491-504, http://dx.doi.org/10.1007/s11356-014-3696-8. [6]

Grigoratos, T. and G. Martini (2014), *Non-exhaust traffic related emissions. Brake and tyre wear PM*, http://dx.doi.org/10.2790/21481. [88]

Guckeisen, F. (2018), *Conference communication*. [188]

Gurgueira, S. et al. (2002), "Rapid increases in the steady-state concentration of reactive oxygen species in the lungs and heart after particulate air pollution inhalation", *Environmental Health Perspectives*, Vol. 110/8, pp. 749-755, http://dx.doi.org/10.1289/ehp.02110749. [101]

Gustafsson, M. (2018), "Review of Road Wear Emissions: A Review of Road Emission Measurement Studies: Identification of Gaps and Future Needs", in Amato, F. (ed.), *Non-Exhaust Emissions*, Academic Press, San Diego, http://dx.doi.org/10.1016/B978-0-12-811770-5.00008-X. [51]

Gustafsson, M. et al. (2009), "Factors influencing PM10 emissions from road pavement wear", *Atmospheric Environment*, Vol. 43/31, pp. 4699-4702, http://dx.doi.org/10.1016/j.atmosenv.2008.04.028. [48]

Gustafsson, M. et al. (2008), "Properties and toxicological effects of particles from the interaction between tyres, road pavement and winter traction material", *Science of the Total Environment*, Vol. 393/2-3, pp. 226-240, http://dx.doi.org/10.1016/j.scitotenv.2007.12.030. [148]

Gustafsson, M. et al. (2015), *Operational measures against PM10 pollution in Stockholm. Evaluation of winter season 2013–2014*, VTI rapport 847, VTI, http://195.198.217.75/en/publications/operational-measures-against-pm10-pollution-in-stockholm-evaluation-of-winter-season-20132014/ (accessed on 20 May 2019). [167]

Gustafsson, M. and C. Johansson (2012), *Road pavements and PM10: Summary of the results of research funded by the Swedish Transport Administration on how the properties of road pavements influence emissions and the properties of wear particles*, Trafikverket, Uppsala. [152]

Hagino, H., M. Oyama and S. Sasaki (2015), "Airborne brake wear particle emission due to braking and accelerating", *Wear*, Vol. 334-335, pp. 44-48, http://dx.doi.org/10.1016/j.wear.2015.04.012. [134]

Hampel, R. et al. (2015), "Long-term effects of elemental composition of particulate matter on inflammatory blood markers in European cohorts", *Environment International*, Vol. 82, pp. 76-84, http://dx.doi.org/10.1016/j.envint.2015.05.008. [223]

Harrison, R. et al. (2012), "Estimation of the contributions of brake dust, tire wear, and resuspension to nonexhaust traffic particles derived from atmospheric measurements", *Environmental Science and Technology*, Vol. 46/12, pp. 6523-6529, http://dx.doi.org/10.1021/es300894r. [10]

Harrison, R. et al. (2018), "Diesel exhaust nanoparticles and their behaviour in the atmosphere", *Proceedings of the Royal Society A: Mathematical, Physical and Engineering Sciences*, Vol. 474/2220, p. 20180492, http://dx.doi.org/10.1098/rspa.2018.0492. [21]

HEI Review Panel on Ultrafine Particles (2013), *Understanding the Health Effects of Ambient Ultrafine Particles HEI Review Panel on Ultrafine Particles. HEI Perspectives 3*, Health Effects Institute, Boston, MA, http://www.healtheffects.org (accessed on 19 May 2019). [22]

Heinrich, J. and R. Slama (2007), "Fine particles, a major threat to children", *International Journal of Hygiene and Environmental Health*, Vol. 210/5, pp. 617-622, http://dx.doi.org/10.1016/j.ijheh.2007.07.012. [87]

Hulskotte, J., G. Roskam and H. Denier van der Gon (2014), "Elemental composition of current automotive braking materials and derived air emission factors", *Atmospheric Environment*, Vol. 99, pp. 436-445, http://dx.doi.org/10.1016/j.atmosenv.2014.10.007. [34]

Hussein, T. et al. (2008), "Factors affecting non-tailpipe aerosol particle emissions from paved roads: On-road measurements in Stockholm, Sweden", *Atmospheric Environment*, Vol. 42/4, pp. 688-702, http://dx.doi.org/10.1016/j.atmosenv.2007.09.064. [170]

ICCT (2018), *European vehicle market statistics 2018/2019*, International Council on Clean Transportation Europe, Berlin, http://eupocketbook.theicct.org (accessed on 7 March 2019). [138]

Iijima, A. et al. (2008), "Emission factor for antimony in brake abrasion dusts as one of the major atmospheric antimony sources", *Environmental Science and Technology*, Vol. 42/8, pp. 2937-2942, http://dx.doi.org/10.1021/es702137g. [36]

Iijima, A. et al. (2007), "Particle size and composition distribution analysis of automotive brake abrasion dusts for the evaluation of antimony sources of airborne particulate matter", *Atmospheric Environment*, Vol. 41/23, pp. 4908-4919, http://dx.doi.org/10.1016/j.atmosenv.2007.02.005. [35]

Jacobson, T. and L. Wågberg (2007), "Developing and upgrading of a prediction model of wear caused by studded tyres and an overview of the knowledge of the factors influencing the wear – Version 3.2.03", *VTI notat*, No. 7-2007, VTI, Linköping, http://www.vti.se/en/publications/developing-and-upgrading-of-a-prediction-model-of-wear-caused-by-studded-tyres-and-an-overview-of-the-knowledge-of-the-factors-influencing-the-wear--version-3203/ (accessed on 20 May 2019). [155]

Janhäll, S. et al. (2016), "Utvärdering av städmaskiners förmåga att reducera vägdammsförrådet i gatu-och tunnelmiljöer i Trondheim", *VTI rapport*, No. 883, VTI, Linköping, http://vti.diva-portal.org/smash/get/diva2:899278/FULLTEXT01.pdf (accessed on 19 May 2019). [196]

Kantamaneni, R. et al. (1996), "The measurement of roadway PM10 emission rates using atmospheric tracer ratio techniques", *Atmospheric Environment*, Vol. 30/24, pp. 4209-4223, http://dx.doi.org/10.1016/1352-2310(96)00131-8. [70]

Kelly, F. (2003), *Oxidative stress: Its role in air pollution and adverse health effects*, http://dx.doi.org/10.1136/oem.60.8.612. [93]

Kettunen, J. et al. (2007), "Associations of Fine and Ultrafine Particulate Air Pollution With Stroke Mortality in an Area of Low Air Pollution Levels", *Stroke*, Vol. 38/3, pp. 918-922, http://dx.doi.org/10.1161/01.STR.0000257999.49706.3b. [23]

Kioumourtzoglou, M. et al. (2014), "The impact of source contribution uncertainty on the effects of source-specific PM2.5 on hospital admissions: A case study in Boston, MA", *Modern Pathology*, Vol. 27/8, pp. 365-371, http://dx.doi.org/10.1038/jes.2014.7. [117]

Kodavanti, U. et al. (2005), "Consistent pulmonary and systemic responses from inhalation of fine concentrated ambient particles: Roles of rat strains used and physicochemical properties", *Environmental Health Perspectives*, Vol. 113/11, pp. 1561-1568, http://dx.doi.org/10.1289/ehp.7868. [102]

Kole, P. et al. (2017), "Wear and Tear of Tyres: A Stealthy Source of Microplastics in the Environment", *International Journal of Environmental Research and Public Health*, Vol. 14/10, p. 1265, http://dx.doi.org/10.3390/ijerph14101265. [159]

Kousoulidou, M. et al. (2008), "Road-transport emission projections to 2020 in European urban environments", *Atmospheric Environment*, Vol. 42/32, pp. 7465-7475, http://dx.doi.org/10.1016/J.ATMOSENV.2008.06.002. [75]

Kreider, M. et al. (2010), "Physical and chemical characterization of tire-related particles: Comparison of particles generated using different methodologies", *Science of the Total Environment*, Vol. 408/3, pp. 652-659, http://dx.doi.org/10.1016/j.scitotenv.2009.10.016. [42]

Kukutschová, J. and P. Filip (2018), "Chapter 6 – Review of Brake Wear Emissions: A Review of Brake Emission Measurement Studies: Identification of Gaps and Future Needs", in *Non-Exhaust Emissions*, http://dx.doi.org/10.1016/B978-0-12-811770-5.00006-6. [125]

Kukutschová, J. et al. (2011), "On airborne nano/micro-sized wear particles released from low-metallic automotive brakes", *Environmental Pollution*, Vol. 159/4, pp. 998-1006, http://dx.doi.org/10.1016/j.envpol.2010.11.036. [3]

Kukutschová, J. et al. (2009), "Wear mechanism in automotive brake materials, wear debris and its potential environmental impact", *Wear*, Vol. 267/5-8, pp. 807-817, http://dx.doi.org/10.1016/j.wear.2009.01.034. [124]

Kupiainen, K., H. Tervahattu and M. Räisänen (2003), "Experimental studies about the impact of traction sand on urban road dust composition", *Science of the Total Environment*, Vol. 308/1-3, pp. 175-184, http://dx.doi.org/10.1016/S0048-9697(02)00674-5. [50]

Lagorio, S. et al. (2006), "Air pollution and lung function among susceptible adult subjects: a panel study", *Environmental health : a global access science source*, Vol. 5, p. 11, http://dx.doi.org/10.1186/1476-069X-5-11. [224]

Lanzinger, S. et al. (2016), "Associations between ultrafine and fine particles and mortality in five central European cities — Results from the UFIREG study", *Environment International*, Vol. 88, pp. 44-52, http://dx.doi.org/10.1016/j.envint.2015.12.006. [24]

Lawrence, S., R. Sokhi and K. Ravindra (2016), "Quantification of vehicle fleet PM10 particulate matter emission factors from exhaust and non-exhaust sources using tunnel measurement techniques", *Environmental Pollution*, Vol. 210, pp. 419-428, http://dx.doi.org/10.1016/j.envpol.2016.01.011. [11]

Lawrence, S., R. Sokhi and K. Ravindra (2016), "Quantification of vehicle fleet PM10 particulate matter emission factors from exhaust and non-exhaust sources using tunnel measurement techniques", *Environmental Pollution*, Vol. 210, pp. 419-428, http://dx.doi.org/10.1016/j.envpol.2016.01.011. [67]

Le Maître, O., M. Süssner and C. Zarak (1998), "Evaluation of Tire Wear Performance", *SAE Technical Paper*, No. 980256, http://dx.doi.org/10.4271/980256. [149]

Lee, P. and P. Filip (2013), "Friction and wear of Cu-free and Sb-free environmental friendly automotive brake materials", *Wear*, Vol. 302/1-2, pp. 1404-1413, http://dx.doi.org/10.1016/j.wear.2012.12.046. [126]

Lee, S. et al. (2013), "Properties of roadway particles from interaction between the tire and road pavement", *International Journal of Automotive Technology*, Vol. 14/1, pp. 163-173, http://dx.doi.org/10.1007/s12239-013-0018-y. [135]

Levy, D. et al. (2001), "Referent selection in case-crossover analyses of acute health effects of air pollution", *Epidemiology*, Vol. 12/2, pp. 186-192, https://journals.lww.com/epidem/Fulltext/2001/03000/Referent_Selection_in_Case_Crossover_Analyses_of.10.aspx#pdf-link (accessed on 20 May 2019). [106]

Lipfert, F. et al. (2006), “PM _{2.5} Constituents and Related Air Quality Variables As Predictors of Survival in a Cohort of U.S. Military Veterans”, *Inhalation Toxicology*, Vol. 18/9, pp. 645-657, http://dx.doi.org/10.1080/08958370600742946. [210]

Lippmann, M. et al. (2013), “National Particle Component Toxicity (NPACT) Initiative: integrated epidemiologic and toxicologic studies of the health effects of particulate matter components.”, *Research report (Health Effects Institute)*, Vol. 177/177, pp. 5-13. [202]

Li, P. et al. (2014), “Association between particulate matter and its chemical constituents of urban air pollution and daily mortality or morbidity in Beijing City”, *Environmental Science and Pollution Research*, Vol. 22/1, pp. 358-368, http://dx.doi.org/10.1007/s11356-014-3301-1. [201]

Li, Y. et al. (2012), “Analysis of impact factors of tire wear”, *JVC/Journal of Vibration and Control*, Vol. 18/6, pp. 833-840, http://dx.doi.org/10.1177/1077546311411756. [142]

Luekewille, A. et al. (2001), “A Framework to Estimate the Potential and Costs for the Control of Fine Particulate Emissions in Europe”, http://pure.iiasa.ac.at/id/eprint/6497/. [136]

Masri, S., C. Kang and P. Koutrakis (2015), “Composition and sources of fine and coarse particles collected during 2002–2010 in Boston, MA”, *Journal of the Air & Waste Management Association*, Vol. 65/3, pp. 287-297, http://dx.doi.org/10.1080/10962247.2014.982307. [81]

McAtee, B. et al. (2009), “Physio-chemical analysis of airborne tire wear particles”, *Toxicology Letters*, Vol. 189, p. S205, http://dx.doi.org/10.1016/j.toxlet.2009.06.621. [47]

Meng, X. et al. (2013), “Size-Fractionated Particle Number Concentrations and Daily Mortality in a Chinese City”, *Environmental Health Perspectives*, Vol. 121/10, pp. 1175-1178, http://dx.doi.org/10.1289/ehp.1206398. [25]

Mosleh, M., P. Blau and D. Dumitrescu (2004), “Characteristics and morphology of wear particles from laboratory testing of disk brake materials”, *Wear*, Vol. 256/11-12, pp. 1128-1134, http://dx.doi.org/10.1016/j.wear.2003.07.007. [131]

Nicholson, K. and J. Branson (1990), “Factors affecting resuspension by road traffic”, *Science of the Total Environment, The*, Vol. 93/C, pp. 349-358, http://dx.doi.org/10.1016/0048-9697(90)90126-F. [175]

Norman, M. et al. (2016), “Modelling road dust emission abatement measures using the NORTRIP model: Vehicle speed and studded tyre reduction”, *Atmospheric Environment*, Vol. 134, pp. 96-108, http://dx.doi.org/10.1016/j.atmosenv.2016.03.035. [183]

Ntziachristos, L. and P. Boulter (2016), “1.A.3.b.vi Road transport: Automobile tyre and brake wear; 1.A.3.b.vii Road transport: Automobile road abrasion”, in *EMEP/EEA air pollutant emission inventory guidebook 2016*, Publications Office of the European Union, Luxembourg. [56]

OECD (2017), *Health at a Glance 2017: OECD Indicators*, OECD Publishing, Paris, https://dx.doi.org/10.1787/health_glance-2017-en. [84]

Ohlwein, S. et al. (2019), “Health effects of ultrafine particles: a systematic literature review update of epidemiological evidence”, *International Journal of Public Health*, http://dx.doi.org/10.1007/s00038-019-01202-7. [26]

Ostro, B. et al. (2007), "The effects of components of fine particulate air pollution on mortality in California: Results from CALFINE", *Environmental Health Perspectives*, Vol. 115/1, pp. 13-19, http://dx.doi.org/10.1289/ehp.9281. [203]

Ostro, B. et al. (2008), "The impact of components of fine particulate matter on cardiovascular mortality in susceptible subpopulations", *Occupational and Environmental Medicine*, Vol. 65/11, pp. 750-756, http://dx.doi.org/10.1136/oem.2007.036673. [204]

Ostro, B. et al. (2015), "Associations of mortality with long-term exposures to fine and ultrafine particles, species and sources: Results from the California teachers study Cohort", *Environmental Health Perspectives*, Vol. 123/6, pp. 549-556, http://dx.doi.org/10.1289/ehp.1408565. [212]

Ostro, B. et al. (2010), "Long-term exposure to constituents of fine particulate air pollution and mortality: Results from the California Teachers Study", *Environmental Health Perspectives*, Vol. 118/3, pp. 363-369, http://dx.doi.org/10.1289/ehp.0901181. [211]

Ostro, B. et al. (2011), "The effects of particulate matter sources on daily mortality: A case-crossover study of Barcelona, Spain", *Environmental Health Perspectives*, Vol. 119/12, pp. 1781-1787, http://dx.doi.org/10.1289/ehp.1103618. [108]

Pachón, J. et al. (2018), "Development and evaluation of a comprehensive atmospheric emission inventory for air quality modeling in the megacity of Bogotá", *Atmosphere*, Vol. 9/2, http://dx.doi.org/10.3390/atmos9020049. [73]

Padoan, E. et al. (2018), "An empirical model to predict road dust emissions based on pavement and traffic characteristics", *Environmental Pollution*, Vol. 237, pp. 713-720, http://dx.doi.org/10.1016/j.envpol.2017.10.115. [158]

Padoan, E. and F. Amato (2018), "Vehicle Non-Exhaust Emissions: Impact on Air Quality", in Amato, F. (ed.), *Non-Exhaust Emissions: An Urban Air Quality Problem for Public Health; Impact and Mitigation Measures*, Academic Press, San Diego, http://dx.doi.org/10.1016/B978-0-12-811770-5.00002-9. [5]

Padoan, E., C. Romè and F. Ajmone-Marsan (2017), "Bioaccessibility and size distribution of metals in road dust and roadside soils along a peri-urban transect", *Science of the Total Environment*, Vol. 601-602, pp. 89-98, http://dx.doi.org/10.1016/j.scitotenv.2017.05.180. [197]

Panko, J., M. Kreider and K. Unice (2018), "Review of Tire Wear Emissions", in *Non-Exhaust Emissions*, http://dx.doi.org/10.1016/b978-0-12-811770-5.00007-8. [59]

Pedersen, M. et al. (2016), "Elemental constituents of particulate matter and newborn's size in eight European cohorts", *Environmental Health Perspectives*, Vol. 124/1, pp. 141-150, http://dx.doi.org/10.1289/ehp.1409546. [225]

Pérez-Peña, M. et al. (2017), "Natural mitigation factor adjustment for re-suspended particulate matter emissions inventory for Bogotá, Colombia", *Atmospheric Pollution Research*, Vol. 8/1, pp. 29-37, http://dx.doi.org/10.1016/j.apr.2016.07.006. [78]

Perricone, G. et al. (2016), "Towards the ranking of airborne particle emissions from car brakes - A system approach", *Proceedings of the Institution of Mechanical Engineers, Part D: Journal of Automobile Engineering*, Vol. 231/6, pp. 781-797, http://dx.doi.org/10.1177/0954407016662800. [140]

Pirjola, L. et al. (2010), "Road dust emissions from paved roads measured using different mobile systems", *Journal of the Air and Waste Management Association*, Vol. 60/12, pp. 1422-1433, http://dx.doi.org/10.3155/1047-3289.60.12.1422. [169]

Pirjola, L. et al. (2009), "Non-exhaust emission measurement system of the mobile laboratory SNIFFER", *Atmospheric Environment*, Vol. 43/31, pp. 4703-4713, http://dx.doi.org/10.1016/j.atmosenv.2008.08.024. [168]

Plachá, D. et al. (2017), "Release of volatile organic compounds by oxidative wear of automotive friction materials", *Wear*, Vol. 376-377, pp. 705-716, http://dx.doi.org/10.1016/j.wear.2016.12.016. [4]

Platt, S. et al. (2017), "Gasoline cars produce more carbonaceous particulate matter than modern filter-equipped diesel cars", *Scientific Reports*, Vol. 7/1, http://dx.doi.org/10.1038/s41598-017-03714-9. [61]

Pohrt, R. (2019), "Tire Wear Particle Hot Spots – Review of Influencing Factors", *Facta Universitatis, Series: Mechanical Engineering*, Vol. 17/1, p. 17, http://dx.doi.org/10.22190/FUME190104013P. [145]

Pulles, T. and D. Heslinga (2007), *The Art of Emission Inventorying TNO I Innovation for Life*. [7]

Raaschou-Nielsen, O. et al. (2016), "Particulate matter air pollution components and risk for lung cancer", *Environment International*, Vol. 87/November 2015, pp. 66-73, http://dx.doi.org/10.1016/j.envint.2015.11.007. [226]

Räisänen, M., K. Kupiainen and H. Tervahattu (2005), "The effect of mineralogy, texture and mechanical properties of anti-skid and asphalt aggregates on urban dust, stages II and III", *Bulletin of Engineering Geology and the Environment*, Vol. 64/3, pp. 247-256, http://dx.doi.org/10.1007/s10064-004-0267-0. [153]

Ramírez, O. et al. (2019), "Physicochemical characterization and sources of the thoracic fraction of road dust in a Latin American megacity", *Science of the Total Environment*, Vol. 652, pp. 434-446, http://dx.doi.org/10.1016/j.scitotenv.2018.10.214. [57]

Ramírez, O. et al. (2019), "Physicochemical characterization and sources of the thoracic fraction of road dust in a Latin American megacity", *Science of the Total Environment*, Vol. 652, pp. 434-446, http://dx.doi.org/10.1016/j.scitotenv.2018.10.214. [198]

Rexeis, M. and S. Hausberger (2009), "Trend of vehicle emission levels until 2020 - Prognosis based on current vehicle measurements and future emission legislation", *Atmospheric Environment*, Vol. 43/31, pp. 4689-4698, http://dx.doi.org/10.1016/j.atmosenv.2008.09.034. [2]

Rhoden, C. et al. (2004), "N-acetylcysteine prevents lung inflammation after short-term inhalation exposure to concentrated ambient particles", *Toxicological Sciences*, Vol. 79/2, pp. 296-303, http://dx.doi.org/10.1093/toxsci/kfh122. [99]

Rohr, A. et al. (2011), "Altered heart rate variability in spontaneously hypertensive rats is associated with specific particulate matter components in Detroit, Michigan", *Environmental Health Perspectives*, Vol. 119/4, pp. 474-480, http://dx.doi.org/10.1289/ehp.1002831. [103]

Roubicek, V. et al. (2008), "Wear and environmental aspects of composite materials for automotive braking industry", *Wear*, Vol. 265/1-2, pp. 167-175, http://dx.doi.org/10.1016/j.wear.2007.09.006. [129]

Sakai, H. (1996), "Friction and Wear of Tire Tread Rubber", *Tire Science and Technology*, Vol. 24/3, pp. 252-275, http://dx.doi.org/10.2346/1.2137522. [151]

Salminen, H. (2014), "Parametrizing tyre wear using a brush2014 tyre mode", p. 68. [143]

Samoli, E. et al. (2016), "Exposure to ultrafine particles and respiratory hospitalisations in five European cities.", *European Respiratory Journal*, Vol. 48/3, pp. 674-682, http://dx.doi.org/10.1183/13993003.02108-2015. [27]

Samoli, E. et al. (2016), "Exposure to ultrafine particles and respiratory hospitalisations in five European cities.", *European Respiratory Journal*, Vol. 48/3, pp. 674-682, http://dx.doi.org/10.1183/13993003.02108-2015. [115]

Sanders, P. et al. (2003), "Airborne brake wear debris: Size distributions, composition, and a comparison of dynamometer and vehicle tests", *Environmental Science and Technology*, Vol. 37/18, pp. 4060-4069, http://dx.doi.org/10.1021/es034145s. [32]

Sanders, P. et al. (2003), "Airborne brake wear debris: Size distributions, composition, and a comparison of dynamometer and vehicle tests", *Environmental Science and Technology*, Vol. 37/18, pp. 4060-4069, http://dx.doi.org/10.1021/es034145s. [37]

Schaap, M. et al. (2009), "Regional Modelling of Particulate Matter for the Netherlands" January, p. 99, http://www.rivm.nl/bibliotheek/rapporten/500099008.pdf. [15]

Schaap, M. et al. (2009), "Regional Modelling of Particulate Matter for the Netherlands" January, p. 99, http://www.rivm.nl/bibliotheek/rapporten/500099008.pdf. [176]

Schauer, J. et al. (2006), "Characterization of metals emitted from motor vehicles.", *Research report (Health Effects Institute)* 133, pp. 1-76; discussion 77-88. [95]

Secretaria del Medio Ambiente de la Ciudad de Mexico (2018), "Inventario de Emisiones de la Ciudad de Mexico 2016", p. 111, http://www.aire.cdmx.gob.mx/descargas/publicaciones/flippingbook/inventario-emisiones-2016/mobile/inventario-emisiones-2016.pdf. [77]

Sehmel, G. (1973), "Particle resuspension from an asphalt road caused by car and truck traffic", *Atmospheric Environment (1967)*, Vol. 7/3, pp. 291-309, http://dx.doi.org/10.1016/0004-6981(73)90078-4. [174]

Simons, A. (2016), "Road transport: new life cycle inventories for fossil-fuelled passenger cars and non-exhaust emissions in ecoinvent v3", *The International Journal of Life Cycle Assessment*, Vol. 21/9, pp. 1299-1313, http://dx.doi.org/10.1007/s11367-013-0642-9. [137]

Sioutas, C., R. Delfino and M. Singh (2005), "Exposure Assessment for Atmospheric Ultrafine Particles (UFPs) and Implications in Epidemiologic Research", *Environmental Health Perspectives*, Vol. 113/8, pp. 947-955, http://dx.doi.org/10.1289/ehp.7939. [28]

Son, J. et al. (2012), "Characterization of fine particulate matter and associations between particulate chemical constituents and mortality in Seoul, Korea", *Environmental Health Perspectives*, Vol. 120/6, pp. 872-878, http://dx.doi.org/10.1289/ehp.1104316. [205]

Stafoggia, M. and A. Faustini (2018), "Impact on Public Health—Epidemiological Studies: A Review of Epidemiological Studies on Non-Exhaust Particles: Identification of Gaps and Future Needs", in Amato, F. (ed.), *Non-Exhaust Emissions*, Academic Press, San Diego, http://dx.doi.org/10.1016/B978-0-12-811770-5.00003-0. [107]

Stafoggia, M. et al. (2017), "Association Between Short-term Exposure to Ultrafine Particles and Mortality in Eight European Urban Areas.", *Epidemiology*, Vol. 28/2, pp. 172-180, http://dx.doi.org/10.1097/EDE.0000000000000599. [29]

Suh, H. et al. (2011), "Chemical properties of air pollutants and cause-specific hospital admissions among the elderly in Atlanta, Georgia", *Environmental Health Perspectives*, Vol. 119/10, pp. 1421-1428, http://dx.doi.org/10.1289/ehp.1002646. [112]

Sun, S. et al. (2016), "Chemical components of respirable particulate matter associated with emergency hospital admissions for type 2 diabetes mellitus in Hong Kong", *Environment International*, Vol. 97, pp. 93-99, http://dx.doi.org/10.1016/j.envint.2016.10.022. [114]

Thorpe, A. and R. Harrison (2008), "Sources and properties of non-exhaust particulate matter from road traffic: A review", *Science of The Total Environment*, Vol. 400/1-3, pp. 270-282, http://dx.doi.org/10.1016/J.SCITOTENV.2008.06.007. [45]

Thorpe, A. et al. (2007), "Estimation of particle resuspension source strength on a major London Road", *Atmospheric Environment*, Vol. 41/37, pp. 8007-8020, http://dx.doi.org/10.1016/j.atmosenv.2007.07.006. [184]

Thurston, G. et al. (2016), "Ischemic heart disease mortality and long-term exposure to source-related components of U.S. fine particle air pollution", *Environmental Health Perspectives*, Vol. 124/6, pp. 785-794, http://dx.doi.org/10.1289/ehp.1509777. [213]

Tiittanen, P. et al. (1999), "Fine particulate air pollution, resuspended road dust and respiratory health among symptomatic children", *European Respiratory Journal*, Vol. 13/2, pp. 266-273, http://dx.doi.org/10.1034/j.1399-3003.1999.13b08.x. [113]

Timmers, V. and P. Achten (2016), "Non-exhaust PM emissions from electric vehicles", *Atmospheric Environment*, Vol. 134, pp. 10-17, http://dx.doi.org/10.1016/j.atmosenv.2016.03.017. [1]

Timmers, V. and P. Achten (2016), "Non-exhaust PM emissions from electric vehicles", *Atmospheric Environment*, Vol. 134, pp. 10-17, http://dx.doi.org/10.1016/J.ATMOSENV.2016.03.017. [178]

Tobías, A. et al. (2018), "Short-term effects of ultrafine particles on daily mortality by primary vehicle exhaust versus secondary origin in three Spanish cities", *Environment International*, Vol. 111, pp. 144-151, http://dx.doi.org/10.1016/J.ENVINT.2017.11.015. [30]

Tonne, C. et al. (2016), "Long-term traffic air and noise pollution in relation to mortality and hospital readmission among myocardial infarction survivors", *International Journal of Hygiene and Environmental Health*, Vol. 219/1, pp. 72-78, http://dx.doi.org/10.1016/j.ijheh.2015.09.003. [110]

Tonne, C. et al. (2016), "Long-term traffic air and noise pollution in relation to mortality and hospital readmission among myocardial infarction survivors", *International Journal of Hygiene and Environmental Health*, Vol. 219/1, pp. 72-78, http://dx.doi.org/10.1016/j.ijheh.2015.09.003. [227]

U.S. Environmental Protection Agency (2019), *National Emissions Inventory (NEI)*, https://www.epa.gov/air-emissions-inventories/national-emissions-inventory-nei (accessed on 19 May 2019). [76]

U.S. Environmental Protection Agency (2011), "13.2.1 Paved Roads", in *AP-42, Fifth Edition, Volume I.* [68]

UNECE (2019), *Particle Measurement Programme*, Transport - Vehicle Regulations, https://wiki.unece.org/pages/viewpage.action?pageId=2523173 (accessed on 15 November 2019). [39]

Valdés, A. et al. (2012), "Elemental concentrations of ambient particles and cause specific mortality in Santiago, Chile: A time series study", *Environmental Health: A Global Access Science Source*, Vol. 11/1, pp. 1-8, http://dx.doi.org/10.1186/1476-069X-11-82. [206]

Vedal, S. et al. (2013), *National Particle Component Toxicity (NPACT) initiative report on cardiovascular effects.*, http://www.ncbi.nlm.nih.gov/pubmed/24377210. [119]

Vedal, S. et al. (2013), *National Particle Component Toxicity (NPACT) initiative report on cardiovascular effects.*, http://www.ncbi.nlm.nih.gov/pubmed/24377210. [214]

Veirh, A. (1992), "A Review of Important Factors Affecting Treadwear", *Rubber Chemistry and Technology*, Vol. 65/3, pp. 601-659, http://dx.doi.org/10.5254/1.3538631. [163]

Venkatram, A. (2000), "A critique of empirical emission factor models: a case study of the AP-42 model for estimating PM10 emissions from paved roads", *Atmospheric Environment*, Vol. 34/1, pp. 1-11, http://dx.doi.org/10.1016/S1352-2310(99)00330-1. [69]

Viman, L. and M. Gustafsson (2015), "Slaggasfalt , delrapport C Slitage och bildning av inandningsbara partiklar (PM 10)". [164]

Von Uexküll, O. et al. (2005), "Antimony in brake pads-a carcinogenic component?", *Journal of Cleaner Production*, Vol. 13/1, pp. 19-31, http://dx.doi.org/10.1016/j.jclepro.2003.10.008. [46]

Wåhlin, P., R. Berkowicz and F. Palmgren (2006), "Characterisation of traffic-generated particulate matter in Copenhagen", *Atmospheric Environment*, Vol. 40/12, pp. 2151-2159, http://dx.doi.org/10.1016/j.atmosenv.2005.11.049. [12]

Wahlström, J. et al. (2017), "Contact Pressure and Sliding Velocity Maps of the Friction, Wear and Emission from a Low-Metallic/Cast-Iron Disc Brake Contact Pair", *Tribology in Industry*, Vol. 39/4, pp. 460-470, http://dx.doi.org/10.24874/ti.2017.39.04.05. [132]

Wahlström, J. et al. (2010), "A pin-on-disc simulation of airborne wear particles from disc brakes", *Wear*, Vol. 268/5-6, pp. 763-769, http://dx.doi.org/10.1016/j.wear.2009.11.014. [139]

Wang, C. et al. (2017), "The influence of the contact features on the tyre wear in steady-state conditions", *Proceedings of the Institution of Mechanical Engineers, Part D: Journal of Automobile Engineering*, Vol. 231/10, pp. 1326-1339, http://dx.doi.org/10.1177/0954407016671462. [144]

Wang, H. et al. (2016), "Global, regional, national, and selected subnational levels of stillbirths, neonatal, infant, and under-5 mortality, 1980-2015: a systematic analysis for the Global Burden of Disease Study 2015", *Lancet*, Vol. 388/10053, pp. 1725-1774, http://dx.doi.org/10.1016/S0140-6736(16)31575-6. [85]

Wang, M. et al. (2014), "Long-term exposure to elemental constituents of particulate matter and cardiovascular mortality in 19 European cohorts: Results from the ESCAPE and TRANSPHORM projects", *Environment International*, Vol. 66, pp. 97-106, http://dx.doi.org/10.1016/j.envint.2014.01.026. [215]

Wang, Y. et al. (2017), "Long-term Exposure to PM2.5 and Mortality Among Older Adults in the Southeastern US", *Epidemiology*, Vol. 28/2, pp. 207-214, http://dx.doi.org/10.1097/EDE.0000000000000614. [216]

Wellenius, G. et al. (2003), *Inhalation of concentrated ambient air particles exacerbates myocardial ischemia in conscious dogs*, http://dx.doi.org/10.1289/ehp.5775. [100]

WHO Regional Office for Europe (2013), *Review of evidence on health aspects of air pollution – REVIHAAP Project*, http://www.euro.who.int (accessed on 20 March 2020). [89]

Willers, S. et al. (2013), "Fine and coarse particulate air pollution in relation to respiratory health in Sweden", *European Respiratory Journal*, Vol. 42/4, pp. 924-934, http://dx.doi.org/10.1183/09031936.00088212. [120]

Willers, S. et al. (2013), "Fine and coarse particulate air pollution in relation to respiratory health in Sweden", *European Respiratory Journal*, Vol. 42/4, pp. 924-934, http://dx.doi.org/10.1183/09031936.00088212. [228]

Wiman, L. et al. (2009), *Prov med olika överbyggnadstyper: Uppföljning av observationssträckor på väg E6, Fastarp–Heberg 1996–2006*, VTI rapport 632, VTI, http://www.vti.se/publikationerProvmedolikaöverbyggnadstyper (accessed on 20 May 2019). [165]

Wolf, K. et al. (2015), "Long-term Exposure to Particulate Matter Constituents and the Incidence of Coronary Events in 11 European Cohorts", *Epidemiology*, Vol. 26/4, pp. 565-574, http://dx.doi.org/10.1097/EDE.0000000000000300. [229]

Zanobetti, A. et al. (2009), "Fine particulate air pollution and its components in association with cause-specific emergency admissions", *Environmental Health: A Global Access Science Source*, Vol. 8/1, http://dx.doi.org/10.1186/1476-069X-8-58. [111]

Zanobetti, A. et al. (2009), "Fine particulate air pollution and its components in association with cause-specific emergency admissions", *Environmental Health: A Global Access Science Source*, Vol. 8/1, http://dx.doi.org/10.1186/1476-069X-8-58. [116]

Zhou, J. et al. (2011), "Time-series analysis of mortality effects of fine particulate matter components in Detroit and seattle", *Environmental Health Perspectives*, Vol. 119/4, pp. 461-466, http://dx.doi.org/10.1289/ehp.1002613. [207]

Zhu, D. et al. (2009), "Fugitive dust emissions from paved road travel in the lake tahoe basin", *Journal of the Air and Waste Management Association*, Vol. 59/10, pp. 1219-1229, http://dx.doi.org/10.3155/1047-3289.59.10.1219. [172]

Žnidarič, A. (2015), *Heavy-Duty Vehicle Weight Restrictions in the EU Enforcement and Compliance Technologies*, ACEA Scientific Advisory Group Report, Brussels, https://www.acea.be/uploads/publications/SAG_23_Heavy-Duty_Vehicle_Weight_Restrictions_in_the_EU.pdf (accessed on 20 May 2019). [146]

zum Hagen, F. et al. (2019), "Study of Brake Wear Particle Emissions: Impact of Braking and Cruising Conditions", *Environmental Science & Technology*, Vol. 53/9, pp. 5143-5150, http://dx.doi.org/10.1021/acs.est.8b07142. [133]

3. The implications of electric vehicle uptake for non-exhaust emissions

This chapter estimates the non-exhaust PM emission factors from electric vehicles and compares these factors with those of internal combustion engine vehicles. Assuming lightweight EVs (i.e. with battery packs enabling a driving range of about 100 miles), the report finds that EVs emit an estimated 11-13% less non-exhaust PM2.5 and 18-19% less PM10 than ICEVs. Assuming that EV models are heavier (with battery packs enabling a driving range of 300 miles or higher), however, the report finds that they reduce PM10 by only 4-7% and increase PM2.5 by 3-8% relative to conventional vehicles. Additional simulations indicate that the uptake of electric vehicles will lead to very marginal decreases in total PM emissions from road traffic in future years. In scenarios where electric vehicles comprise 4% and 8% of the vehicle stock in 2030, their penetration reduces PM emissions by 0.3%-0.8% relative to current levels.

The direct and indirect implications of vehicular emissions on the environment and human health indicate that current transportation systems based on the use of conventional vehicles are unsustainable from social, environmental and economic perspectives. Electric vehicles are widely regarded as a solution to many of the negative impacts of their conventional counterparts. Given their potential to reduce local air pollution and greenhouse gas emissions, consumers, businesses, and governments are increasingly supportive of electric vehicles (Requia et al., 2018[1]), which has led to rising shares of new vehicle sales around the world.

According to the IEA Global EV Outlook 2018 (IEA, 2018[2]), sales of new electric vehicles, including battery electric vehicles (BEVs), plug-in hybrid electric vehicles (PHEVs) and fuel-cell electric vehicles (FCEVs) passed 1 million units in 2017, 54% more than in 2016. More than half of new electric vehicles were sold in China, where their market share amounted to 2.2% in 2017. Twice as many cars were sold in China as in the United States, the second-largest electric car market.

Growth in the EV market has been driven by technological improvements that improve performance and reduce costs, as well as by policy support. To the extent that technological improvements are widely available, differences in EV uptake across markets is best explained by differing degrees of policy support in place in these markets. The largest EV markets by volume (China) and sales share (Norway), for example, are both characterised by highly supportive policy environments. This is true for light-duty vehicles (LDVs) as well as for buses and two-wheelers.

Looking to the future, strong policy signals in favour of EVs include electric car mandates in China and California, as well as the European Union's recent proposal on carbon dioxide emissions standards for 2030 (IEA, 2018[3]). Electrification targets announced by a number of countries and major cities worldwide also point to continued growth in EV uptake in the coming years. The IEA (2018[3]) foresees two possible scenarios of EV penetration worldwide. In the New Policies Scenario, which takes into account existing and announced policies, the number of electric light-duty vehicles on the road reaches 125 million by 2030. Should policy ambitions continue to rise to meet climate goals and other sustainability targets, as in the EV30@30 Scenario, then the number of electric LDVs on the road could be as high as 220 million in 2030, consisting of 130 million battery electric and 90 million plug-in hybrid vehicles, respectively.

3.1. Evidence on the impact of electric vehicle use on particulate emissions

3.1.1. Impacts on particulate emissions levels

Since BEVs do not emit tailpipe emissions, the adoption of these vehicles is generally viewed as a highly effective measure for improving air quality. Although increasing the market share of EVs is an important part of achieving environmental goals, their implications for non-exhaust emissions remain less well-understood than their implications for exhaust emissions.

In a recent review, Requia et al. (2018[1]) assessed 4734 studies on the impact of a shift to greater EV use. Of the 65 studies that fulfilled the inclusion criteria for the review, the authors concluded that while the benefits of EVs with respect to exhaust emissions of a number of air pollutants are well-established, less evidence exists regarding the impact of EV use on PM emissions: these impacts appear to be particularly dependent on context.[1] Since Requia et al. (2018[1]), PM10 and PM2.5 emissions have been studied in 11 papers 16 papers, respectively. Some studies find that EVs offer moderate potential for reductions in PM emissions.[2]

In Ireland, Alam et al., (2018[4]) addressed the co-benefits of climate change mitigation policies to reduce the air pollution (PM2.5) and climate change (CO2) impacts of passenger cars, using a scenario-based approach, disaggregating road traffic PM2.5 in exhaust and brake, tyre and road abrasion. The results revealed that CO2 emissions continuously decreased in the projection period, however, reductions of PM2.5 reversed from the year 2028 due to increases in the non-exhaust component of PM2.5 emissions. Under the two alternative scenarios, a 9-15% reduction in PM2.5 could be achieved by 2035. The analysis suggests that non-exhaust PM2.5 was found to have a larger share of total emissions (as much as 34 times that of exhaust emissions) in 2035 in a scenario in which passenger cars with alternative drivetrains comprised a major part of the vehicle fleet. In the Yangtze River Delta region in China, Ke et al. (2017[5]) estimated that a scenario with 20% of private light-duty passenger vehicles and 80% commercial passenger vehicles electrified with BEV could reduce average total PM2.5 concentrations by 0.4 to 1.1 $\mu g/m^3$.

3.1.2. Determinants of PM emissions impacts

Vehicle weight

Heavier vehicles require greater amounts of energy for acceleration and deceleration, implying greater wear rate of brakes and tyres (Carslaw, 2006[6]). The recent UK government Survey "Call for Evidence on non-exhaust emissions" acknowledged that data on tyre wear from EVs was lacking or not publically available. Nonetheless, many respondents assumed that increased EV weight would lead to increased tyre wear, and possibly higher particulate emissions, although no direct evidence of this was provided.

Van Zeebroek and De Ceuster (2013[7]) compared the weight (mass in running order) of 20 battery electric passenger cars to the average weight of conventional vehicles in the same vehicle segment, finding that EVs are 22% heavier than the average of their market segments. However, comparing EVs to the average passenger car in a category is complicated by a number of issues (see also Timmers and Achten (2018[8])). First, there are various classification systems available. This study used the EURO market segment classification, but vehicles can also be classified using the US EPA Size Class or EURO NCAP Class, which would produce different results. Second, EVs do not always fit well into a specific class. Finally, and most importantly, the vehicles in any vehicle class will vary significantly even within the class. They will have a range of dimensions, engine sizes, and features that renders isolating the impact of weight differences on PM emissions problematic.

Another method of comparing the weight of EVs to ICEVs is by comparing EVs with their equivalent conventional models. This avoids classification problems and ensures that the vehicles are as similar as possible. Timmers and Achten (2016[9]) used this method to compare the mass in running order of nine EVs and their ICEV counterparts. On average, they found the difference in weight to be 24% and assume that road and tyre wear increase linearly with vehicle weight.

The most appropriate comparison would be between vehicles that share identical specifications in all respects except for their drivetrains. However, EVs and ICEVs often have different specifications in terms of materials used, range, top speed, trailer load, types of tyres, and brakes, among others. Moreover, the increased weight due to the addition of battery pack depends on a number of characteristics (battery density, efficiency and km range) which vary from one segment to another and are also expected to evolve in the future. Finally, there is no evidence that two vehicles with the same size and shape but different weights have different emission factors for road dust resuspension.

Hooftman et al. (2016[10]) assumed that BEVs had 10% higher emissions from tyre wear due to their increased weight and tyre type, but they do not specify the assumptions underlying this estimation. Other studies have assumed no difference in non-exhaust emissions between BEVs and ICEVs (Requia et al., 2018[1]; Soret, Guevara and Baldasano, 2014[11]; Huo et al., 2015[12]).

Regenerative braking

Regenerative braking systems (RBS) are energy recovery mechanisms that slow a vehicle by converting its kinetic energy into a form which can be either used immediately or stored until needed. In these systems, the electric motor uses the vehicle's momentum to recover energy that would be otherwise lost to the brake discs as heat. This contrasts with friction braking systems, where the excess kinetic energy is converted to heat by friction in the brakes. In addition to improving the overall efficiency of the vehicle, RBS can greatly extend the life of the braking system, as its parts do not wear as quickly.

On hybrid and electric vehicles, pressing the brake pedal has very different effects, as the strategy followed is mostly oriented to maximising the amount of energy recuperated through regenerative braking, i.e. using the electric circuits in reverse to transform kinetic energy into deceleration. The amount of regenerative energy that a system can produce is strictly related to the maximum power of the installed electric motor(s) and electronics, and to the capacity of the battery to receive the energy without degrading. Above a certain battery size, the energy of a braking event can be recovered, except in the case this happens with the battery still fully charged. It is therefore safe to assume, that fully electric vehicles have extremely low brake emissions (the pads are used mainly to keep the vehicle at a standstill). Hybrid vehicles also have relatively low brake wear emissions, proportional to the level of hybridisation (micro hybrids show practically no advantage from this point of view, since the added mass is likely to compensate for the reduced energy to be dissipated). Vice versa, for RBS-equipped vehicles with large batteries, vehicle mass has a low to negligible influence on brake wear.

Several estimates of the impact of RBS on brake wear PM emissions exist in literature. The Platform for Electro-Mobility (2016[13]) claims that RBS reduce brake wear by 25-50%. Van Zeebroek and De Ceuster (2013[7]) assume that regenerative braking should reduce the PM emissions associated with brake wear by 50%. Timmers and Achten (2016[9]) assume a zero brake wear emissions from RBS-equipped vehicles, and Barlow (2014[14]) also suggests that regenerative braking produces virtually no brake wear. Hooftman et al. (2016[10]) state that EVs require about two-thirds (66%) less braking activity than ICEVs due to RBS. Their analysis is based on the service times of brake pads on Teslas, BMW i3s, and Nissan Leafs, which demonstrates that on average, the brake pads of these EVs last roughly two-thirds longer than those on diesel/petrol vehicles. They note that this outweighs the additional wear due to the vehicle's mass. Ligterink et al. (2014[15]) assume regenerative braking reduces wear by up to 95%. Del Duce et al. (2016[16]) report that brake wear emissions fall by 80% for EVs, based on a report by Althaus and Gauch (2010[17]). Nopmongcol et al. (2017[18]) estimated a 25% reduction of brake wear.

Road dust resuspension

Out of many studies evaluating the relative environmental burden of BEVs and ICEVs, only a handful have analysed PM10 (Kantor et al., 2010[19]; Huo et al., 2013[20]; Nichols, Kockelman and Reiter, 2015[21]; Huo et al., 2015[12]; Peng et al., 2018[22]; Nopmongcol et al., 2017[18]; Wu and Zhang, 2017[23]; Hooftman et al., 2016[10]; Timmers and Achten, 2016[9]), and of these, only six considered non-exhaust emissions. Road dust resuspension was included in only three studies. As evidenced in Section 2, road dust resuspension is currently understood to be the main source of non-exhaust PM10 emissions for road vehicles. This is confirmed both by emission inventories (Pachón et al., 2018[24]; Secretaria del Medio Ambiente de la Ciudad de Mexico, 2018[25]; DICTUC, 2007[26]; U.S. Environmental Protection Agency, 2019[27]), which consider primary particulates, as well as by source apportionment studies (Padoan and Amato, 2018[28]) which assess secondary PM from vehicle exhaust emissions.

Given its importance as a source of non-exhaust PM10 emissions, road dust resuspension should be taken into account in vehicle emissions assessments. As evidenced by the literature inventoried in this report, non-exhaust emissions from road dust resuspension have been neglected in most studies to date (Van Zeebroeck and De Ceuster, 2013[7]; Hooftman et al., 2016[10]; Requia et al., 2018[29]). An exception is Soret et al. (2014[11]), who include an emission factor for resuspension of 88 mg/vkm, adjusted for rainfall but invariant to vehicle class. Timmers and Achten (2016[9]) have also corrected a base road dust EF of 40 mg/vkm used for ICEV, increasing it by 24% on the assumption of a linear relationship between vehicle weight and resuspension emissions. As already seen in Section 2, a relationship between vehicle weight and road dust emission factor is questionable as only aerodynamic features (size and shape) should affect resuspension from paved roads.

Differences in findings are driven by differences in PM fractions of primary and secondary emissions, the emission processes under consideration, as well as the methodologies used for their estimation. A review of this literature reveals a number of factors that determine the amount of particulate matter emitted by BEVs vs. ICEVs.

Secondary aerosols

Secondary aerosols (SA) are formed in the atmosphere by gas-particle conversion processes such as nucleation, condensation and heterogeneous chemical reactions (Ziemann and Atkinson, 2012[30]; Zhang et al., 2007[31]; Carlton, Wiedinmyer and Kroll,

2009[32]). Secondary aerosols are therefore not included in emission inventory and their contribution can only be estimated through PM chemical speciation (offline or online) or by air quality modelling. Only eight studies accounted for secondary PM from ICEVs when comparing their environmental burden with that of BEVs, using air quality modelling (Nopmongcol et al., 2017[18]; Ke et al., 2017[5]; Razeghi et al., 2016[33]; Tobollik et al., 2016[34]; Tessum, Hill and Marshall, 2014[35]; Li et al., 2016[36]; Soret, Guevara and Baldasano, 2014[11]).

Air quality models still have difficulties, however, in reproducing observed particulate matter (PM) concentration levels. This is mostly due to a poor representation of the organic aerosols fractions—primary and notably secondary—limiting the capability to assess the full air quality impact of ICEVs. Despite the substantial number of studies conducted during the last decades, the source apportionment of the secondary organic aerosols (SOA) fraction remains difficult, due to the complexity of the physicochemical processes involved. The selection and use of appropriate approaches are a major challenge for the atmospheric science community.

3.2. Calculating primary and secondary PM from exhaust

Primary PM emissions

For ICEVs, EURO 6-temp emission factors for primary exhaust emissions of PM10 and PM2.5 are taken from (Ntziachristos and Samaras, 2018[37]), which is a widely used reference for emission reporting in EU.

Secondary inorganic aerosol (SIA) formation

While natural sources (seas and volcanoes) dominate SIA at a global scale, SIA at the urban scale are mainly due to anthropogenic (combustion) sources. Given the low-sulphur content of current fuels used in road transport in most regions of the world (CCAC, 2016[38]), the road traffic contribution to SIA is generally comprised of NH_4NO_3 (ammonium nitrate) formation from NO_x (vehicles) and NH_3 (mainly from agriculture) emissions. This report provides a range of estimates of SIAs from exhaust emissions using the LOTOS-EUROS source apportionment tool applied to European countries (as has been done for the Netherlands in Hendriks et al. (2013[39])). LOTOS-EUROS is a CTM model incorporating a “labelling” tool, which involves tracking specific emissions from the source to the receptor, thus allowing for source apportionment analysis of secondary aerosols. The main advantage of this approach with respect to receptor models like PMF, is that the full (modelled) NH_4NO_3 is apportioned, while PMF is typically unable to do so. Source apportionment analysis was performed for European countries over one year (2018), which provided nitrate and elemental carbon (EC) concentrations (μg/m^3) from LDV for each country. This allows for the estimation of a range of gas-to-particle conversion rates over a quite heterogeneous geographical domain, i.e. covering different climatic conditions and anthropogenic source types. The range for SIA emission factors was calculated as:

$$maxSIA_{ij} - minSIA_{ij} = \left(max\frac{NO3_i}{EC_i} - min\frac{NO3_i}{EC_i}\right) * \frac{NOx_j}{NOx_{fleet}} * 1.29$$

where $NO3_i/EC_i$ is the ratio between nitrate and elemental carbon due to LDV emissions for i^{th} country, NOx_j/NOx_{fleet} is the ratio between the NOx emission factor for the jth vehicle type (e.g. diesel EURO6-temp) and the average NOx emission factor for the whole EU fleet, estimated based on Ntziachristos and Samaras (2018[37]) for emission factors, CARB

(2020[40]) for age composition and OICA (2020[41]) for fuels/classes distribution. The constant 1.29 is the molecular mass ratio between ammonium nitrate and nitrate.

Secondary organic aerosols (SOA) formation

Similarly to SIA, SOA are known to account for a significant fraction of airborne PM, with considerable impacts on air quality. The contribution of SOA to organic aerosols (OA) reaches up to 80% under certain atmospheric conditions (Carlton, Wiedinmyer and Kroll, 2009[32]). Most organic aerosols (OA) in urban and rural atmospheres are speculated to be secondary in nature but their exact chemical composition remains uncertain (Shrivastava et al., 2007[42]; Zhao et al., 2013[43]). In contrast with SIA, SOA are formed from both biogenic (i.e. naturally occurring) and anthropogenic gaseous emission sources, even at the urban scale (Griffin et al., 1999[44]; Vidhi and Shrivastava, 2018[45]). Several methodologies currently used assess SOA levels and composition, including the elemental carbon (EC) tracer method, chemical mass balance method (CMB), SOA tracer method, radiocarbon (14C) measurement and positive matrix factorization (PMF). Another group of studies uses simulation chambers in which SOA formation is reproduced under controlled conditions (Platt et al., 2017[46]).

In this report, we compiled the chemical factor profile of 26 PMF analyses carried out in the US in which authors were able to separate between emissions from gasoline LDVs and diesel HDVs (e.g. (Kim and Hopke, 2004[47]; Kim et al., 2003[48]; Kim, Hopke and Edgerton, 2004[49]; Wang et al., 2012[50]; Zhao and Hopke, 2006[51]; Gildemeister, Hopke and Kim, 2007[52]; Lee and Hopke, 2006[53]). We then applied the EC tracer method, applying an average primary OC/EC ratio of 3.7 for gasoline and 0.5 for diesel, respectively, considering the age distribution of US fleet in 2000 and ratios of organic matter to elemental carbon (OM/EC ratios) from Ntziachristos and Samaras (2018[37]). Compiling these factor profiles, we found median values for secondary-to-primary organic carbon (SOC/POC) ratios of 0 (i.e. no formation of SOC) for diesel and 0.35 for gasoline emissions, respectively. We then multiplied the SOC by a factor of 1.5, following Aiken et al. (2008[54]), in order to convert SOC to SOA.

Estimates of SIA and SOA assume that the area of study as representative of a global situation, which is not likely given that secondary aerosol formation does not depend linearly on gaseous precursors and is heavily affected by local conditions such as air temperature, relative humidity and ambient concentrations of various precursors. There are limitations to each approach. SIA could be underestimated given that only modelled nitrate is apportioned and that secondary sulphate is not included (relevant for countries using high-sulphur diesel (CCAC, 2016[38])). SOA estimates are affected by errors from a possible inaccurate apportionment of OC. Moreover, in the United States, diesel is used almost exclusively by HDVs which may have a different OM/EC ratio than LDVs (the category used in (Ntziachristos and Samaras (2018[37])). We also assume SOC/POC ratios to be same between EURO6 vehicles and the pre-2000 fleet.

3.3. Calculating primary PM from non-exhaust sources

This section develops a methodological approach to compare non-exhaust emissions between battery electric and internal combustion vehicles. The comparison is performed for three vehicle categories: passenger cars (PCs), sport utility vehicles (SUVs) and light commercial vans (LCVs). These categories correspond to the following European Nomenclature for Reporting (NFR) categories: “Medium cars,” “Large-SUV-Executive,” and “Light Commercial Vehicles < 3.5 t (LCV).” Assumptions regarding vehicle weights follow those estimated by the Argonne National Laboratory from updated vehicle specifications for the GREET Vehicle-Cycle model (Argonne National Laboratory, 2019[55]).

The benchmark ICEVs considered are diesel and gasoline EURO6d-temp vehicles. Estimates of UFP particle numbers are not addressed given the scarcity of data and the considerable uncertainty regarding EF estimates from non-exhaust processes (Amato, 2018[56]). Additional assumptions used in the calculation of non-exhaust emission factors are reviewed in the subsequent sections.

Internal combustion engine vehicles

For ICEVs, base emission factors for primary non-exhaust emissions of PM10 and PM2.5 for brake wear, tyre wear and road wear are taken from Ntziachristos & Boulter (2016[57]), which is a widely used reference for emission reporting in the EU.[3] PM10 emission factors for road dust resuspension are calculated as the median of the lower bounds of observed ranges in the literature for light duty vehicles, corresponding to 0.009 g/vkm for LDV. Because the LDV category includes PCs, SUVs and LCVs, we performed a least squares fit model, using fleet-averaged emission factor data from two studies in Barcelona and Zurich (Amato et al., 2012[58]; Bukowiecki et al., 2010[59]) and assuming that the distribution of these vehicle types in these locations is similar to that in the metropolitan area of Milan (ACI Automobile Club d'Italia, 2019[60]).

When applied to current assumptions regarding each vehicle type, this analysis yields road dust EFs of 0.0083, 0.0099, and 0.0113 g/vkm for PC, SUV and LCV respectively. All of these values are significantly lower than the 0.040 g/vkm used by Timmers and Achten (2016[9]) or the 0.088 g/vkm used by Soret et al. (2014[11]). The reason for this more conservative choice is driven by the large variability observed in the literature, which reflects the large number of factors influencing EFs (vehicle speed, weight and road dust loading among others, see Section 2). Given that the highest values were found where additional sources of road dust are present (e.g. dust sources on the roadside, road shoulders, sanding/salting and use of studded tyres), road dust loadings appear to be most responsible for the variability in EFs in the literature. The estimate of non-exhaust EF used in this analysis can therefore be considered a lower bound, as it does not take into account additional sources of road dust emissions that are likely to be present in certain regions.

We base the PM2.5 component of road dust emissions on the PM10 estimate via the application of a mean PM2.5/PM10 ratio of 0.34 (standard deviation of 0.27) that characterises road dust contributions, as found in the literature (Chan et al 1999; (Achilleos et al., 2016[61]; Chan et al., 2008[62]; Cheng et al., 2015[63]; Srimuruganandam and Shiva Nagendra, 2012[64]; Gummeneni et al., 2011[65]; Guttikunda et al., 2013[66]; Perrone et al., 2012[67]; Almeida et al., 2005[68]; Amato et al., 2009[69]; Amato et al., 2014[70]).

Battery electric vehicles

Emission factors for BEVs are calculated based on evidence about the quantitative relationships between various vehicle characteristics and the PM emissions generated by brake, tyre, and road wear, and road dust resuspension. As described in Section 1, vehicle weight is the main determinant of wear emissions. In a first step therefore, quantitative relationships between vehicle weight and each non-exhaust emissions generation process are estimated based on the available literature. Emission factors are then calculated by applying the assumed weight of BEVs in each vehicle category to these estimated relationships (see Table 3.1 and Table 3.2)

A lack of robust quantitative evidence characterises the literature concerning the relationship between brake wear and vehicle weight. This relationship was therefore estimated using existing estimates of brake wear emission factors for medium-sized cars and LCVs, assuming their respective mean weights according to the GREET model (Argonne National Laboratory, 2019[55]).

The relationship between vehicle weight and tyre wear is estimated using a range of values found in the literature. Emission factors are first estimated using a linear relationship, similar to (Chen and Prathaban, 2013[256]; Aatmeeyata, Kaul and Sharma, 2009[257]; Wang et al., 2017[258]; Li et al., 2012[259]; Simons, 2016[260]). They are also estimated using a non-linear relationship based on results from Salminen (2014[261]) and Ngeno and Mohammadi (2015). In the absence of a functional form proposed, a power-law function is used, following the approach for brake wear as described in Table 3.1 and Table 3.2

No robust relationships for road wear emission factors as a function of ve hicle weight were found in the literature. Although a power law of 4 has been proposed for HDV loads (ACEA, 2015), applying this relationship to LDVs is not recommended. Following EMEP/EEA, all vehicle classes are therefore assumed to have the same road wear emission factors. For road dust resuspension, the OLS model described in Table 3.1 and Table 3.2 estimate 19% and 36% higher road dust EFs for SUV and LCV categories relative to PCs, likely due to their larger size.

Table 3.1 Estimation methods used in the calculation of PM2.5 non-exhaust emissions for BEVs

Source	Estimation Method	
Brake wear	$0.25 * 2x10^{-7} * Weight_j^{\ 1.290}$ Model estimated using EF values for PC and LDV from Ntziachristos and Boulter (2016[57]) (0.0029 g/km and 0.0046 g/km, respectively) and weights for vehicle classes *j* from (Argonne National Laboratory, 2019[55]). A 75% reduction in brake wear from RBS is also assumed.	
Tyre wear	Model 1 $3x10^{-7}\ Weight_j^{\ 1.326}$ Power law model estimated using EF values for PC and LDV from Ntziachristos and Boulter (2016[57]) (0.0064 g/km and 0.0101 g/km, respectively) and weights for vehicle classes *j* from (Argonne National Laboratory, 2019[55]).	Model 2 For PCs and SUVs: $0.0031 * Weight_j$ For LCVs: $0.0035 * Weight_j$ Linear model estimated using EFs from Ntziachristos and Boulter (2016[57]) and weights for vehicle classes *j* from (Argonne National Laboratory, 2019[55]).
Road wear	N/A Values are taken from Ntziachristos and Boulter (2016[57]) (0.0041 for all vehicle classes)	
Road dust resuspension	$0.34 * EF_j^{PM10}$ A ratio of $PM_{2.5}/PM_{10}$ emissions from road dust is applied to EF_j^{PM10}, the PM10 EF from road dust suspension for vehicle class *j* (last row in Table 3.1), according to the mean found in the literature (Chan et al 1999; Achilleos et al 2016; Wahlin et al 2006; Cheng et al 2015; Srimuruganandam and Shiva Nagendra 2012a and 2012b; Gummeneni et al 2011; Guttikunda et al., 2013; Perrone at al., 2012; Almeida et al., 2005; Amato et al., 2009b and 2014a).	

Note: Base EFs are assumed the same for diesel and gasoline-fuelled vehicles. Tables 3.5, 3.7, and 3.9 in (Ntziachristos and Boulter, 2016[57]) contain estimates of the mass fraction of TSP (gPM/gTSP) and Tables 3.4, 3.6, and 3.8 in (Ntziachristos and Boulter, 2016[57]) contain estimates of TSP emission factors (gTSP/vkm). See Table 3.3 for weight assumptions.

Table 3.2 Estimation methods used in the calculation of PM10 non-exhaust emissions for BEVs

Source	Estimation Method	
Brake wear	$0.25 \times 6x10^{-7} \times Weight_j^{1.290}$ Model is estimated using EF values for PC and LDV from Ntziachristos and Boulter (2016[57]) (0.0074 and 0.0015 g/km, respectively) and weights for vehicle classes j from (Argonne National Laboratory, 2019[55]). A 75% reduction in brake wear from RBS is also assumed following the mean of the estimates in the literature.	
Tyre wear	Model 1 $4x10^{-7}\ Weight_j^{1.326}$ Power law model estimated using EF values for PC and LDV from Ntziachristos and Boulter (2016[57]) (0.0064 and 0.0101 g/km, respectively) and weights for vehicle classes *j* from (Argonne National Laboratory, 2019[55]).	Model 2 For PCs and SUVs: 0.0044 * $Weight_j$ For LCVs: 0.0049 * $Weight_j$ Linear model estimated using EFs from Ntziachristos and Boulter (2016[57]) and weights for vehicle classes *j* from (Argonne National Laboratory, 2019[55]).
Road wear	N/A Values are taken from Ntziachristos and Boulter (2016[57]) for ICEV vehicles (0.0075 for all vehicle classes)	
Road dust resuspension	Final EFs are calculated for each class based on an optimisation tool that minimises the difference between observed total LDV emissions per day at three locations (Bukowiecki et al., 2010[59]; Amato et al., 2012[71]) and the sum of emissions per day from different vehicles categories, assuming a distribution of PCs, SUVs, and LCVs according to vehicle stock estimates in Milan (ACI Automobile Club d'Italia, 2019[60]).	

Note: Base EFs are assumed to be the same for diesel and gasoline-fuelled vehicles. Tables 3.5, 3.7, and 3.9 in (Ntziachristos and Boulter, 2016[57]) contain estimates of the mass fraction of TSP (gPM/gTSP) and Tables 3.4, 3.6, and 3.8 in (Ntziachristos and Boulter, 2016[57]) contain estimates of TSP emission factors (gTSP/vkm). See Table 3.3 below for weight assumptions.

Table 3.3 Vehicle weight assumptions (kg)

Vehicle class	ICEV	BEV 100	Difference	BEV 300	Difference
PC	1453	1517	+4 %	1949	+34 %
SUV	1775	1866	+5 %	2437	+37 %
LCV	2051	2185	+6 %	2904	+41 %

Source: (Argonne National Laboratory, 2019[55])

The extra weight of BEVs with respect to ICEVs, relevant for the calculation of brake and tyre wear emission factors, is based on updated vehicle specifications for the GREET Vehicle-Cycle model developed by the Argonne National Laboratory (2019[55]) . Both BEVs with a 100-mile range (BEV 100) and a 300-mile range (BEV 300) are considered in the analysis. BEVs with a longer range are heavier due to the weight of the battery. Lighter weight BEVs with a shorter range are between 4% and 6% heavier than ICEVs, while heavier BEVs are between 34 and 41% heavier than ICEVs across vehicle classes.

Other estimates in the literature have placed the difference within this range, at around 20-25% (Van Zeebroeck and De Ceuster, 2013[7]; Timmers and Achten, 2016[9]).

3.4. Particulate matter emitted by conventional and electric vehicles

3.4.1. Total PM emission factors

Estimations of exhaust and non-exhaust emission factors for passenger cars (PCs), SUVs, and LCVs are listed in Table 3.4 and Table 3.5. Between 95 and 98% of primary PM10 emissions come from non-exhaust sources and between 74 and 96% of total (primary + secondary) PM10 are emitted by EURO 6-temp ICEV. These shares are similarly high for PM2.5: 88-96% of primary PM2.5 emissions come from non-exhaust sources and 65-93% of total PM2.5 are emitted by ICEVs. The non-exhaust share of total PM is generally lower for diesel ICEVs than gasoline since the contribution of diesel to secondary aerosols is higher than that of gasoline. There are small differences between vehicle categories, with 90.6% of PM10 and 85% of PM2.5 from ICEV PCs originating from non-exhaust sources, 93% and 88% for SUVs and 95% and 91% for LCVs.

Table 3.4 PM2.5 emission factors across EURO-6-temp and BEV vehicle classes (g/vkm)

		PC				SUV				LCV			
		Diesel	Gasoline	BEV 100	BEV 300	Diesel	Gasoline	BEV 100	BEV 300	Diesel	Gasoline	BEV 100	BEV 300
Non-exhaust	low	0.0121	0.0121	0.0100	0.0115	0.0133	0.0133	0.0113	0.0135	0.0165	0.0165	0.0134	0.0164
	high	0.0165	0.0165	0.0147	0.0169	0.0193	0.0193	0.0174	0.0206	0.0226	0.0226	0.0200	0.0241
Exhaust (total)	low	0.0020	0.0017			0.0020	0.0017			0.0013	0.0013		
	high	0.0088	0.0026			0.0088	0.0026			0.0071	0.0020		
Primary		0.0015	0.0016			0.0015	0.0016			0.0009	0.0012		
Secondary													
SOA			0.0003				0.0003				0.0002		
SIA	low	0.0005	0.0001			0.0005	0.0001			0.0004	0.0001		
	high	0.0073	0.0010			0.0073	0.0010			0.0062	0.0008		
Total PM	low	0.0141	0.0137	0.0100	0.0115	0.0153	0.0150	0.0113	0.0135	0.0178	0.0178	0.0134	0.0164
	high	0.0253	0.0192	0.0147	0.0169	0.0281	0.0219	0.0174	0.0206	0.0297	0.0246	0.0200	0.0241
Percent non-exhaust	low	85.7%	87.8%			86.9%	88.9%			92.6%	92.9%		
	high	65.3%	86.3%			68.7%	88.2%			76.1%	91.9%		

Table 3.5 PM10 emission factors across EURO 6-temp ICEV and BEV vehicle classes (g/vkm)

		PC				SUV				LCV			
		Diesel	Gasoline	BEV 100	BEV 300	Diesel	Gasoline	BEV 100	BEV 300	Diesel	Gasoline	BEV 100	BEV 300
Non-exhaust PM	low	0.0296	0.0296	0.0243	0.0270	0.0346	0.0346	0.0281	0.0317	0.0404	0.0404	0.0326	0.0376
	high	0.0296	0.0296	0.0244	0.0276	0.0349	0.0349	0.0286	0.0333	0.0404	0.0404	0.0326	0.0388
Exhaust PM (total)	low	0.0033	0.0018			0.0033	0.0018			0.0024	0.0014		
	high	0.0103	0.0028			0.0103	0.0028			0.0084	0.0022		
Primary		0.0015	0.0016			0.0015	0.0016			0.0009	0.0012		
Secondary			0.0003				0.0003				0.0002		
SOA													
SIA	low	0.0018	0.0002			0.0018	0.0002			0.0015	0.0002		

	high	0.0088	0.0012			0.0088	0.0012			0.0075	0.0010		
Total PM	low	0.0328	0.0317	0.0243	0.0270	0.0378	0.0367	0.0281	0.0317	0.0428	0.0420	0.0326	0.0376
	high	0.0399	0.0327	0.0244	0.0276	0.0452	0.0379	0.0286	0.0333	0.0488	0.0428	0.0326	0.0388
Percent non-exhaust		90.1%	93.4%			91.4%	94.3%			94.4%	96.2%		
		74.1%	90.6%			77.2%	92.0%			82.8%	94.5%		

3.4.2. Non-exhaust PM emission factors

Estimated PM2.5 and PM10 emission factors from non-exhaust sources are reported in Tables 3.4 and 3.5, respectively. Estimates indicate that both lighter weight and heavier weight BEVs emit less PM10 than their ICEV counterparts. However, this is not the case for PM2.5. Electric vehicles with a longer range, and therefore a higher weight, emit more PM2.5 than ICEV vehicles across all vehicle classes depicts these results graphically and Table 3.8 shows the relative differences in particulate matter emitted between BEVs and gasoline-fuelled ICEVs for each vehicle class.

Table 3.6 PM2.5 emission factors from non-exhaust sources across ICEV and BEV vehicle classes (g/vkm)

		PC			SUV			LCV		
		ICEV	BEV 100	BEV 300	ICEV	BEV 100	BEV 300	ICEV	BEV 100	BEV 300
Brake wear		0.0029	0.0006	0.0009	0.0031	0.0008	0.0012	0.0046	0.0010	0.0015
Tyre wear	low	0.0045	0.0047	0.0060	0.0055	0.0058	0.0075	0.0071	0.0076	0.0100
	high	0.0045	0.0050	0.0069	0.0061	0.0065	0.0093	0.0071	0.0080	0.0117
Road wear		0.0041	0.0041	0.0041	0.0041	0.0041	0.0041	0.0041	0.0041	0.0041
Road dust		0.0028	0.0028	0.0028	0.0034	0.0034	0.0034	0.0038	0.0038	0.0038
Total non-exhaust	low	0.0121	0.0100	0.0115	0.0133	0.0113	0.0135	0.0165	0.0134	0.0164
	high	0.0165	0.0147	0.0169	0.0193	0.0174	0.0206	0.0226	0.0200	0.0241

Note: Emission factors for BEV100 and BEV300 are calculated using the weight estimates for BEVs with a range of 100 and 300 miles, respectively (Argonne National Laboratory, 2019[55]). The amount of PM from non-exhaust sources produced by gasoline and diesel vehicles are assumed to be the same.
Source: Authors' calculations, see Table 3.1

Table 3.7 PM10 emission factors from non-exhaust sources across ICEV and BEV vehicle classes (g/vkm)

		PC			SUV			LCV		
		ICEV	BEV 100	BEV 300	ICEV	BEV 100	BEV 300	ICEV	BEV 100	BEV 300
Brake wear		0.0074	0.0019	0.0026	0.0093	0.0025	0.0035	0.0115	0.0030	0.0044
Tyre wear	low	0.0064	0.0066	0.0086	0.0078	0.0082	0.0108	0.0101	0.0107	0.0144
	high	0.0064	0.0067	0.0092	0.0081	0.0087	0.0124	0.0101	0.0108	0.0156
Road wear		0.0075	0.0075	0.0075	0.0075	0.0075	0.0075	0.0075	0.0075	0.0075
Road dust		0.0083	0.0083	0.0083	0.0099	0.0099	0.0099	0.0113	0.0113	0.0113
Total non-exhaust	low	0.0296	0.0243	0.0270	0.0346	0.0281	0.0317	0.0404	0.0326	0.0376
	high	0.0296	0.0244	0.0276	0.0349	0.0286	0.0333	0.0404	0.0326	0.0388

Note: Emission factors for BEV100 and BEV300 are calculated using the weight estimates for BEVs with a range of 100 and 300 miles, respectively (Argonne National Laboratory, 2019[55]). The amount of PM from non-exhaust sources produced by gasoline and diesel vehicles is assumed to be the same.
Source: Authors' calculations, see Table 3.2.

Figure 3.1. ICEV and BEV non-exhaust PM emission factors by vehicle class

PM2.5 (left) and PM10 (right)

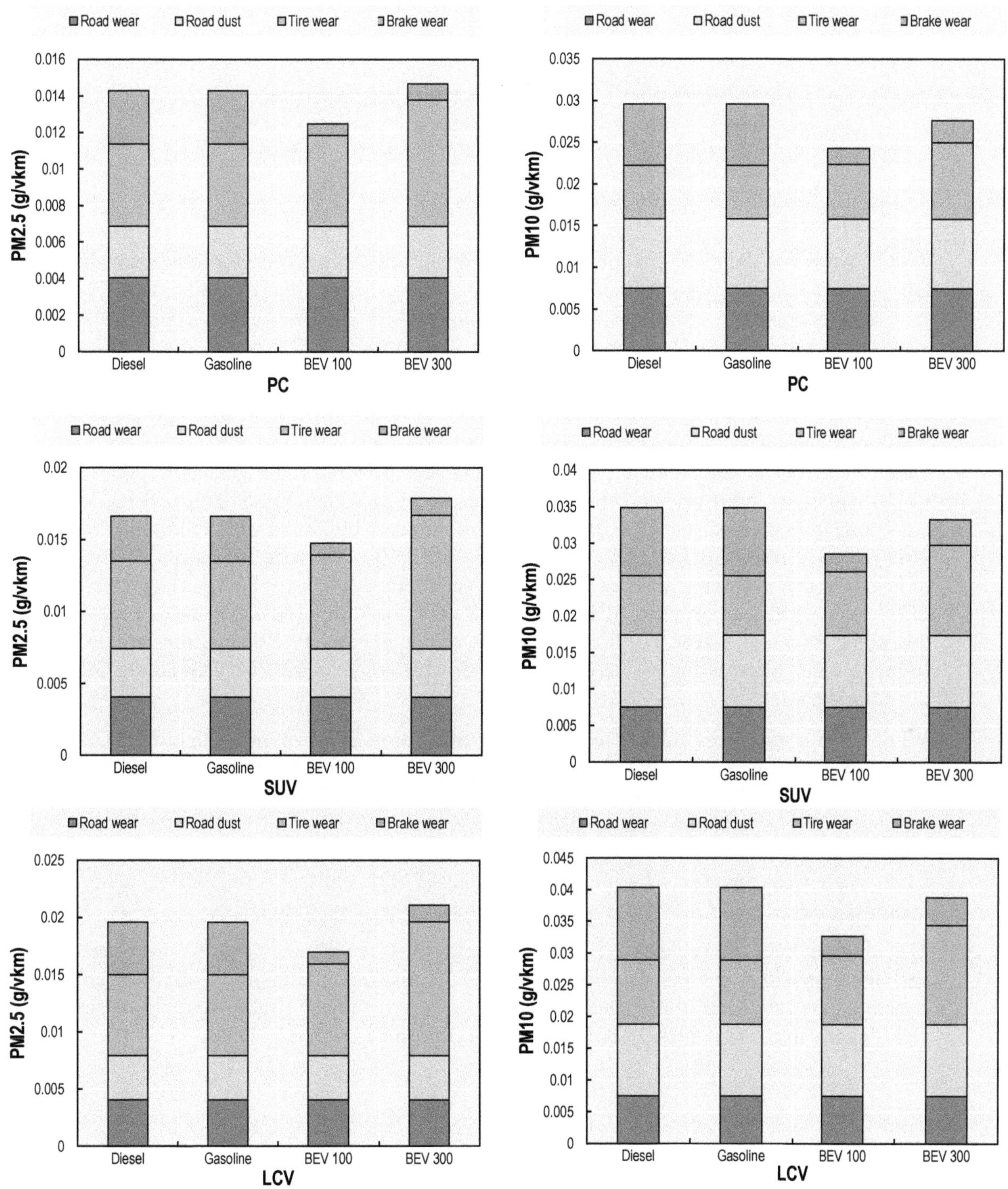

Note: Emission factors for BEV 100 and BEV 300 are calculated using the conventional weight estimates for a BEV with a range of 100 and 300 miles, respectively (Argonne National Laboratory, 2019).
Source: Authors' calculations, see Table 3.1 and Table 3.2.

Table 3.8 Net change in total non-exhaust emission factors of BEVs relative to gasoline ICEVs (percentage)

		PC	SUV	LCV
PM2.5	BEV 100	-12.8	-11.2	-13.3
	BEV 300	+2.6	+7.5	+7.8
PM10	BEV 100	-17.8	-18.0	-19.3
	BEV 300	-6.5	-4.5	-5.5

Note: Reductions are calculated on the basis of the estimated relationship between vehicle weight and tyre wear according to Model 1 described in Table 3.1 and Table 3.2.
Source: Author's calculations.

Results show that reductions in non-exhaust emission factors are greater for lighter weight BEVs than for heavier weight BEVs. Indeed, BEV 100 vehicles are estimated to emit 11-19% less non-exhaust emissions than their conventional gasoline-fuelled counterparts across all vehicle classes. However, this is not the case for BEV 300 vehicles. Heavier EVs lead to marginal reductions in PM10 emissions of 4.5-6.5%, and increase PM2.5 emissions across all vehicle classes by 2.6-7.8%.

As shown in Figure 3.2, the relative importance of the sources of non-exhaust emissions varies by drivetrain and vehicle class. Road dust resuspension is the greatest source of PM10 emissions in all vehicle categories, representing 28% and 30-35% of total PM10 emissions from non-exhaust for ICEVs and BEVs, respectively. Road wear represents 19-25% of PM10 emissions for ICEVs and 19-31% for BEVs. Tyre wear represents 22-25% of PM10 from non-exhaust sources for ICEV vehicles, and 27-40% for BEVs. The greatest difference in composition across ICEVs and BEVs is the portion of non-exhaust emissions that come from brake wear. For ICEVs, 25-28% of non-exhaust PM10 emissions are due to brake wear, whereas for BEVs, only 8-11% of total non-exhaust PM10 emissions are due to brake wear.

While road dust makes up a significantly smaller proportion of non-exhaust PM2.5 emissions, the same general patterns hold for changes in the composition of non-exhaust emissions across ICEV and BEV vehicle categories for PM2.5. Road dust comprises an estimated 20% of total non-exhaust PM2.5 emissions for ICEVs, and 18-23% for BEVs. Road wear is responsible for 21-28% of non-exhaust PM2.5 for ICEVs and 19-32% for BEVs. Tyre wear represents 40-56% of non-exhaust PM2.5 emissions for BEVs. Finally, brake wear represents 19-23% of PM2.5 non-exhaust emissions from BEVs.

Moving from BEV100 vehicles to BEV300 vehicles shifts the composition of non-exhaust emissions toward tyre wear, especially for PM2.5 emissions, the majority of which are generated by tyre wear for all vehicle classes and drivetrains. Brake wear decreases significantly in BEVs relative to ICEVs due to regenerative braking systems.

Figure 3.2. Relative share of non-exhaust emission factors for ICEV and BEV vehicle classes (percent)

PM2.5 (top) and PM10 (bottom)

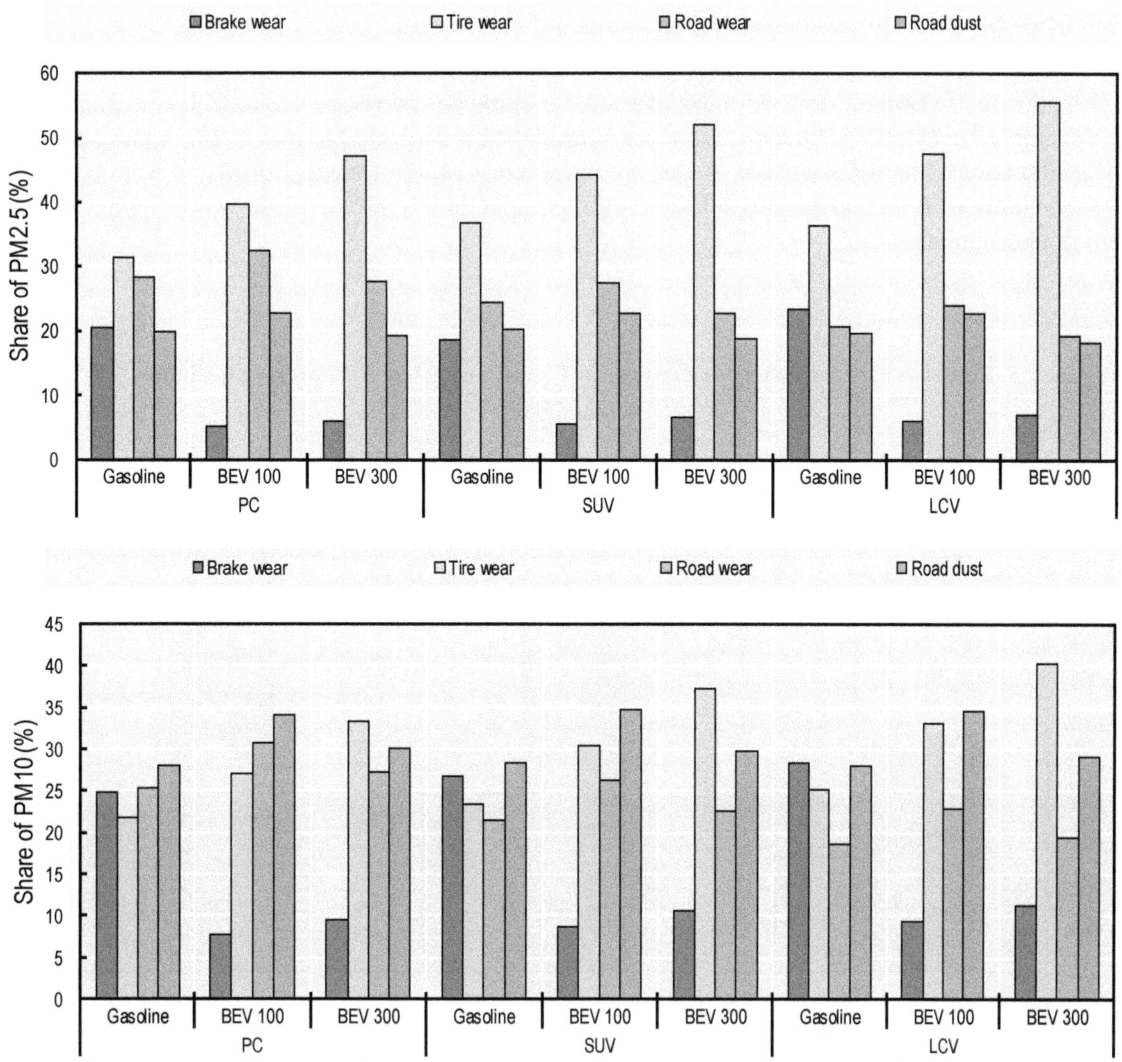

Note: Calculated on the basis of tyre wear emission factors estimated according to Model 2 as described in Tables 3.1 and 3.2. The relative shares of non-exhaust emission sources are similar for gasoline and diesel vehicles.
Source: Author's calculations.

3.4.3. Projections of particulate emissions from non-exhaust sources

On the basis of the emission factor estimates above[4] and projections for global vehicle stocks, this section presents estimates of non-exhaust emissions rates per kilometre travelled by the global vehicle fleet (tonnes/km) and annual non-exhaust emissions between 2017 and 2030. In 2017, the global vehicle fleet emitted an estimated 38.1 tonnes of PM10 per kilometre travelled, or 571,881 tonnes, assuming an annual mileage of 15,000 km/vehicle. Projected emissions are estimated for two scenarios based on different assumptions about electric vehicle uptake following the previous penetration scenarios of 4% and 8% uptake in 2030, similar to those projected by IEA's New Policies Scenario and EV30@30 Scenario (IEA, 2019).

In both scenarios, increasing travel demand causes non-exhaust emissions to rise substantially from 2017 to 2030. However, the reductions in PM emissions made possible by a doubling of electric vehicle uptake over this period are slight. The amount of non-exhaust emissions emitted per kilometre by the global vehicle fleet in 2030 is estimated to be 58.1 tonnes PM10 with a 4% uptake of electric vehicles and 57.2 tonnes PM10 with an uptake of 8%. This amounts to 871,500 and 858,000 tonnes of total PM10, respectively.

Results are even less significant for PM2.5 emissions: global emissions in 2017 are estimated to amount to 18.5 tonnes of PM2.5 emitted per kilometre travelled by the global vehicle fleet, or 277,500 tonnes in total. Emissions are projected to rise to 28.3 tonnes per kilometre with an EV uptake of 4%, amounting to 424,500 tonnes globally. Assuming a doubling of EV uptake leads to PM2.5 emissions of 28.0 tonnes per kilometre or 420,000 tonnes globally.

Figure 3.3. Emission rate estimates for the year 2017 and projected 2030 under alternative EV uptake scenarios

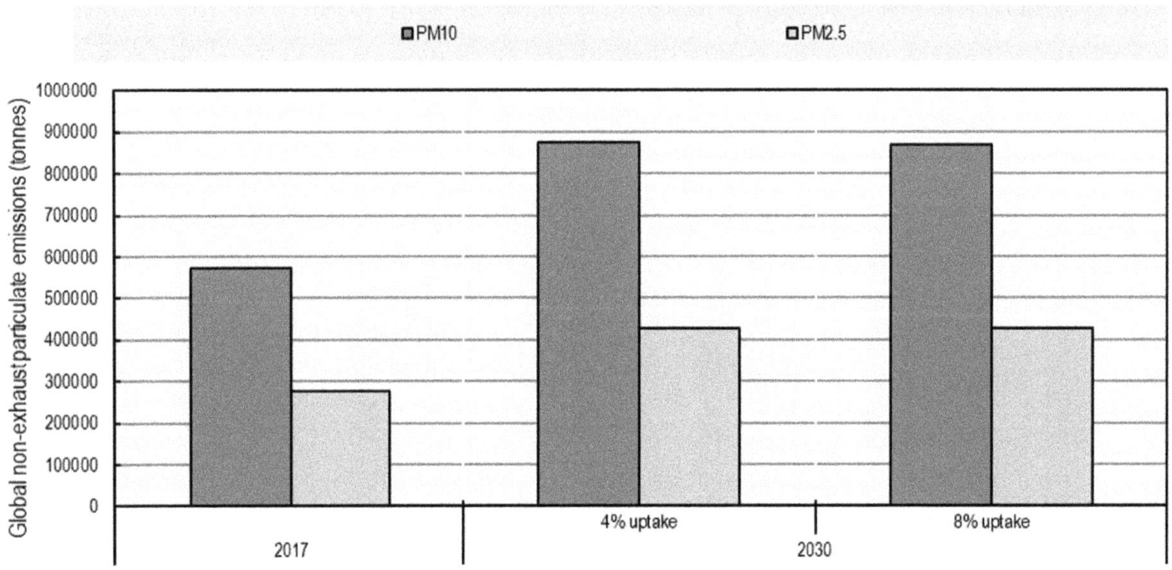

Source: Author's calculations. Projections of non-exhaust emissions are made on the basis of the emission factors estimated above and on projections for vehicle stocks. Emission factors from road wear are assumed to be unchanging from 2017 to 2030. Global vehicle fleet projections are based on those used by the IEA, and the electric vehicle penetration scenarios of 4% and 8% uptake are based on the New Policies Scenario and EV30@30 scenarios developed by the IEA (2019[72]). The annual distance travelled by each vehicle is assumed to be 15,000 km.

Other data available also permits an evaluation of the impact of BEV uptake in two specific cities: Milan, Italy, and Santiago, Chile. Following the previous projection, BEV uptake scenarios of 4% and 8% are used. Assuming that current EV technologies will not change until 2030 (e.g. battery weight), these simulations also indicate a minimal impact of BEV uptake on total particulate emissions from non-exhaust sources. In Milan (based on emission inventories from INEMAR and AMAT for 2014), an uptake of 4% and 8% leads to reductions of 0.4% and 0.8% for PM10 emissions and 0.3% and 0.7% for PM2.5 emissions. In Santiago, high road dust emission factors and a lower percentage of diesel cars in the vehicle fleet lead to a negligible reduction of non-exhaust PM emissions with the uptake of BEVs (≤0.1%).

3.4.4. Influencing factors and implications for policy

Relative to conventional gasoline-fuelled vehicles, electric vehicles emit 11-19% less PM10. Reductions in PM2.5 emissions are only observed for lightweight BEVs, which generate 11.2-13.3% less PM2.5 from non-exhaust sources. Heavier BEVs, in contrast, generate 2.6-7.8% more PM2.5 than their conventional counterparts. Moreover, projections of global PM emissions rates from non-exhaust sources show that emissions are set to increase, even when considering a relatively high level of electric vehicle penetration by that year.

For EVs, the most important source of PM2.5 emissions is by tyre wear, and the most important sources of PM10 are more evenly spread between tyre, road wear and road dust resuspension. For both drivetrain types, tyre wear increases with vehicle weight. The share of non-exhaust emissions from brake wear falls sharply for EVs relative to ICEVs due to regenerative braking. Uncertainty regarding emission factors remains, however, due to a lack of experimental data on various sources of wear, and the estimations reported here rely on a number of assumptions based on the available evidence (see Tables 3.1 and 3.2).

A number of other factors beyond those considered in the reported estimates could also affect the amount of particulate matter emitted by EVs in real world driving conditions. The higher fuel economy of BEVs may, for example, have a rebound effect of increased travel demand, which could further undermine projected PM emissions reductions, especially if it draws travel demand away from non-motorised modes. EV use can also contribute to traffic congestion. While congestion is known to increase exhaust emissions, its impact on non-exhaust emissions is not clear given that a higher braking frequency (i.e. higher brake wear) could be offset by lower average speed (i.e. lower tyre and road wear and lower resuspension). If, could also reduce the benefits of EVs with respect to PM emissions, as heavier BEVs are estimated to emit more PM2.5 than their conventional counterparts.

Given that PM, and PM2.5 in particular, is the most harmful pollutant for public health, it is clear that the widespread adoption of EVs will not eliminate air pollution concerns due to road traffic and that policies addressing non-exhaust emissions are warranted. The body of literature is too limited to assess whether the change in composition of the PM emissions generated from ICEVs vs. EVs has implications for the risk of mortality and morbidity associated with exposure to these emissions. More research is needed on the relative risk associated with each traffic source and PM component, as well as possible non-linearities in health impacts at different PM exposure levels.

[1] The vast majority of studies have focused on CO_2 emissions (51 papers), followed by NOx (32 papers), VOCs (18 papers), SO_2 (17 papers), and CO (15 papers).

[2] A number of studies have evaluated the impact of EV uptake on well-to-wheel and lifecycle PM emissions (Peng et al., 2018[22]; Kantor et al., 2010[19]; Tessum, Hill and Marshall, 2014[35]; Huo et al., 2015[12]). This report focuses on particulate emissions during a vehicle's use phase, i.e. only the particulate matter emitted when the vehicle is being driven.

[3] These estimates are characterised by uncertainty on the order of ±50% (Ntziachristos and Boulter, 2016[57]). Ongoing activities by the UN GRPE-PMP (Particle Measurement Program) and the Horizon 2020 EU-funded LOWBRASYS project, as well as the California Air Resources Board, will soon produce updated estimates for brake wear emission factors.

[4] Assuming an uptake of BEV100 vehicles and an average annual mileage of 15,000 km per vehicle.

References

Achilleos, S. et al. (2016), "Spatial variability of fine and coarse particle composition and sources in Cyprus", *Atmospheric Research*, Vol. 169, pp. 255-270, http://dx.doi.org/10.1016/j.atmosres.2015.10.005. [61]

ACI Automobile Club d'Italia (2019), *Stock vehicles in the metropolitan area of Milan.* [60]

Aiken, A. et al. (2008), "O/C and OM/OC ratios of primary, secondary, and ambient organic aerosols with high-resolution time-of-flight aerosol mass spectrometry", *Environmental Science and Technology*, Vol. 42/12, pp. 4478-4485, http://dx.doi.org/10.1021/es703009q. [54]

Alam, M. et al. (2018), "Analysing the Co-Benefits of transport fleet and fuel policies in reducing PM2.5 and CO2 emissions", *Journal of Cleaner Production*, Vol. 172, pp. 623-634, http://dx.doi.org/10.1016/j.jclepro.2017.10.169. [4]

Almeida, S. et al. (2005), "Source apportionment of fine and coarse particulate matter in a sub-urban area at the Western European Coast", *Atmospheric Environment*, Vol. 39/17, pp. 3127-3138, http://dx.doi.org/10.1016/j.atmosenv.2005.01.048. [68]

Althaus, H., M. Gauch and Empa (2010), "Comparative Life Cycle Assessment in Mobility (in Germany)", p. 162, https://www.empa.ch/documents/56122/458579/LCA-Mobilitaetsvergleich_Bericht.pdf/824aec56-3393-439e-8bc9-d1a365041e4d. [17]

Amato, F. (ed.) (2018), *Non-exhaust emissions: an urban air quality problem for public health ; impact and mitigation measures*, Elsevier, SAN DIEGO, https://www.elsevier.com/books/non-exhaust-emissions/amato/978-0-12-811770-5. [56]

Amato, F. et al. (2014), "Trends of road dust emissions contributions on ambient air particulate levels at rural, urban and industrial sites in southern Spain", *Atmospheric Chemistry and Physics*, Vol. 14/7, pp. 3533-3544, http://dx.doi.org/10.5194/acp-14-3533-2014. [70]

Amato, F. et al. (2012), "Emission factors from road dust resuspension in a Mediterranean freeway", *Atmospheric Environment*, Vol. 61, http://dx.doi.org/10.1016/j.atmosenv.2012.07.065. [58]

Amato, F. et al. (2012), "Emission factors from road dust resuspension in a Mediterranean freeway", *Atmospheric Environment*, Vol. 61, pp. 580-587, http://dx.doi.org/10.1016/j.atmosenv.2012.07.065. [71]

Amato, F. et al. (2009), "Spatial and chemical patterns of PM10 in road dust deposited in urban environment", *Atmospheric Environment*, Vol. 43/9, pp. 1650-1659, http://dx.doi.org/10.1016/j.atmosenv.2008.12.009. [69]

Argonne National Laboratory (2019), *GREET vehicle-cycle model Series 2*, https://greet.es.anl.gov (accessed on 17 December 2019). [55]

Barlow, T. (2014), "Briefing paper on non-exhaust particulate emissions from road transport", *Transport Research Laboratory.* [14]

Bukowiecki, N. et al. (2010), "PM10 emission factors for non-exhaust particles generated by road traffic in an urban street canyon and along a freeway in Switzerland", *Atmospheric Environment*, Vol. 44/19, pp. 2330-2340, http://dx.doi.org/10.1016/j.atmosenv.2010.03.039. [59]

California Air Resources Board (2020), *Fleet Database*, https://arb.ca.gov/emfac/fleet-db (accessed on 23 April 2020). [40]

Carlton, A., C. Wiedinmyer and J. Kroll (2009), "A review of Secondary organic aerosol (SOA) formation from isoprene", *Atmospheric Chemistry and Physics*, Vol. 9/14, pp. 4987-5005, http://dx.doi.org/10.5194/acp-9-4987-2009. [32]

Carslaw, D. (2006), "New Directions: A heavy burden for heavy vehicles: Increasing vehicle weight and air pollution", *Atmospheric Environment*, Vol. 40/8, pp. 1561-1562, http://dx.doi.org/10.1016/j.atmosenv.2005.11.039. [6]

CCAC (2016), *Cleaning up the Global On-road Diesel Fleet*, Climate and Clean Air Coalition, UNEP. [38]

Chan, Y. et al. (2008), "Apportionment of sources of fine and coarse particles in four major Australian cities by positive matrix factorisation", *Atmospheric Environment*, Vol. 42/2, pp. 374-389, http://dx.doi.org/10.1016/j.atmosenv.2007.09.030. [62]

Cheng, Y. et al. (2015), "PM2.5 and PM10-2.5 chemical composition and source apportionment near a Hong Kong roadway", *Particuology*, Vol. 18, pp. 96-104, http://dx.doi.org/10.1016/j.partic.2013.10.003. [63]

Del Duce, A., M. Gauch and H. Althaus (2016), "Electric passenger car transport and passenger car life cycle inventories in ecoinvent version 3", *International Journal of Life Cycle Assessment*, Vol. 21/9, pp. 1314-1326, http://dx.doi.org/10.1007/s11367-014-0792-4. [16]

DICTUC (2007), *Actualización del Inventario de Emisiones de Contaminantes Atmosféricos en la Región Metropolitana: Escenario 2010*, Report to the Comisión Nacional del Medio Ambiente Región Metropolitana, Santiago, Chile, https://www.cepal.org/ilpes/noticias/paginas/3/36023/DICTUC2007-Inventario2010.pdf (accessed on 20 May 2019). [26]

Electro-mobility, P. (2016), "Briefing: Non-Exhaust Emissions of Electric Cars", http://dx.doi.org/10.1016/j.atmosenv.2016.03.017. [13]

Gildemeister, A., P. Hopke and E. Kim (2007), "Sources of fine urban particulate matter in Detroit, MI", *Chemosphere*, Vol. 69/7, pp. 1064-1074, http://dx.doi.org/10.1016/j.chemosphere.2007.04.027. [52]

Griffin, R. et al. (1999), "Organic aerosol formation from the oxidation of biogenic hydrocarbons", *Journal of Geophysical Research Atmospheres*, Vol. 104/D3, pp. 3555-3567, http://dx.doi.org/10.1029/1998JD100049. [44]

Gummeneni, S. et al. (2011), "Source apportionment of particulate matter in the ambient air of Hyderabad city, India", *Atmospheric Research*, Vol. 101/3, pp. 752-764, http://dx.doi.org/10.1016/j.atmosres.2011.05.002. [65]

Guttikunda, S. et al. (2013), "Receptor model-based source apportionment of particulate pollution in Hyderabad, India", *Environmental Monitoring and Assessment*, Vol. 185/7, pp. 5585-5593, http://dx.doi.org/10.1007/s10661-012-2969-2. [66]

Hendriks, C. et al. (2013), "The origin of ambient particulate matter concentrations in the Netherlands", *Atmospheric Environment*, Vol. 69, pp. 289-303, http://dx.doi.org/10.1016/j.atmosenv.2012.12.017. [39]

Hooftman, N. et al. (2016), "Environmental analysis of petrol, diesel and electric passenger cars in a Belgian urban setting", *Energies*, Vol. 9/2, pp. 1-24, http://dx.doi.org/10.3390/en9020084. [10]

Huo, H. et al. (2015), "Life-cycle assessment of greenhouse gas and air emissions of electric vehicles: A comparison between China and the U.S.", *Atmospheric Environment*, Vol. 108, pp. 107-116, http://dx.doi.org/10.1016/j.atmosenv.2015.02.073. [12]

Huo, H. et al. (2013), "Climate and environmental effects of electric vehicles versus compressed natural gas vehicles in China: A life-cycle analysis at provincial level", *Environmental Science and Technology*, Vol. 47/3, pp. 1711-1718, http://dx.doi.org/10.1021/es303352x. [20]

IEA (2019), *Global EV Outlook 2019: Scaling-up the transition to electric mobility*, IEA, Paris, https://webstore.iea.org/download/direct/2807?fileName=Global_EV_Outlook_2019.pdf (accessed on 17 June 2019). [72]

IEA (2018), *Global EV Outlook 2018: Towards Cross-Modal Electrification*, IEA, Paris, https://doi.org/10.1787/9789264302365-en (accessed on 18 June 2018). [2]

IEA (2018), *Global EV Outlook 2018: Towards cross-modal electrification*, International Energy Agency, Paris, https://dx.doi.org/10.1787/9789264302365-en. [3]

Kantor, I. et al. (2010), "Air quality and environmental impacts of alternative vehicle technologies in Ontario, Canada", *International Journal of Hydrogen Energy*, Vol. 35/10, pp. 5145-5153, http://dx.doi.org/10.1016/j.ijhydene.2009.08.071. [19]

Ke, W. et al. (2017), "Well-to-wheels energy consumption and emissions of electric vehicles: Mid-term implications from real-world features and air pollution control progress", *Applied Energy*, Vol. 188, pp. 367-377, http://dx.doi.org/10.1016/j.apenergy.2016.12.011. [5]

Kim, E. and P. Hopke (2004), "Improving source identification of fine particles in a rural northeastern U.S. area utilizing temperature-resolved carbon fractions", *Journal of Geophysical Research D: Atmospheres*, Vol. 109/9, http://dx.doi.org/10.1029/2003JD004199. [47]

Kim, E., P. Hopke and E. Edgerton (2004), "Improving source identification of Atlanta aerosol using temperature resolved carbon fractions in positive matrix factorization", *Atmospheric Environment*, Vol. 38/20, pp. 3349-3362, http://dx.doi.org/10.1016/j.atmosenv.2004.03.012. [49]

Kim, E. et al. (2003), "Incorporation of parametric factors into multilinear receptor model studies of Atlanta aerosol", *Atmospheric Environment*, Vol. 37/36, pp. 5009-5021, http://dx.doi.org/10.1016/j.atmosenv.2003.08.035. [48]

Lee, J. and P. Hopke (2006), "Apportioning sources of PM2.5 in St. Louis, MO using speciation trends network data", *Atmospheric Environment*, Vol. 40/SUPPL. 2, pp. 360-377, http://dx.doi.org/10.1016/j.atmosenv.2005.11.074. [53]

Ligterink, N., U. Stelwagen and J. Kuenen (2014), *Emission factors for alternative drivelines and alternative fuels*, http://dx.doi.org/10.13140/RG.2.1.2655.4483. [15]

Li, N. et al. (2016), "Potential impacts of electric vehicles on air quality in Taiwan", *Science of the Total Environment*, Vol. 566-567, pp. 919-928, http://dx.doi.org/10.1016/j.scitotenv.2016.05.105. [36]

Nichols, B., K. Kockelman and M. Reiter (2015), "Air quality impacts of electric vehicle adoption in Texas", *Transportation Research Part D: Transport and Environment*, Vol. 34, pp. 208-218, http://dx.doi.org/10.1016/j.trd.2014.10.016. [21]

Nopmongcol, U. et al. (2017), "Air Quality Impacts of Electrifying Vehicles and Equipment Across the United States", *Environmental Science and Technology*, Vol. 51/5, pp. 2830-2837, http://dx.doi.org/10.1021/acs.est.6b04868. [18]

Ntziachristos, L. and P. Boulter (2016), "1.A.3.b.vi Road transport: Automobile tyre and brake wear; 1.A.3.b.vii Road transport: Automobile road abrasion", in *EMEP/EEA air pollutant emission inventory guidebook 2016*, Publications Office of the European Union, Luxembourg. [57]

Ntziachristos, L. and Z. Samaras (2018), "1.A.3.b.i, 1.A.3.b.ii, 1.A.3.b.iii, 1.A.3.b.iv Passenger cars, light commercial trucks, heavy-duty vehicles including buses and motor cycles", in *EMEP/EEA air pollutant emission inventory guidebook 2016 – Update Jul. 2018*, https://www.eea.europa.eu/publications/emep-eea-guidebook-2016/part-b-sectoral-guidance-chapters/1-energy/1-a-combustion/1-a-3-b-i. [37]

OICA (2020), *Production Statistics*, http://www.oica.net/production-statistics/ (accessed on 23 April 2020). [41]

Pachón, J. et al. (2018), "Development and evaluation of a comprehensive atmospheric emission inventory for air quality modeling in the megacity of Bogotá", *Atmosphere*, Vol. 9/2, http://dx.doi.org/10.3390/atmos9020049. [24]

Padoan, E. and F. Amato (2018), "Vehicle Non-Exhaust Emissions: Impact on Air Quality", in Amato, F. (ed.), *Non-Exhaust Emissions: An Urban Air Quality Problem for Public Health; Impact and Mitigation Measures*, Academic Press, London, UK, http://dx.doi.org/10.1016/B978-0-12-811770-5.00002-9. [28]

Peng, W. et al. (2018), "Potential co-benefits of electrification for air quality, health, and CO 2 mitigation in 2030 China", *Applied Energy*, Vol. 218/October 2017, pp. 511-519, http://dx.doi.org/10.1016/j.apenergy.2018.02.048. [22]

Perrone, M. et al. (2012), "Sources of high PM2.5 concentrations in Milan, Northern Italy: Molecular marker data and CMB modelling", *Science of the Total Environment*, Vol. 414, pp. 343-355, http://dx.doi.org/10.1016/j.scitotenv.2011.11.026. [67]

Platt, S. et al. (2017), "Gasoline cars produce more carbonaceous particulate matter than modern filter-equipped diesel cars", *Scientific Reports*, Vol. 7/1, http://dx.doi.org/10.1038/s41598-017-03714-9. [46]

Razeghi, G. et al. (2016), "Episodic air quality impacts of plug-in electric vehicles", *Atmospheric Environment*, Vol. 137, pp. 90-100, http://dx.doi.org/10.1016/j.atmosenv.2016.04.031. [33]

Requia, W. et al. (2018), "How clean are electric vehicles? Evidence-based review of the effects of electric mobility on air pollutants, greenhouse gas emissions and human health", *Atmospheric Environment*, Vol. 185/May, pp. 64-77, http://dx.doi.org/10.1016/j.atmosenv.2018.04.040. [1]

Requia, W. et al. (2018), “How clean are electric vehicles? Evidence-based review of the effects of electric mobility on air pollutants, greenhouse gas emissions and human health”, *Atmospheric Environment*, Vol. 185, pp. 64-77, http://dx.doi.org/10.1016/J.ATMOSENV.2018.04.040. [29]

Secretaria del Medio Ambiente de la Ciudad de Mexico (2018), “Inventario de Emisiones de la Ciudad de Mexico 2016”, p. 111, http://www.sedema.cdmx.gob.mx. [25]

Shrivastava, M. et al. (2007), “Sources of organic aerosol: Positive matrix factorization of molecular marker data and comparison of results from different source apportionment models”, *Atmospheric Environment*, Vol. 41/40, pp. 9353-9369, http://dx.doi.org/10.1016/j.atmosenv.2007.09.016. [42]

Soret, A., M. Guevara and J. Baldasano (2014), “The potential impacts of electric vehicles on air quality in the urban areas of Barcelona and Madrid (Spain)”, *Atmospheric Environment*, Vol. 99, pp. 51-63, http://dx.doi.org/10.1016/j.atmosenv.2014.09.048. [11]

Srimuruganandam, B. and S. Shiva Nagendra (2012), “Application of positive matrix factorization in characterization of PM<inf>10</inf>and PM<inf>2.5</inf>emission sources at urban roadside”, *Chemosphere*, Vol. 88/1, http://dx.doi.org/10.1016/j.chemosphere.2012.02.083. [64]

Tessum, C., J. Hill and J. Marshall (2014), “Life cycle air quality impacts of conventional and alternative light-duty transportation in the United States”, *Proceedings of the National Academy of Sciences*, Vol. 111/52, pp. 18490-18495, http://dx.doi.org/10.1073/pnas.1406853111. [35]

Timmers, V. and P. Achten (2018), “Non-Exhaust PM Emissions From Battery Electric Vehicles”, in *Non-Exhaust Emissions*, http://dx.doi.org/10.1016/b978-0-12-811770-5.00012-1. [8]

Timmers, V. and P. Achten (2016), “Non-exhaust PM emissions from electric vehicles”, *Atmospheric Environment*, Vol. 134, pp. 10-17, http://dx.doi.org/10.1016/j.atmosenv.2016.03.017. [9]

Tobollik, M. et al. (2016), “Health impact assessment of transport policies in Rotterdam: Decrease of total traffic and increase of electric car use”, *Environmental Research*, Vol. 146, pp. 350-358, http://dx.doi.org/10.1016/j.envres.2016.01.014. [34]

U.S. Environmental Protection Agency (2019), *National Emissions Inventory (NEI)*, https://www.epa.gov/air-emissions-inventories/national-emissions-inventory-nei (accessed on 19 May 2019). [27]

Van Zeebroeck, B. and G. De Ceuster (2013), *Elektrische auto zorgt voor evenveel fijn stof als conventionele auto*. [7]

Vidhi, R. and P. Shrivastava (2018), “A review of electric vehicle lifecycle emissions and policy recommendations to increase EV penetration in India”, *Energies*, Vol. 11/3, http://dx.doi.org/10.3390/en11030483. [45]

Wang, Y. et al. (2012), “Multiple-year black carbon measurements and source apportionment using Delta-C in Rochester, New York”, *Journal of the Air and Waste Management Association*, Vol. 62/8, pp. 880-887, http://dx.doi.org/10.1080/10962247.2012.671792. [50]

Wu, Y. and L. Zhang (2017), “Can the development of electric vehicles reduce the emission of air pollutants and greenhouse gases in developing countries?”, *Transportation Research Part D: Transport and Environment*, Vol. 51, pp. 129-145, http://dx.doi.org/10.1016/j.trd.2016.12.007. [23]

Zhang, Q. et al. (2007), “Ubiquity and dominance of oxygenated species in organic aerosols in anthropogenically-influenced Northern Hemisphere midlatitudes”, *Geophysical Research Letters*, Vol. 34/13, http://dx.doi.org/10.1029/2007GL029979. [31]

Zhao, W. and P. Hopke (2006), *Source investigation for ambient PM 2.5 in Indianapolis, IN*, http://dx.doi.org/10.1080/02786820500380297. [51]

Zhao, Y. et al. (2013), “Sources of organic aerosol investigated using organic compounds as tracers measured during CalNex in Bakersfield”, *Journal of Geophysical Research Atmospheres*, Vol. 118/19, pp. 11388-11398, http://dx.doi.org/10.1002/jgrd.50825. [43]

Ziemann, P. and R. Atkinson (2012), *Kinetics, products, and mechanisms of secondary organic aerosol formation*, http://dx.doi.org/10.1039/c2cs35122f. [30]

4. Policy responses to tackle particulate matter from non-exhaust emissions

This chapter identifies currently available technological solutions to reduce non-exhaust PM emissions from wear and road dust resuspension and reviews policy measures that have an effect on non-exhaust emissions. The chapter then develops a framework for the design of an efficient public policy instrument to address non-exhaust emissions. Finally, it provides an overview of the main uncertainties and data gaps on non-exhaust emissions and proposes next steps for moving forward in better understanding and mitigating PM emissions from non-exhaust sources. Given the high proportion of non-exhaust emissions generated by tyre wear, priority should be placed on measures that seek to reduce PM emissions from this source in particular, namely vehicle lightweighting and regulations on tyre composition. Priority should also be placed on conducting research to better understand the mitigation potential of different policy options.

Few policy measures currently target non-exhaust emissions. Two broad approaches can be taken to reduce non-exhaust emissions from road traffic, namely either lowering emission factors or reducing vehicle-kilometres travelled.[1] Exceptions come in the form of regulations regarding brake and tyre material, and mitigating measures such as street washing that are taken in some areas. To the extent that supply-side regulations may require extended approval processes, policy measures that reduce vehicle-kilometres travelled can yield more immediate impacts in terms of mitigating non-exhaust emissions.

Section 4.1 describes existing measures to reduce non-exhaust emissions by lowering emission factors and by reducing vehicle-kilometres travelled. Section 4.2 discusses how policymakers can better address non-exhaust emissions from road transport and proposes a framework to guide the design of a pricing instrument addressing non-exhaust emissions specifically. Section 4.3 discusses the work that remains to be done in order to implement the proposed measures. Table 4.1 provides a broad overview of some of the measures that can address non-exhaust emissions from road transport.

Table 4.1. Policy Measures to address non-exhaust emissions

Type of measure	Scale of implementation		
	International	*National*	*Subnational/Local*

Market-based instrument		**Non-exhaust emissions charge** [BTRD]	**Include EVs in road pricing** [BTRD]
Regulation	• Standardise the measurement of non-exhaust emissions [BTRD] • Regulate the content of brake and tyre materials [BT]	• Include vehicle weight as determinant of vehicle taxes and fees [BT] • RBS in ICEVs [B] • Restrictions on studded tyre use [TR]	• UVARs differentiated by brake, tyre, road characteristics [BTRD] • Vehicle weight limitations in city centres [BT] • Traffic flow measures to ease congestion [BTRD]
Management measures			• Road washing and dust binding [D] • Minimise sanding and salting [TRD]
Soft measures	• Eco-labelling [BTR]	• **Communication campaigns** [BTRD]	

Note: Measures in bold incentivise both a reduction in EFs and in vehicle-kilometres travelled. Superscripts denote non-emissions source targeted, where B, T, R and D indicate brake wear, tyre wear, road wear, and road dust resuspension, respectively. UVAR: urban vehicle access regulation.

4.1. Review of existing measures that reduce non-exhaust emissions

The "avoid, shift, improve" conceptual framework used to categorise strategies to reduce exhaust emissions from road transport (SUTP, 2019[1]) can also be applied to non-exhaust emissions.

Strategies to "improve" vehicle emission factors are covered in Section 4.1.1, which reviews the types of regulations in place and currently available technologies that reduce non-exhaust emission factors. Section 4.1.2. reviews policy strategies to reduce overall demand for vehicle-kilometres travelled through measures to "avoid" unnecessary car travel and "shift" to less emissions-intensive modes. It should be noted that many of the measures presented in these sections are not motivated by the objective of reducing non-exhaust emissions. Rather, reductions in non-exhaust emissions happen to occur as a side-benefit of other targeted objectives.

4.1.1. Reducing vehicle kilometres travelled

To date, other negative externalities associated with car use, namely those issuing from exhaust emissions and congestion, have been the primary motivation behind measures aiming to reduce the number of vehicle kilometres driven. This section presents an overview of such policies that are currently in place, although the specific features of their implementation can vary considerably. Given that these policies target all vehicle emissions and are not unique to non-exhaust emissions, there is extensive precedent for their use. This review is not intended to be exhaustive with respect to these policies; for more comprehensive reviews, see (UNESCAP, 2017[2]; CIVITAS, 2019[3]; UN ECE, 2016[4]; Rupprecht Consult (editor), 2012[5]; Rye and Ison, 2008[6]).

Reducing demand for private vehicle travel can be accomplished by a variety of measures that increase the relative attractiveness of public transport and non-motorised modes relative to private vehicles. These measures can consist of disincentives for private vehicle ownership and use, i.e. measures that raise their costs and/or inconvenience, as well as incentives for alternative modes (e.g. public transit, walking, and biking).

Disincentives for car ownership and use can be pecuniary or regulatory in nature. Pecuniary disincentives for car ownership can be one-time or reoccurring, and include purchase taxes, registration fees, and annual taxes. Disincentives for car use come in the form of operational costs, including taxes on fuel (and increasingly carbon), flat rate distance-based charges, congestion pricing, and parking pricing. Currently, few pecuniary measures differentiate the costs of passenger car use by the determinants of the marginal damages from non-exhaust emissions (e.g. vehicle weight). In some countries (e.g. Norway and Sweden), owning heavier cars is discouraged through vehicle registration fees and annual taxes that are based in part on vehicle weight (Svenningsen et al., 2019[7]). While fuel charges indirectly incentivise the use of lighter weight vehicles by virtue of the fact that such vehicles use less fuel, all else equal, explicit weight-based use charges do not exist for passenger vehicles. Although weight-based disincentives for LCV use are in place in some regions (ACEA, 2019[8]), these charges are not sensitive to other determinants of marginal damages of non-exhaust emissions such as population exposure.

In addition to increasing the cost of using private vehicles, regulatory measures can also make private motor vehicle use less convenient. Examples of regulations that seek to limit car use include urban access restrictions (e.g. low emission zones), vehicle bans based on vehicle age or technology (e.g. bans on diesel and heavy duty vehicles), license plate limitations (e.g. even/odd criteria during pollution spikes), and parking regulations, including limiting parking supply. Parking restriction policies can, for example, prohibit parking for non-resident vehicles in specific areas of the city or expand the size of the areas requiring paid parking. A time-trend analysis of parking restrictions on the number of circulating vehicles/working day in central Barcelona showed a decrease of vehicles from 2005 to 2015 of close to 10% (Querol et al., 2018[9]).

Urban vehicle access restrictions (UVARs) come in a number of forms and have been adopted by a growing number of cities in recent years (e.g. Stockholm, London, Milan, Paris and Madrid) with the primary goal of reducing congestion and exhaust emissions. In addition, the implementation of low emission zones which prohibits the access of more polluting vehicles to city centres, may have an indirect effect on the number of vehicles entering the urban area, and thus on non-exhaust emissions (Holman, Harrison and Querol, 2015[10]).While UVARs are generally motivated by the need to comply with air quality standards for NO2 and reduce congestion in city centres, an additional benefit arises from the reduction of non-exhaust emissions.

In Madrid, an analysis of the number of cars in circulation during a NOx pollution peak revealed an average decrease in traffic volume of 17% in the centre of the city when a license-plate-based access restriction was in force, and an average decrease in the NO2/SO2 ratio of 13% (Querol et al., 2018[9]). A successful case of congestion charging is that of Stockholm, where a congestion charging scheme led to a 30% reduction in circulating vehicles, as well as a 5-13% reduction in NOx and a 14-20% reduction in PM10, which is partially attributable to lower non-exhaust emissions (Johansson, Burman and Forsberg, 2009[11]; Johansson, 2016[12]).

Electric vehicles are often exempt from access restrictions and road charging schemes. In some cases, even some less emission-intensive ICEVs (such as hybrid vehicles) are exempt. The exemption of EVs and other alternative fuel vehicles from road pricing measures (e.g. in London, Oslo, Milan and Palermo) decreases the effectiveness of these schemes in reducing vehicle-kilometres, and therefore non-exhaust emissions and congestion. The effectiveness of these schemes can be particularly lower if travel demand shifts do no only occur from ICEVs to EVs, but also from public and non-motorised transport. In such cases, the net environmental benefit of the measures may be lower or even negative. Given a basic knowledge of the determinants of non-exhaust emissions, it is clear that EVs should not be exempt from restrictions or pricing instruments seeking to reduce these emissions. In Stockholm and Liverpool, for example, EVs are not exempt from city tolls. Rather than provide a uniform incentive for EV use by exempting them from measures seeking to reduce motor vehicle use, such charges should be differentiated with respect to the amount of non-exhaust emissions they produce.

Incentives to increase the uptake of public transit and non-motorised modes include improving the coverage, frequency, comfort, information provision, and payment systems of public transit services. Integrating ticketing will encourage multi-modal use of public transit systems. According public transport vehicles priority in express lanes will reduce travel times for these modes. Better quality and more well-connected infrastructure for non-motorised modes, such as protected bike lanes, sidewalks, and priority pedestrian crosswalks increase the attractiveness of using these modes in urban areas. In the long term, developing compact urban areas can also contribute to reducing the number and length of trips taken in private vehicles by reducing the distances required to access amenities (CIVITAS, 2019[3]). New forms of high-occupancy shared mobility services also have potential to reduce demand for total vehicle kilometres (ITF, 2016[13]; CIVITAS, 2019[3]).

Bike sharing programs have also been shown to be an effective strategy for increasing the mode share of cycling in urban areas, and new forms of on-demand, high occupancy public transport hold promise for drastically reducing demand for vehicle kilometres travelled (ITF, 2016[13]). The provision of park and ride facilities and incentives for carpooling can also reduce the number of vehicle kilometres driven if private vehicles are no longer used for entire trips, but instead used as a feeder to public transit. Various financial incentives, including offering subsidies for bicycle purchases, making public transport costs eligible to be tax deductible, or engaging private companies in plans to co-finance the use of public transport or soft modes for their staff, will increase the relative attractiveness of these modes.

It should also be noted that some existing measures targeting exhaust emissions could have a negative impact on non-exhaust emissions, such as freight consolidation measures to maximise the amount of freight-tonnes transported per kilometre driven. Given the importance of vehicle weight on non-exhaust emissions, is not clear whether consolidating freight will tend to increase or decrease net non-exhaust emissions. Traffic calming measures also have the potential to reduce non-exhaust emissions insofar as they reduce frequency and rates of acceleration and deceleration. Most importantly, however, the analysis and evidence gathered in this report indicate that a key strategy of urban development plans, namely indiscriminate incentives to electrify private vehicle fleets, will not be an effective strategy for reducing non-exhaust emissions.

4.1.2. Improving emission factors

Measures to improve emission factors can come in the form of regulations on materials or manufacturing processes, or in the form of pricing mechanisms that effectively incentivise the development of technologies that are otherwise cost-prohibitive. This section summarizes the range of technological solutions currently available to reduce non-exhaust emissions, the main regulations in place, as well as a number of other types of traffic management measures that can be used to lower emissions potentials. Technologies to reduce emission factors generally address the vehicle itself (brake system and tyres), but other technologies designed to reduce road wear and the resuspension of road surface particles are also reviewed in the section on management measures. Due to the high degree of geographic and temporal variability in non-exhaust emissions from road dust resuspension, measures to address them are most relevant on an as-needed basis at local scales rather than via more generalised instruments.

Regulatory measures

Vehicle lightweighting and HDV weight limitations

The evidence presented in this report indicates that vehicle weight is an important driver of non-exhaust emissions. Given that electric vehicles are considerably heavier than their conventional counterparts, vehicle lightweighting should be considered an important regulatory tool for addressing the non-exhaust particulate matter emitted by ICEVs and BEVs alike.

The mean vehicle weight of passenger cars in the EU has risen by 10% over the last 15 years (ICCT, 2018[14]) and similar trends are observed in other regions. Currently, most automobile bodies are made of steel plates, with lighter components comprising only 30% of their weight. In terms of material changes, high-strength steel and aluminum alloy have seen rapid advancements in recent years. Other lightweight materials in development include porcelain, plastic, fiberglass and carbon fiber. Lifecycle analyses can identify the potential environmental trade-offs involved in reducing vehicle weight, such as those generated by the use of more resource-intensive materials, and the GHG emissions and other pollutants released in the production and disposal of light weight vehicle parts (e.g. .

Beyond the fact that lighter weight vehicles are typically more fuel efficient than heavier weight vehicles, added incentives to produce and purchase lighter vehicles remain limited, especially for passenger cars. In several countries, however, vehicle taxes (e.g. road taxes and circulation fees) are a function of vehicle weight (ACEA, 2019[8]). Evidence indicates that while reducing the weight of passenger cars is currently cost-effective, this is not the case for LCVs (ITF, 2017[15]). Efforts to account for and internalise the benefits that lightweighting yields in terms of non-exhaust emission reductions could make it a cost-effective mitigation policy. Regulation to reduce the maximum weight allowed for vehicle type approval could also be considered (see Section 3.2).

The average load of HDVs has also been increasing in recent decades, a trend that has been driven by economic growth and the roll out of the new vehicle technologies that made such an expansion possible (Žnidarič, 2015[16]). Many municipalities have established vehicle weight restrictions for vehicles circulating in urban areas. A number of German cities implement lorry transit bans to reduce emissions and traffic. In Germany, the emissions reduction potential of circulation restrictions based on vehicle weight strongly depends on the proportion of lorries in the traffic flow, as well as on how well the measure is enforced and on compliance rates (UBA, 2015[17]). The maximum emissions reduction potentials are found to be 20% for NOx, 10% for NO2, 10% for PM10 and 7% for black soot. Across cities, dates, and compliance levels, theoretical reduction potentials ranged from 1.2-16.7%.

In Barcelona, vehicle weight limits depend on the number of road lanes. For one-lane roads, regulations prohibit vehicles weighing more than 12 tonnes during the day and more than 18 tonnes at night. On two-lane roads vehicles weighing more than 18 tonnes are prohibited during the day, and more than 44 tonnes at night. The one-lane historic city centre road is not accessible to vehicles over 7.5 tonnes. These measures have led to dramatic changes, reducing the number of heavy goods vehicles by 97.5% during cordon hours and by 97% over 24 hours. The number of heavy goods vehicles using this road per month in 2009 was less than the daily average in 2006.

Brake and tyre manufacturing regulations

The most important worldwide regulations affecting brake and tyre production are summarized in Grigoratos (2018[18]). These include the asbestos ban, the REACH and REACH-like regulations, the European regulation on the classification, labeling and packaging of chemical substances and mixtures (CLP Regulation), as well as regulations related to restrictions on the use of particular trace elements and heavy metals. Table 4.2 provides a brief overview of the regulations related to brake composition and the countries where these regulations were applied in 2018.

Table 4.2. Brake composition related regulations worldwide

Regulation	Country
Asbestos ban	Algeria, Argentina, Australia, Bahrain, Brunei, Chile, Egypt, EU*, FYROM, Gabon, Gibraltar, Honduras, Iceland, Iraq, Israel, Japan, Jordan, Korea, Kuwait, Mauritius, Monaco, Mozambique, New Caledonia, New Zealand, Norway, Oman, Qatar, Saudi Arabia, Serbia, South Africa, Switzerland, Turkey, Uruguay, USA*
REACH regulation	EU
REACH-like regulation	Albania, Australia, Brazil*, Canada, China, Chinese Taipei, FYROM, Hong Kong (China), Iceland, India, Indonesia*, Israel, Japan, Korea, Malaysia, Mexico, Norway, Philippines, Serbia, South Africa*, Switzerland, Taiwan, Thailand, Turkey*, UAE, USA*, Vietnam*
End of Life Vehicles Directive	EU
Senate Bill regulations	California (SB 346), Washington (SB 6557), Rhode Island (SB H7997), and New York State
CLP Regulation	EU

Note: Not applied in every member state or applied with some modifications.
Source: Grigoratos (2018[18]).

Trace and heavy metals content restrictions

Regulations regarding the use of trace elements and heavy metals in vehicle manufacturing have also had implications for the composition of brake systems and tyres. In Europe, the End of Life Vehicles directive requires that "Member States shall ensure that materials and components of vehicles put on the market after 1 July 2003 do not contain Lead (Pb), Hexavalent Chromium (Cr VI), Cadmium (Cd) and Mercury (Hg)" (EC, 2000[19]). The objective of the directive is to prevent waste from vehicles and promote the reuse, recycling and recovery of end-of-life vehicles and components, improving thus environmental performance for all operators involved.

Although similar federal regulations do not exist in the US, a number of US states have also adopted regulations regarding the use of heavy metals in brake friction materials. California (SB 346), Washington State (SB 6557), Rhode Island State (SB H7997) and New York State (SB A10871) have passed laws which limit the weight percentage of specific constituents within a friction material. In addition to the heavy metals that are restricted in Europe (chromium, lead, cadmium and mercury) special attention has also been paid to copper in brake systems in the US. The issue began in the early 1990s when cities south of San Francisco were having trouble meeting Clean Water Act requirements to reduce copper in urban run-off. After it was found that brake wear accounted for 35-60% of the copper in the area's urban run-off, legislators adopted measures to reduce the amount of copper used to manufacture brake systems. The legislation requires manufacturers to acquire and report third party verification of compliance level, label brakes with their compliance levels, and retest and recertify the materials used to make brakes every three years.

Table 4.3. Heavy metals restrictions enforced in California and Washington State and date of implementation for each level of regulation

	Jan 2014	Jan 2021	Jan 2025
Copper	No limit	5.0% wt	0.5% wt
Chromium (VI), Lead, Mercury	0.1% wt	0.1% wt	0.1% wt
Cadmium	0.01% wt	0.01% wt	0.01% wt
Nickel, Antimony, Zinc	Currently none – Monitored and maybe regulated in the future		

In Europe, the REACH regulation (Regulation 1907/2006) aims to improve the protection of human health and the environment through better and earlier identification of the intrinsic properties of chemical substances. This is done by the four processes of REACH, namely the Registration, Evaluation, Authorisation and Restriction of chemicals. The general principle of REACH regulation is "No data, no market". Practically speaking, this means that if a substance has not been registered for a specific application, it must not be used. Under REACH, the substances in a product must be registered if "the substances are intended to be released from the produced or imported article(s) during normal and reasonable foreseeable conditions of use." However, because the release of particles from tyres, rubber belts, brake linings and discs is not considered to be intended, no registration of their chemical components is required. An exception to this rule is products that contain Substances of Very High Concern (SVHC) in the quantity of 0.1% or more by weight, which should be reported.

One group of substances relevant to the manufacture, import, supply and use of tyres which is subject to REACH restrictions is polycyclic aromatic hydrocarbons (PAHs). PAHs include over 100 different chemicals that are formed during the incomplete burning of coal, oil and gas, garbage, or other organic compounds. PAHs are known for their carcinogenic, mutagenic and teratogenic properties and have been used in the production of tyres. REACH Annex XVII has placed a restriction on the use of 8 PAHs in tyres and extender oils (oils added to tyres during the manufacturing process).

Regulations have also been applied in countries including China, Malaysia, and Korea. Despite the similar concept of these regulations with REACH regulations, a number of differences exist regarding the timing of notifications/registrations, the threshold values applied, the availability of exemptions, and the communication in the supply chain (Grigoratos, 2018[18]).

The automotive industry has also developed tools to support compliance with the REACH regulations and the End of Life Vehicles directive. The International Material Data System (IMDS) is an on-line system used by the automobile industry that collects, maintains, analyzes and archives information on materials used for automotive components. IMDS entry is obligatory for recycling rate management, management of substances of concern, and REACH compliance. It therefore supports compliance with the obligations placed on automobile manufacturers and suppliers by national and international standards, laws and regulations, scientific findings and risk assessments, as reflected in the Global Automotive Declarable Substance List (GADSL). The GADSL is the result of a year-long global effort of representatives from the automotive, automotive parts supplier and chemical/plastics industries. The list reflects regulated substances used in the automobile and chemical industries in Japan, Europe, and the U.S. (American Chemistry Council, 2019[20]). Suppliers are required to comprehensively manage substances of concern and to make continuous efforts to reduce use in accordance with GADSL. In the IMDS system, suppliers are required to request parts and materials from automotive producers via the IMDS website, which provides a repository of up to 9,000 vehicle components and the substances they are made of.

Asbestos bans

Asbestos was historically used as a friction material in brake linings, disc brake pads, and clutch facings in vehicles because of its unique fire resistance and wear properties. Asbestos has since proven to be associated with occupational diseases, including respiratory problems (Stayner et al., 2008[21]), mesothelioma (Lemen, 2004[22]), and lung cancer (Program, 2005[23]). For this reason, the manufacturing of asbestos containing friction materials including brake pads has ceased in many places worldwide, with positive effects on ambient air quality.

In Europe, the asbestos-free directive (Council Directive 83/477/EEC on the protection of workers from the risks related to exposure to asbestos at work) was introduced with the aim of protecting workers against risks to their health arising or likely to arise from exposure to asbestos at work. In that context, many European Member States have introduced total bans in the use of asbestos for the production of brake pads, while there are still some countries where the compliance with this directive has not been verified (IBAS, 2019[24]).

In the United States, brake friction materials are not covered by US Environmental Protection Agency asbestos regulations at the federal level. Legislation has been enacted in California (SB 346) and Washington (SB 6557) to eliminate the use of several toxic chemicals, including asbestos, in brake pads, drum linings, and heavy-duty brake blocks since 2014. More recent bills have prohibited the production, import, transfer, provision, or use of asbestos or any material containing more than 0.1% asbestos by weight. In practice this constitutes a total asbestos ban because 0.1% is below the detection limit of existing measurement methodologies. Despite the global trend towards total asbestos bans, some countries including China, Russia, India and the United States still permit the use of asbestos in some applications (IBAS, 2019[24]).

Studded tyre restrictions

Many countries regulate the use of studded tyres, although this is generally to reduce expenditure on road maintenance rather than the damages associated with non-exhaust emissions. Restrictions come in a number of forms, including restrictions on the type of tyres that can be used (e.g. Spain, where tyres with studs above 2mm are prohibited), the speeds that can be driven using studded tyres (e.g. Ireland, where the maximum speed allowed for cars with studded tyres is 96-112 km/hr depending on the roadway), the conditions under which they can be used (e.g. Turkey, where they are only allowed for use on ice-covered roads), and the vehicles which can use them (e.g. in Austria studded tyres are only permitted on vehicles <3.5t GVW).

Many countries combine various criteria and apply them on a seasonal basis. Switzerland allows the use of studded tyres on vehicles <7.5t GVW in winter-spring months (max. speed 80 km/h) on snow-covered roads. Norway, Denmark, Lithuania and Sweden (with some exceptions) allow them during winter-spring, but Norway levies a charge for their use. France restricts the use of studded tyres to vehicles <3.5t GVW and to winter-spring months allowing a maximum speed of 90 km/h.

As a regulation targeting a specific technology, these measures appear to be effective. In Hornsgatan (Sweden), a combination of reduced traffic volume and reduced use of studded tyres reduced road wear by an estimated 72% (Norman et al., 2016[25]). Given that studded tyres constitute an important safety measure in the countries where they are used, and given that their use is generally less prevalent in urban areas where population exposure is high, their relevance as a measure to target non-exhaust emissions in these areas is limited.

Available technologies

Regenerative braking systems

Motors in electric cars are designed not only for acceleration, but also for deceleration. When the brake pedal is pressed in the generator mode, the motor works in the reverse direction in order to recharge the battery. Regenerative braking systems (RBS) increase the range of BEVs as well as the fuel economy of HEVs by recuperating some of the energy normally lost as heat when braking using conventional friction brakes. An additional benefit of regenerative braking systems is that they significantly reduce brake wear emissions. While regenerative braking can be sufficient for most daily use brake applications, the combined use of regenerative braking and friction braking will remain necessary in the near future for safety reasons (AUDI AG, 2016[26]), as emergency stops still require the use of the latter.

Estimates of the brake wear emissions reductions made possible by RBS range from 25% to 100%. Regenerative braking has been reported to reduce brake wear by 25-50% (Platform for Electromobility, 2016[27]). Van Zeebroeck and De Ceuster (2013[28]) assume that regenerative braking reduces the PM emissions associated with brake wear by 50%. Timmers and Achten (2016[29]) assume zero brake wear emissions for electric vehicles, i.e. a 100% reduction. Hooftman et al. (2016[30]) state that EVs require about two-thirds (66%) less friction braking action than ICEVs due to regenerative braking. Their analysis is based on the service times of brake pads on Teslas, BMW i3s, and Nissan Leafs, which on average last roughly two-thirds longer than those on diesel/petrol vehicles. They note that the savings made possible by regenerative braking outweighs the additional wear due to the higher mass of electric vehicles. Barlow (2014[31]) suggested that regenerative braking produces virtually no brake wear, and (Ligterink, Stelwagen, & Kuenen (2014[32]) assume regenerative braking reduces wear by up to 95%. Based on a report by Althaus and Gauch (2010[33]), Del Duce et al. (2014) report that brake wear emissions are 80% lower for EVs than ICEVs. Nopmongcol et al. (2017[34]) assume a 25% reduction in brake wear with the use of regenerative braking. Observed reductions in particle number concentrations range from 66-99% (Augsburg and Hesse, 2018[35]).

Although regenerative braking systems are one of the most promising technologies for reducing non-exhaust emissions from brake wear in terms of their cost-effectiveness, they are currently only used in electric and hybrid-electric vehicles. Therefore, although electric vehicle manufacturers are constantly developing more technologically advanced and light weight RBS, the penetration of these systems in vehicle fleets will grow only as fast as that of electric and hybrid-electric vehicles. For this reason, industry should be encouraged to explore the extent to which RBS could be easily incorporated in ICEVs, e.g. via kinetic energy recovery systems. However, some trade-offs of RBS have been pointed out. If friction brake systems on vehicles with RBS are slow to reach bedded conditions, this could result in increased brake wear emissions when they are used. Additionally, if brake disc pads are degraded with the little use they receive in conjunction with RBS, rusted surfaces could lead to poor bedding conditions and higher brake wear.

Friction braking systems

While regenerative braking and driver assistance systems are aimed at preventing brake wear emissions by minimising the use of friction braking, a number of measures aim to reduce the amount of particle wear produced from the friction and heat that occur during the braking process itself. These technological measures mainly consist of physico-chemical modifications of the composition of rotors and pads, although the design of the brake system (geometry, ventilation, clamp, etc.) is also important. Composition changes should be evaluated carefully since they may involve trade-offs in terms of the types and relative toxicity of particles generated: for example, one modification may reduce the mass of particles emitted but increase their number, or may reduce the metallic particulates but increase the organic content of PM.

The EU funded LOWBRASYS project aims to test a novel and low-emission brake system that will reduce micro and nanoparticles from brake wear by at least 50% (Kousoulidou, Perricone and Grigoratos, 2019[36]). The project addresses both particulate emissions in the typical micrometer ranges, which are important for PM *mass* reduction, as well as ultrafine particles of less than 0.1 micrometers, which are important for particulate *number* reduction. A number of different technologies are considered, the most well-developed of which are the use of novel material formulations for brake pads and discs, the design of environmentally friendly braking strategies that optimise vehicle braking action, and technologies for capturing PM particles near their source. The interaction of new surface combinations must be rigorously tested and a clear, transparent procedure should be followed to ensure that the use of new braking materials do not have negative impacts on human health. For this reason, the LOWBRASYS project received a 6 month extension in order to explore further configurations of new pads and execute additional toxicity tests (Kousoulidou, Perricone and Grigoratos, 2019[36]). The LOWBRASYS technology is a candidate to become Best Available Technology (BAT) and serve as a basis to support the preparation of robust measurement standards and legislations on non-exhaust PM emissions, which is not addressed by any current EU legislation.

Box 4.1. The LOWBRASYS project

The LOWBRASYS project tests a novel and low-emission brake system designed to reduce micro and nanoparticles generation by at least 50%. The main objectives of the project are to:

1. Develop novel environmentally friendly material formulations for brake pads and discs used in passenger cars.
2. Develop software functions for dynamic assisted braking strategies and develop a human-machine interface (HMI) smart dashboard.
3. Develop new technology for capturing particles near the braking system.
4. Use life cycle costing, life cycle assessment and comprehensive cost-benefit analysis to assess the financial costs and environmental benefits of proposed new material formulations vs. existing formulations.
5. Pursue an improved understanding of brake wear emissions on the basis of particle numbers vs particle mass concentrations.
6. Environment: the project had demonstrated to have the potential to improve air quality (lowering PM emissions), prevent ecosystem impacts and waste, and increase resource efficiency.
7. Propose a roadmap for the development and implementation of brake wear emissions regulation in Europe, emphasising the need to prioritise the development of a methodology for sampling and measuring brake wear particles followed by a testing period in order to accurately measure real-world brake wear emissions.

The project considered a series of different technologies, the most important being the introduction of novel material formulations for brake pads and discs, the development of environmental friendly braking strategies that optimise the vehicle braking action and reduce the particle emissions and the development of breakthrough technology for capturing particles near the PM source. The project concluded that no single technology was able to reduce PM emissions by 50%. Rather, a multitude of different technologies was needed to achieve this reduction. A conclusion of the project is that further development is required to advance the proposed solutions from prototype-level technologies to market ready applications. In this context, the UNECE- GRPE PMP IWG recognizes the need for prioritizing the development of a suitable methodology for sampling and measuring brake wear particles followed by a testing period in order to accurately measure real-world brake wear PM and PN EFs.

Source: Kousoulidou, Perricone, & Grigoratos (2019[36])

Brake disc composition, coating and treatment

Brake discs made of gray cast iron represent the majority of brake rotors produced today because their manufacturing process is well understood, but most of all, they are very inexpensive to produce. Some improvements can nevertheless be made to reduce the brake wear and particle emissions they generate.

Some manufacturers have discussed adding titanium in the range of 0.1%-0.25% by weight to high-carbon cast iron brake discs to improve their hardness and reduce wear (Sichuan Province Vanadium and Titanium Brake Ltd., 2014[37]). Molybdenum has also been suggested as an additive to cast iron rotors to increase their wear resistance. Early evidence suggests that an addition of up to 1.5 wt% to the iron cast is feasible and results in wear improvement without affecting other characteristics (Piwowarsky, 2013[38]). Patterson, Standke, & Kocheisen (2013[39]) have also found that additional molybdenum reduces wear. Shangdong Hong MA Construction Machinery Co. (2014[40]) has presented a new disc material composed of a high-carbon, low-silicon cast iron containing niobium. According to the inventors, increasing niobium by 0.1-0.3 wt% improves strength at high temperatures and resistance to wear. However, these materials have not been widely introduced to the market because the addition of titanium or molybdenum increases production costs, which, under current policy conditions, is difficult to justify in the manufacturing of braking systems.

Gray cast iron disc coatings

Disc coatings are a very promising mitigation measure from a technological point of view, but the additional costs entailed (EUR 100 or more per disc) currently prohibit their market entry. Mayer and Lembach (2012[41]) describe a layer concept to improve the wear resistance of brake discs. A protective layer is made of an iron-based matrix alloy (chromium or nickel), as well as hard materials (carbides or ceramic oxides). Between the cast iron base body and the protection layer, a so-called sealing layer helps bond the friction surface layer. Mayer and Lembach (2013[42]) also discuss the use of a 10-55mm thick anti-wear layer on the rubbing ring of a brake rotor composed of a metal alloy or ceramic material. An integrated wear indicator could alert drivers when this protection layer is worn out. The indicator material would be made of a colored, black or white ceramic material, or a woven or braided fabric and could also consist of mineral pigments. A wear-indicating element in combination with a wear-reducing surface coating is also presented in Dupuis (2013[43]). In this case the wear indicator consists of a raised portion between the friction ring and the surface coating that runs around the ring in the form of a wavy line. These indicator proposals could be very useful in optimising the wear of brake rotors, which are characterised by low mass loss due to hardened surface coatings, making it difficult to gauge the extent of their wear.

Qihong (2011[44]) present a cast iron disc with a surface-hardened layer composed of hard ceramic particles and a nodular cast iron. Although its thickness of 2e5 mm could lead to crack or delamination processes over lifetime, the patent for the disc contends that it enhances the rotor by a factor 4.6. Another coated brake disc patent is presented by Keith (2009[45]), who introduces a dual-coating to enhance the wear performance of the rubbing ring as well as the corrosion prevention of the hat of the rotor. The rubbing ring is first prepared by roughening of the surface followed by the deposit of a 20-30 mm thick bond coat layer of adhesion-promoting material composed of nickel or a nickel-alloy. Next, a wear-reducing friction surface coating is applied. The layer can be made of pure alumina material or alumina alloy material. The finished layer thickness should be in the range of 100-400 mm, preferably between 150 and 250 mm. Finally, the rotor hat is also coated to protect it from corrosion. Özer and Lampke (2012[46]) also describe a thermal spray coating material to wear reduction purposes. A ceramic powder (30-35 wt%) and a metallic powder mixture (65-70 wt%) are considered. The ceramic powder is composed of reinforced particles of aluminum oxide, zirconium oxide, and titanium oxide, while the metallic powder mixture consists of zinc alloy (25-30 wt%) and iron alloy (70-75 wt%). These proposed spray coatings are designed to be economical and extend the service life of the cast iron base body. Lembach and Mayer (2012[41]) also describe design of a wear-reducing surface coating, the thickness of which varies according to the cooling channel and fin design. Because the base body material and the coating are characterised by different thermal expansion coefficients, mechanical strains are likely to occur when a coating of uniform thickness is used. This can lead to cracks in the coating or even to delamination, and cause hot spots that lead to brake judder. The authors therefore recommend a thicker coating in the area of the cooling channels where the thermal expansion is smaller.

For commercial vehicles, Khambekar et al. (2004[47]) describe a non-ceramic metallic coating for application to cast iron brake rotors and its production method and provide a number of recommendations regarding the cast iron composition of the base body. The metallic character of the layer optimises adherence to the cast iron base body relative to ceramic composites. The authors recommend a roughening of the friction ring surface as a pretreatment, after which the coating is applied via a thermal spray coating method that leads to reactions of the metallic elements with the cast iron. This reduces not only general wear, but also wear that occurs at high temperatures. A preferred composition of the coating consists of 16% of Chrome and a steel alloy. In addition, the composition of the base body of the rotor should be modified in the way that a molybdenum content of 6-8% and a chrome content of less than 5% are considered. The authors predict that service life will double with the use of a 0.7mm thick coating. For a brake rotor with a diameter of 430 mm and a weight of 25 kg, this would require 250-450 grammes of coating composite per rubbing ring.

Treatments for gray cast iron rotor discs

In addition to coating methods, ferritic nitrocarburizing (FNC) is a thermochemical treatment method that is also designed to protect cast iron rotors from corrosion and to increase their hardness in order to improve wear performance. The application of the FNC method is detailed in Hanna (2009), among others, and Riefe et al. (2011[48]) have found that it reduces brake wear. FNC-treated brake rotors currently have a very high market penetration among passenger cars in North America, but other markets remain dominated by the use of conventional gray cast iron rotors. The FNC method involves no coating, rather it enriches the disc with nitrogen and carbon and uses a "metallic" diffusion layer and "ceramic" compound layer. The diffusion layer is dominated by iron-nitrides and is four to five times harder than the gray cast iron basic material and the compound layer is characterized by the generation of nitrides and carbides and a hardness factor that is five times higher than cast iron.

FNC works well with adhesive friction mechanisms, which means that non-asbestos organic (NAO) brake pads are the best for use in combination with FNC rotors (Riefe, Holly and Learman, 2011[48]). However, it should be noted that coefficients of friction have been found to fall by 10%-15% using FNC (Riefe, Holly and Learman, 2011[48]; AUDI AG, 2016[26]). The use of low steel or UNECE-compliant brake linings would mean higher friction levels, but greater wear, removing almost 80% of the compound layer after 2000 km. FNC treatments cost less than coatings (approximately EUR 10 per disc). Although coatings and treatments such as FNC appear to be the most promising approaches for improving brake wear, the additional manufacturing costs they entail remain a barrier for further market penetration.

Aluminum Brake Discs

Although gray cast iron brake rotors have many advantages, other base materials have gained attention for automotive applications in the last 20 years. Brake discs made of aluminum represent a promising technology for future brake systems because they reduce not only weight but also mechanical wear. They are, however, at least EUR 50 more expensive than gray cast iron discs.

Özer (2009[49]) describes an aluminum metal matrix compound (Al-MMC) brake rotor composed of a metal matrix made of AlSi2O with 15-25 wt% silicon carbide. A spray-forming adds other hard particles 3-50 mm in diameter, which can be made of Al2O3, SiO2, TiO2, SiC, tungsten carbide, boron carbide, titanium nitride, or/and titanium diboride. In total, the percentage of hard material particles is 45 wt%. Lampke and Özer (2013[50]) provide more details on the production process of this type of aluminum brake rotor. Hino and Miyashita (1984) also propose an aluminum brake rotor designed to have high abrasion resistance and generate less brake pad wear, which is accomplished through the addition of a ceramic antiwear material and/or a solid lubricant to an aluminum hypereutectic silicon alloy. The ceramic material consists of Al2O3, SiC, or SiN4 and comprises 3-20 wt% of the rotor. A solid lubricant such as graphite could also be added, though in an amount not exceeding 5 wt%.

Lower surface roughness has also been identified as strategy for reducing brake pad wear. To this end, Lampke and Özer (2012[51]) propose a brake rotor base body made of aluminum in combination with a prefabricated steel wear protection layer matching the dimensions of the friction ring. This combination allows for improved wear resistance, corrosion resistance, and thermal load carrying capacity. Smolen (1991[52]) also proposes an aluminum rotor with a ceramic protection layer that is applied to the braking surface at a thickness of 0.33-0.50 mm. The coating consists of aluminum oxide, aluminum titanium, and magnesium zirconate. Because the coating acts as a heat reflector, it prevents the rotor from attaining excessive temperatures that could crack or disintegrate the disc. In addition to improvements related to thermal performance, the ceramic coating is also expected to decrease wear.

Rotors made of aluminum, especially reinforced Al-MMC, constitute a very promising approach to reduce brake wear and particle emissions. Even if issues surrounding their material and manufacturing costs remain (e.g. the critical temperature limit of around 400°C), Al-MMC rotor concepts are expected to become increasingly relevant in the future due to their lighter weight and lower brake wear. The ongoing market penetration of hybrid and full electric vehicles could help overcome the drawbacks associated with their low temperature limits, because regenerative braking generally lowers the maximum operating temperature reached when friction braking is employed.

Ceramic Brake Discs

Ceramic composite brake discs, also known as ceramic brake discs, are another technology that can reduce wear and brake particle emissions. Originally designed for high-performance applications, this type of brake rotor has also demonstrated significantly better wear performance due to its high hardness (Kienzle and Kratschmer, 2007[53]; Johnson, 2009[54]; James, Murdie and Walker, 2002[55]). In terms of their design, they are comprised of a multilayer structure consisting of carrier bodies and friction layers that are both reinforced with carbon fibers. Although a great deal of effort has been expended to improve the manufacturing process of ceramic brake discs, their production is still very time- and energy-consuming, and the level of automation is lower compared with that of cast iron discs, which leads to significantly higher production costs (400 € to 600 € per disc). For this reason, although ceramic brake rotors can be an effective technology for reducing brake wear emissions, their future use is expected to be limited to niche applications such as high-performance sports cars.

Titanium Brake Discs

Other research has shown that titanium also has advantageous properties as a brake rotor material. Muthukannan, et al. (2014[56]) discuss the use of titanium made brake rotors (laser nitrided Ti-6Al-4V, Ti-LSN) and compare the performance of commercial gray cast iron with untreated titanium alloy. They find that untreated titanium alloy exhibits significantly higher wear rates and volume losses, presumably due to poor resistance to abrasion processes and severe plastic deformations. Laser treated titanium material, in contrast, shows a much better wear performance in all operating conditions and its frictional behaviour is comparable to that of cast iron. No adapted lining material was used in this test, suggesting that wear-reducing potential may be even greater than that measured in the study. However, similarly to ceramic brake discs, the use of titanium material remains limited, mostly appropriate for niche applications because of the high material and manufacturing costs. Given that the technology is currently in the pre-development stage, no estimation of their manufacturing costs is currently possible.

The EU-funded REBRAKE project indicates that it is possible to design a disc brake system for a European standard car that reduces PM10 emissions by at least 32% using a standard European pad and a heat-treated rotor. A further reduction to 65 wt% PM10 emissions can be achieved with NAO pad material and a heat-treated disc. The treatment consists in heating the disc to 860 °C for 2 h under controlled atmospheric pressure. Subsequent oil quenching and tempering for 4 h at 180 °C increases the hardness of the cast iron from an initial 210 ±10 Brinell hardness number (HB) to 473 ±25 HB.

Brake pad composition

The second friction partner, the brake pad, also represents a source for remediation measures to reduce brake wear emissions. Because the pad is always considered as the weak partner of the friction couple, most approaches focus on increasing the hardness and mechanical strength of the lining material. Currently, additional costs for these approaches are not expected to exceed 10 € to 20 € per pad.

Given the recent implementation restrictions on the use of heavy metals in brake pads in California (Senate Bill (SB) 346), Washington (SB 6557), Rhode Island State (SB H7997), and New York State (SB A10871), as well as further restrictions foreseen in the coming years, OEMs and after-market manufacturers are in the process of eliminating the use of a number of toxic chemicals (Cu, Cr (VI), Pb, Hg and Cd) in brake pads, drum linings, and heavy-duty brake blocks. Nickel, antimony and zinc could be affected by similar restrictions in the future. Several studies, such as the REBRAKE project, have however found that eliminating or reducing the copper content of brake pads reduces their friction coefficient and increases particulate emissions. A potential substitute for copper is Barite, which is normally used as a filler and supposedly non-hazardous (Konduru et al., 2014[57]; Loza et al., 2016[58]). Barite ore is commonly available, easier to extract, more cheaply mined, and more quickly processed than many other commodities.

Zhao (2013[59]) proposes a brake pad composed of composite ceramic fibers that are designed to be soluble, decomposable, and can be used as reinforcing fibers. The authors emphasize that the fibers do not affect human health and generate low environmental impacts. They also state that the use of a soft ceramic fiber protects the rotor disc from excessive wear. Similar to other brake pad designs, the composite ceramic brake pad consists of a lining matrix and a backing plate made of steel. Bowei (2009[60]) discusses a non-metallic ceramic brake pad for automotive applications, recommending the use of a ceramic binder (10-20 wt%) with a modified aluminium sodium silicate to improve heat resistance and wear in high temperature operating conditions.

Limited attention has been paid to the release of organic compounds from brake pads, despite the fact that these compounds represent a significant part of brake pad formulations (Plachá et al., 2017[61]). The high temperatures and pressures on involved in friction braking cause a thermal decomposition of the organic and carbonaceous components of brake pads, or thermal fade (Yun, Filip and Lu, 2010[62]). The thermal degradation of organic (polymer matrix) brake pads begins at approximately 150°C, and maximum mass loss due to the oxidative thermal degradation of organic components occurs above 300°C (Křístková et al., 2004[63]; Kukutschová et al., 2010[64]), when thermally less stable components of brake pads (e.g., phenolic resin, rubber, graphite, coke) interact with ambient gases and oxygen (Kukutschová et al., 2009[65]) or undergo pyrolysis (Plachá et al., 2017[61]). This process releases very fine amorphous carbon particles and volatile organic compounds, including formaldehyde, that have significant implications for human health (World Health Organization, 2000[66]; WHO, 2006[67]). Metals and their oxides can also catalyze the degradation process of phenol-formaldehyde resin (Křístková et al., 2004[63]). Nano-vermiculite has been proposed as a replacement for phenolic resin as binder in order to enhance the thermal stability and wear resistance of brake pads. Another advantage of vermiculite is that it is currently considered to be a non-carcinogenic material, as it has not yet been shown to have an effect on human health.

Recent findings also shed light on the potential of a new generation of reinforced mineral fibers with varying lengths and aspect ratios (length/diameter) to reduce brake disc and pad wear (Santamaria Razo and Persoon, 2016[68]). An increase in fiber length is associated with a decrease in friction, but an increase in frictional stability. This leads to decreased disc wear and decreased vibration when braking, and the longer the mineral fibers, the better the wear performance. These new fibers have been shown to operate properly under nearly the entire range of temperature conditions which imply improved wear performance.

In summary, changes to brake pad composition have large potential for brake wear reduction. Given the wide range of materials available and the possible trade-offs entailed by different compositions (e.g. with respect to friction performance, noise, vibration, etc.), brake pad options deserve careful consideration on a case-by-case basis. Because every vehicle build has unique design and performance requirements, a general and market-wide adoption of any one specific brake pad composition is unlikely (Gramstat, 2018[69]).

Brake dust capturing systems

Another way to reduce brake wear emissions is to install specialised devices on vehicles to collect emitted particles. Brake particle collection systems have not been introduced to the market, neither from OEMs (original equipment manufacturer), nor as aftermarket solutions. Brake particle collecting systems patented so far include absorbers, adhesives, magnets or collector devices that use the rotational air flow of the rotor or additional fans. Several experimental studies have already been carried out with promising results.

The LOWBRASYS Project is working on a technology for capturing particles near the brake system in order to reduce PM10 emissions by 10% (Kousoulidou, Perricone and Grigoratos, 2019[36]). However, the efficiency of this technology with regard to ultrafine nanoparticles is unknown and practical uncertainties remain regarding its production on a large scale. The limited amount of space generally available in the wheel and wheel house also limits the possibilities for introducing additional components such as fans, impellers, pipes, and filter boxes. Interactions of the collecting devices with the brake are also possible, especially at the high temperatures reached during braking events (up to 700°C), which could impact the collecting devices. Last but not least, possible side-effects regarding noise and vibration should be considered. Rotating parts, especially with direct (frictional) contact with the brake rotor, might cause or at least aggravate noise and vibration issues, such as brake squeal or brake judder. Although standardised costs are not yet available for brake particle capturing systems, they are likely to fall in a range of EUR 50-100.

Box 4.2. Lead wheel weights

Lead wheel weights (LWW) are attached to the rims of automobile wheels in order to balance the tyres. These weights can come loose and fall off. LWW that fall from vehicles can be abraded and ground into tiny pieces by vehicle traffic resulting in higher lead content in fugitive dust along urban roadways, a potentially significant source of human lead exposure in urban environments (Root, 2000). Most wheel weights enter use via commercial tyre dealers and automotive repair and maintenance shops (USGS, 2006[70]; ECCC, 2013[71]).

Several countries have made it illegal to sell, manufacture or install LWW and some major tyre manufacturers and leading retail organizations have voluntarily removed LWW from their operations or are transitioning away from lead. Automobiles imported into Canada from Japan and the EU are equipped with non-lead wheel weights, consistent with the manufacturers national requirements (Government of Canada, 2017[72]).

Despite regulatory action in Europe and by some US States, and a decade of voluntary initiatives encouraging the use of alternatives, LWWs are still used in significant quantities in several countries as for example in North America. There have been various voluntary initiatives to reduce or eliminate the use of LWWs in North America. For example, the US EPA launched its 'National Lead-Free Wheel Weight Initiative' in August 2008 (US EPA, 2008[73]). It was developed as "a partnership among federal agencies, states, wheel weight manufacturers, retailers, tyre manufacturers, automobile trade associations and environmentalists" to encourage "the transition from the use of lead for wheel weights to lead-free alternatives." The Tire Industry has also developed an Environmental Best Practices report which describes procedures to follow in transitioning away from LWWs and the precautions that should be followed to ensure the proper handling, management and recycling of existing LWWs (TIA, 2008[74]).

The most common alternative material is steel, but other non-toxic alternatives are also being used, including high-density polymers in specialty applications, and aluminum and zinc alloys. Costs for non-lead wheel weights would comprise a small percentage of the costs of new vehicles and new tyre purchases. According to the California EPA, lead or zinc wheel weights lost on the roadway have much higher potential impacts to human health or the environment compared to steel (California EPA, 2011[75]). The substitution of zinc for lead weights poses a burden shift as the losses during use are more harmful to the environment than lead. Considering the assumptions outlined above, the impacts from lead- or zinc-based wheel weight losses to roadways, greatly exceed their manufacturing impacts. Therefore, steel appears to be the preferred alternative for clip-on weights due to its comparatively low toxicity and reasonable environmental impacts from manufacturing activity.

A transition to steel weights would raise the total costs of wheel weights deployment by about 0.25%. On the basis of an economic cost-benefit analysis of a potential lead weight phase-out, Campbell et al. (2018[76]) concluded that the social benefits from a regulated requirement for non-lead wheel weights exceeded anticipated costs to the industry.

Source: USGS (2006[70]), ECCC (2013[71]), Government of Canada (2017[72]), US EPA (2008[73]), TIA (2008[74]), California EPA (2011[75]), Campbell et al. (2018[76]).

Driver Assistance Systems

Evidence suggests that smooth traffic flows with fewer stop-and-go patterns generate fewer non-exhaust emissions than more congested traffic flows (Gruden, 2008[77]). Driver Assistant Systems (DAS) can give drivers feedback with the aim of increasing the efficiency of their driving style, making these systems relevant for the reduction of brake and tyre wear emissions. The more these systems can intervene to increase efficiency without requiring action on the part of the driver, the greater their assumed positive impacts on efficiency (Guckeisen, 2018[78]). A number of technologies are currently in use by original equipment manufacturers (Gramstat, 2018[69]; Guckeisen, 2018[78]) but no studies exist quantifying their effectiveness in terms of reduced non-exhaust emissions. For example, the predictive efficiency assistant (PEA) uses GPS-system data (topography, bends, speed limits, etc.) and vehicle sensors (cameras, radar, etc.) to inform the driver in advance about an upcoming need to decelerate.

The LOWBRASYS project implemented software functions for dynamic assisted braking on passenger car vehicles to develop a human-machine (HMI) smart dashboard interface. Adaptive cruise control (ACC) autonomously maintains a constant speed using longitudinal dynamic control. Under ACC, deceleration is preferentially carried out by free-wheeling, motor braking, or recuperation (in the case of an RBS) rather than friction braking, and acceleration is used on an as-needed basis. Lane departure warning (LDW) is a mechanism designed to warn the driver when the vehicle begins to move out of its lane on freeways and arterial roads (unless a turn signal is on in that direction). These systems are designed to minimize accidents by addressing the main causes of collisions including driver error, distractions and drowsiness. Adaptive navigation systems record data during driver's typical daily commute to learn routes, road gradients, curves, and breaking points. The system also uses a camera to visualise the roadway. Once the system learns the route, it can optimize power use to be more efficient during the trip, helping to reduce emissions and improve fuel economy.

All these types of DAS significantly reduce the use of friction braking. Rychlak (2010[79]) examines how DAS can optimise driving through a curve. This requires a measurement of the curve characteristics and the calculation of a drive scenario that reduces CO2 emissions, tyre abrasion and brake dust. A number of technologies are required for this task. In addition to "environment-to-car" communication, "car-to-car" communication is also required to complete the data transfer factor and optimize driving (Integreen, 2012[80]; UR:BAN, 2013[81]). It is expected that the combination of sophisticated assistance systems (ACC, active curve assists and lane departure assists), together with a sophisticated data transfer (Car2X communication) comes close to the requirements needed to enable autonomous driving and can lower brake wear emissions insofar as it limits the usage of friction brakes only for emergency braking or long mountain descents. Importantly, drivers must also feel comfortable using DAS to improve safety and reduce emissions manufacturers (Gramstat, 2018[69]; Guckeisen, 2018[78]). Estimating the costs of DAS is a complex task due to the variety of sensor systems available (e.g. on board vs. off board), but driving feedback applications could be implemented quite easily and cost-effectively (EUR 10-20 per application) (Gramstat, 2018[69]).

Local-level traffic and road management measures

Traffic flow measures

Traffic speed limitation is a common policy measure to improve safety as well as to reduce emissions from vehicles both on highways and in city centres. While its effects on air quality have been studied mostly in the context of exhaust emissions, there is some evidence on its effectiveness in reducing non-exhaust emissions. In Berlin, lowering the speed limit from 50 to 30 km/h, combined with effective enforcement, resulted in a decrease in traffic-related PM concentration of 25%-30% (and 5% of total ambient PM concentration). The traffic-related NO2 concentration at the curbside also fell by 15%-25% and the total concentration fell by 7%-12% (Lutz, 2013[82]). These results were achieved by synchronizing the traffic lights to ensure smooth traffic flow at 30 km/h (i.e., at closer to a constant speed rather than an average of stop-and-go speeds) (Casanova and Fonseca, 2012[83]). According to the Copert emission model, in contrast, which uses average vehicle speeds, reducing average traffic speed from 50 to 30 km/h increases both exhaust PM and NO2 emissions (Int Panis et al., 2011[84]).

A drawback of speed limitation policies is that they require a high level of enforcement (European Commission, 2019[85]). A DSA called Intelligent Speed Assistance (ISA) could be an important in-vehicle measure for tackling speeding. The EU-funded project SpeedAlert has been working on the definitions, classifications and standardisation requirements for a European application of a speed limit information and warning system.[2] The SafeMap project (in the framework of the French-German DEUFRAKO-programme) is also working on a feasibility study and a field trial with a system to inform drivers of a safe speed at a particular location (T'Siobbel, 2005).

Insofar as it reduces travel times, however, improving traffic flow may induce additional demand for travel by private vehicles in the long run. This risk should be managed in an integrated manner in mobility plans to ensure that the expected air quality benefits of traffic management measures continue to be delivered in the long term.

Measures to reduce road dust resuspension

Chemical dust suppressants have been used on unpaved roads and in the minerals industry to suppress dust for a long time in some countries. Since the 90s, they have also been used on paved roads in Norway, Finland, Sweden, and Austria (among other countries), both in tunnels and on open roads. Dust suppressants are sprayed onto the road surface, where the particles that come into contact with it are bound, reducing their capability of becoming airborne when agitated by the wind, tyre action, or vehicle turbulence. Dust suppressants also lower the freezing point of precipitation.

Many different types of dust suppressants have been tested around the world. In Europe, the focus has been on the use of hygroscopic compounds that absorb water when relative humidity exceeds 50%, namely magnesium chloride, calcium chloride, calcium magnesium acetate (CMA), and potassium formate. CMA has been the subject of tests on paved roads in Sweden (Norman and Johansson, 2006[86]), Austria (AIRUSE, 2016[87]), Germany (Reuter, 2010[88]) and the United Kingdom (Barratt et al., 2012[89]). Other studies have been conducted in Sweden, Finland, and Norway (Gustafsson, 2013[90]; Gustafsson, Jonsson and Ferm, 2010[91]). In general, effective dust suppression has been shown to require repeated applications and treatment over large areas. In Sweden and Austria, where road dust emissions represent a major contributor to PM10 levels, the application of CMA led to a decrease of the daily mean PM10 by up to 35% on a highway, and 5-20% in the city, with decreases of up to 40-70% measured during certain hours. The studies carried out in Germany and the United Kingdom could not detect a significant PM10 decrease on typical urban roads. When decreases in PM10 decrease are found, they tend to be short lived (lasting a few hours), which suggests that the effectiveness of CMA in binding deposited particles is closely related to the degree of road moisture.

In Barcelona, the application of CMA and magnesium chloride on a typical urban road had no significant impact on air quality (Amato et al., 2014[92]). In contrast with Sweden,

Austria and Norway, the ineffectiveness of these measures in Mediterranean regions is likely due to faster decreases in moisture from the evaporation induced by higher levels of solar radiation. Böhner et al. (2011[93]) have also indicated that road dust binding agents are only effective when the relative air humidity is at least 35%. In addition, it is noteworthy that the sites where CMA or magnesium chloride were found to have an effect were characterized by very high road dust loads (studded tyres, road sanding, and industrial dust).

Box 4.3. On-board dust filtering

A recent invention to address road dust emissions comes in the form of an active filtering system installed in the undercarriage of a vehicle. This system has been deployed in electric vehicles by the Deutsche Post DHL. The filter is installed in the lower part of the body at the level of the rear axle, so that no valuable cargo space is lost, and fans are installed behind the filters, enabling the vehicle to filter fine dust from the ambient air even when idling. Particle filters are equipped with sensors to monitor their efficiency. Information is collected on filtration performance, the volume of purified air, the concentration of particulate matter and meteorological data. The data can then be sent to the cloud with a web interface for evaluation.

Source: Heise Online (2017[94])

Street sweeping

Evidence indicates that street sweeping alone (without water) does not improve air quality in the short term due to the inability of sweepers to effectively catch particles of diameters below 10 µm (Amato et al., 2009[95]). However, this does not mean that in the long term street sweeping is not beneficial for air quality, due to the removal of larger particles, which could eventually be ground into smaller particulate matter. Vacuum sweepers are preferable to simple mechanical sweepers. However, because road sweepers have the potential to increase local PM10 concentrations due to the resuspension induced by the operating vehicle itself, vacuum sweepers should be equipped with water spraying and particle filters at the vacuum air exhaust.

Street washing

Water on road surfaces reduces the mobility of road dust, making street washing a potentially effective measure for mitigating non-exhaust dust resuspension. When water adheres to deposited particles, it increases their mass and surface tension forces, decreasing their likelihood of becoming airborne, especially as the cohesion of wetted particles often persists after the water has evaporated due to the formation of aggregates.

The effectiveness of street washing in reducing road dust has been quantified in a number of studies worldwide. In Düsseldorf, street washing twice a week reduced daily mean PM10 concentrations by about 2 mg/m3 on a busy road (John et al., 2006[96]). In Stockholm, street washing of roadside next to a highway ramp in favorable weather reduced road dust concentrations by 6% (Norman and Johansson, 2006[97]). Additionally, while the control site exceeded 50 mg/m3 on 12 occasions, the test site exceeded this amount on 10 occasions. Street washing was also found to be beneficial in the Netherlands, where its effectiveness varied depending on local conditions such as pavement material, weather conditions, and particle solubility (Keuken, Denier van der Gon and van der Valk, 2010[98]). In Madrid, Karanasiou et al. (2011[99]) found that the mass contribution from road dust was 2 µg/m3 lower on days that street washing was implemented, corresponding to a 15% reduction of road dust mass contribution relative to days when the road was left untreated.

In Finland, pressurized washing lowered PM10 emission levels by 15-60% (Kupiainen et al., 2011[100]). The effect was found to be highest immediately after treatment and dependent on the water pressure, the volume of water used, and the orientation of the nozzles in the pressure washer. The study found that the effectiveness of street washing is not only dependent on the characteristics of the cleaning equipment and washing method, but also on the frequency of cleaning and the amount of road dust, leading to a recommendation that street washing be considered where street dust levels are high and constitute the dominant source of PM10. Street washing functionalities can be incorporated into street sweepers or manually applied by hoses. An interesting case is that of some Korean cities, where some municipalities have employed self-cleaning road systems to tackle road dust emissions. The systems are generally operated twice a day during the summer. In the event of a heat wave, the system operates three times a day. The self-cleaning road system in Daegu has led to an estimated 5-15% drop in PM10 emissions (Kim, Jung and Kim, 2014[101]).

Street washing was found to reduce the road dust mobility by more than 90% in Spain and 60%-80% in Germany depending on the particle size and methodology applied (Amato et al., 2009[95]). The water volumes required for effective street sweeping may vary according to road dust loading. Although little investigated, an application rate of at least 1 litre per square meter is generally recommended. Road dust emissions levels have been shown to recover to 99% of pre-washing levels after 24 hours in Spain and 72 hours in the Netherlands (Amato et al., 2012b), as the moistening effect of water is more important than actual particle removal (wash off) in determining emissions levels. Given that peak emission period tends to be between 7 and 9am, the available evidence indicates that road washing will be most effective if performed in the early morning hours (4-5 AM) (AIRUSE, 2016[102]). Non-drinking water should ideally be used for street washing purposes, and possible trade-offs may exist regarding increased pollutants in sewage systems and natural waterways.

Within the AIRUSE LIFE project, street washing was also tested on industrial roads (Amato et al., 2016[103]). The interest in industrial sites was related to the higher PM emissions due to high road dust loadings. The paved road was located within the ceramic industrial cluster of L'Alcora (Spain). Road dust loadings (below 10 µm) were within 20-40 mg/m2, much above the general range in European cities of 1-6 mg/m2. Given such high road dust loadings, street washing was intensive (27 L/m2 phreatic water flow was used). Daily mean PM10 concentrations decreased by 18.5% on the day of the cleaning. However, this reduction was short lived, being reduced to only 2.2% on the day after cleaning. The main PM10 decrease occurred from 7 to 11 AM, which corresponds to 5 h after the start of cleaning activities. Although short lived, this decrease is sufficient to produce a significant reduction in daily mean PM10 concentrations (Amato et al., 2016[103]).

Box 4.4. The Barcelona street washing case

In Barcelona's city centre, the effect of a combined cleaning procedure consisting of vacuum-assisted broom sweeping and manual washing was tested. Averaging the daily mean concentration of PM10 over the 24 h following each cleaning event and on dry days, a mean decrease of 3.7-4.9 mg/m3 (7-10% of curbside concentrations) was found (Amato et al., 2014). Based on these results, the City Council implemented specific measures for improved road washing in the Air quality Plan 2015-2018. The measures include:

- Improve the state of road pavements
- Wash at 5 AM, in order to maximize effectiveness
- Wash the entire width of the road rather than the outer lanes only
- Prioritize high traffic roads
- Increase the frequency of washing during PM pollution episodes.
- Avoid the use of blowers for road cleaning

Source: City of Barcelona (2019[104])

Ideally, washing should be performed whenever road dust emissions are expected to be particularly high. The frequency of washing should therefore be optimized according to (1) local resources, (2) rain forecast (washing will be less effective within 24 h of rainfall), and (3) the episodic spikes in road dust (e.g. transported from the desert). If not all roads can be washed given resource constraints, a few roads should be selected for treatment to maximise the impact. The efficacy of road washing depends highly on several factors such as (1) climatic conditions, (2) road dust loadings, (3) frequency of washing, (4) road surface material, (5) portion and length of the road that is washed, and (6) relevance of other sources of PM.

Another set of measures are those aimed at reducing dust deposition, i.e. road dust loading. Trucks carrying dusty loads could be required to cover these loads, and trucks exiting building sites could be required to have their wheels and undercarriages washed. Reducing the amount of unpaved roads in urban areas and adopting the best available technologies to reduce dust generation during building activities, e.g. stockpiles, handling, loading/unloading) could also reduce road dust (EU, 2003[105]; Holman, 2014[106]; Regional Government of Styria Austria, 2006[107]; Environment Canada, 2005[108]; Swiss Agency for the Environment, 2004[109]; Greater London Authority, 2006[110]).

4.2. New strategies to target non-exhaust emissions

Stringent fuel efficiency regulations have succeeded in significantly reducing the vehicle exhaust PM emissions in recent decades. The evidence presented in Section 3 shows, however, that one of the most promising technological solutions for reducing exhaust emissions – namely the widespread penetration of electric vehicles – will not yield significant reductions in non-exhaust emissions. Given that the vast majority of all road transport PM emissions will come from non-exhaust sources in the coming years, similar attention should now be given to non-exhaust PM emissions.

Although the complete elimination of non-exhaust PM emissions is probably not realistic in the foreseeable future given that friction processes are inherent in acceleration and deceleration, the reduction of these emissions and the social costs associated with them is possible. PM from non-exhaust sources can be reduced by decreasing vehicle-kilometres travelled and lowering the amount of non-exhaust PM emitted per kilometre driven. A robust understanding of emission factors, their drivers, and the effectiveness of measures to reduce them will be necessary before being able to comprehensively assess the costs and benefits of various policy options. The analysis that follows is applied from a partial equilibrium perspective, as it does not consider potential trade-offs between reducing non-exhaust emissions and impacts on other environmentally-related outcomes.

This section reviews available policy options that can be used to reduce non-exhaust emissions. Policy instruments for addressing other environmental externalities include regulatory instruments, market-based instruments, as well as soft measures to encourage voluntary action on the part of producers and consumers. Section 4.2.1 discusses the relevance of an optimally-designed market-based instrument in the form of a charge designed to internalise the social costs associated with non-exhaust emissions. Section 4.2.2. identifies measures that can improve non-exhaust emission factors. Caveats and further considerations with respect to these policy options are also presented.

4.2.1. Reducing vehicle kilometres travelled

As reviewed in Section 4.1.2, a number of measures can be taken to reduce vehicle-kilometres travelled. To date, however, these measures have not targeted the reduction of non-exhaust emissions specifically, instead focusing on other negative externalities such as congestion and greenhouse gas emissions. Given the evidence presented in Sections 2 and 3, and in view of economic theory regarding the efficient internalisation of the costs of negative externalities, this section presents a framework for the design of a market-based instrument that addresses the negative externalities arising from non-exhaust emissions specifically.

The adverse impacts to human health entailed by non-exhaust emissions constitute the most significant negative externality associated with their generation and the main reason why policies targeting these emissions are needed. As these impacts can be considered a form of market failure, pricing instruments designed to internalise these external costs are an efficient, i.e. cost-effective, strategy to reduce emissions to optimal levels. At these levels, the marginal social benefit of an additional unit of emissions is equal to the marginal social cost of the damages associated with it (van Dender, 2019[111]; Parry et al., 2014[112]).[3] Importantly, economic efficiency only achieved if the charge targets the correct source of the negative externality in question and accurately reflects environmental damages. Equity issues stemming from the potential regressive distributional effects of the charge can be addressed through targeted compensatory mechanisms using part of the resulting fiscal dividends (Parry et al., 2014[112]).

Although non-exhaust emissions are primarily proportional to distance travelled, rather than fuel used, they also depend on factors other than distance travelled, namely vehicle weight, size, acceleration/deceleration speeds, road moisture, and road dust loading, as established in Section 2. The external cost per unit of non-exhaust emissions, moreover, depends on the number of people who are exposed to the PM caused by them. As such, a purely distance-based charge does not take into account the fact that the damages caused by non-exhaust emissions vary according to two important determinants of the magnitude of external costs, namely the characteristics of the vehicle, the area in which it travels, and the road surfaces.

To more accurately reflect these variations in marginal damages, therefore, charges designed to address the externalities from non-exhaust emissions should be differentiated according to the determinants of the marginal social costs they incur. A charge on non-exhaust emissions from road transport activity should drive both improvements in emission factors, as well as reductions in vehicle-kilometres driven (Parry et al., 2014[112]; van Dender, 2019[111]). An efficient non-exhaust emissions charge will be equal to the emission factor of a vehicle (g/vkm) times the marginal social cost of these emissions (EUR/g):

$$C_{ia} = f(E_i, D_a) \quad (1)$$

where C_{ia} is the per-kilometre charge for vehicle *i* in area *a*, E_i is the non-exhaust emission factor of vehicle *i* in grammes per kilometre, and D_a is the marginal damage cost of non-exhaust emissions per gramme in area *a*. Importantly, this charge differs from a flat per-kilometre charge because it is differentiated with respect to the determinants of the marginal external cost of non-exhaust emissions, namely by the characteristics of the vehicle and the area in which it operates.[4] The emission factor E is indexed by the vehicle *i* and the marginal damage is indexed by area *a*:

$$E_i = f(w_i, b_i, t_i) \quad (2)$$

$$D_a = f(p_a, c_a) \quad (3)$$

Where the emission factors are determined by w_i, which represents the vehicle weight, b_i the relevant brake characteristics, and t_i the tyre characteristics.[5] Marginal damages D_a are a function of p_a, the population density of an area and c_a, the level of congestion. Because the purpose is to take into account population exposure, the definition of each area would ideally be informed by, for example, measures of population density, the general proximity of buildings to roadways, and travel via soft modes that is undertaken (where mode shares are not available, the extent of soft-mode infrastructure available could be used as a proxy). Following EU standards for CO2 emissions, for example, the charge could vary according to whether travel took place in urban, suburban, or rural areas, or on motorways. If marginal damages are found to depend on the ambient air quality, this could be reflected by a scale parameter that increases the charge for all vehicles when air quality is already poor.

This type of charge combines the spatial and temporal specificities of a congestion charge with the distance-based characteristic of a flat per-kilometre charge in order to accurately reflect variations in the marginal social damages entailed by non-exhaust emissions. The specific form that these functions should take will rely on more extensive evidence than currently exists regarding the drivers and impacts of non-exhaust emissions. Their design will notably require the establishment of reliable estimates of marginal damages based on emission factors and health impacts (see Section 3.3). To the extent that the implementation of this instrument makes vehicles with lower non-exhaust emission factors more attractive to consumers, it theoretically also incentivises manufacturers to produce vehicles and vehicle parts (mainly tyres and brakes) with lower emission factors if these emissions factors are made known to prospective consumers.

The fact that non-exhaust PM emissions can also contain larger particles than exhaust PM emissions (i.e. they settle more rapidly, thus affecting a smaller area), means that the need to prioritise densely populated areas is even greater for measures targeting non-exhaust emissions than for measures targeting exhaust emissions. The design of a pricing instrument targeting non-exhaust emissions should involve context-specific evidence on emission factors, health impacts, as well as any insights arising from the previous implementation of distance-based charges. The implementation of such an instrument would realistically need to be automated, for example based on GPS data (as suggested in van Dender (2019[111])). Additional considerations that should be taken into consideration in the design of such a measure are provided in Section 4.3.3.

Goodkind et al. (2019[113]) estimate marginal damages of primary and secondary PM2.5 from exhaust emissions, as well as from road dust resuspension, but not from direct wear sources (Table 4.4). They also assume no difference in health impacts across different PM2.5 species, and value mortality only. Fann, Baker, and Fulcher (2012[114]) also estimate the benefits of reducing primary PM as well as secondary PM from exhaust sources, reporting benefits of 2015 USD 400,000, 81,000, and 21,000 per tonne of PM avoided.[6] To date, no studies have estimated the marginal damages associated with exposure to non-exhaust emissions specifically.

Table 4.4. Median marginal damages of PM2.5 emissions from road transport

(thousand 2011 USD per tonne)

	Light petrol vehicles	Heavy petrol vehicles	Light diesel vehicles	Heavy diesel vehicles	Dust: paved roads	Dust: unpaved roads
Primary PM2.5	122.44	88.97	116.53	83.97	64.43	34.72
Secondary PM2.5						
VOC	7.18	6.25	7.49	5.96	0	0
NH3	73.58	61.20	68.44	50.69	0	0
SO2	24.32	22.61	24.4	22.54	0	0
NOx	12.55	11.72	13.37	12.54	0	0

Source: Goodkind et al. (2019[113])

4.2.2. Improving emission factors

Given the importance of vehicle weight as a determinant of non-exhaust emissions, vehicle lightweighting should be considered an important regulatory tool for addressing the non-exhaust particulate matter emitted by both ICEVs and BEVs. Reducing vehicle weight will lead to less brake, tyre, and perhaps also road wear. In addition to the maximum allowed weight for selected roads, other measures to reduce HDV overloading include improved enforcement mechanisms and higher fines (Žnidarič, 2015[16]). Overloading of goods vehicles has been estimated to cost the UK over GBP 50 million a year (2003 PPP) through the additional wear and tear that it creates on roads and bridges. Overloaded drive axles are the biggest single cause of excessive wear and tear on roads in the country (UK Department for Transport, 2003[115]).

In a similar way as increasing stringency has led to improved fuel efficiency, regulations on the materials that make up brake pads, brake rotor discs, and tyres have led to reductions in the toxicity of PM emissions. Regulations regarding not only the toxicity of brake and tyre materials, but also their durability would more directly target the amount of particulate matter emitted from tyres and non-regenerative braking systems. Nevertheless, regulations affecting brake and tyre composition such as asbestos bans, REACH, CLP, and restrictions on the use of trace elements and heavy metals should continue to be adopted in countries where they are not yet implemented. These regulations should also become increasingly stringent both in terms of the minimum concentration thresholds they require and in the number of toxic components they consider. Particular attention should be given to heavy metals and organic compounds of known toxicity. Given the nascency of the evidence regarding the health impacts of non-exhaust emissions, efforts should also be undertaken to make regulations more easily adaptable to emerging scientific evidence.

More generally, continued technological development, supported by incentives for innovation to further reduce emission factors, will contribute to reducing non-exhaust emissions. Policies favouring vehicle lightweighting should be put in place. Driver assistant systems are another existing technology that can influence driver behaviour to be more efficient so as to reduce non-exhaust emissions from brake and tyre wear. Sophisticated DAS can include sensors for rotor temperature and tyre pressure, as they are important parameters for brake and tyre emissions, respectively. The more these systems reach automated driving, taking the human driver out of the loop, the more effective they will be in reducing non-exhaust emissions.

The cost-effectiveness of road management measures, such as dust binding and street washing, should be evaluated on a case-by-case basis. The use of dust suppressants, for example, should involve a consideration of potential environmental trade-offs, including damage to vegetation and human health and contamination of soil and ground water. Other potential side-effects include reducing road friction and corrosion to highway infrastructure such as bridges and the road surfaces. In areas where water is scarce, street washing may not be cost-effective.

Eco-labelling of brakes and tyres can be a useful element of regulations to increase consumer awareness about the negative impacts of non-exhaust emissions. As a first step, eco-labelling can reflect the content of toxic components, as is already practiced in the US states of California and Washington. Ultimately, eco-labelling could be implemented in the same way as CO2 emissions labelling, which is mandatory in the EU, although this would rely on the development of a standardized measurement protocol for non-exhaust emissions.

4.3. Knowledge gaps and an agenda for future research

Evident challenges exist with respect to developing policies to internalise the externalities of non-exhaust emissions. These include measuring non-exhaust emissions, measuring and valuing exposure to non-exhaust emissions, and designing and implementing the policy. For example, the implementation of a charge on non-exhaust emissions in road transport is predicated on being able to quantify the marginal damages associated with these emissions as well as establishing a robust understanding of the quantitative nature of the relationship between the various drivers of non-exhaust emissions (e.g. vehicle weight) on which emission factors (and thus the charge amount) would be based. As evident in Section 2, considerable uncertainty remains with respect to these relationships.

4.3.1. Measuring and sourcing non-exhaust emissions

First, standardized methodologies to measure brake, tyre and road wear emissions will need to be developed in order to design, implement, and enforce the policies presented in the previous section. There is currently a lack of such standardized measurement methods that use reliable sampling equipment and have the capacity to replicate real-world conditions. This has a direct influence on the quality and harmonization of emissions inventorying, air quality modelling and projections, since the values available in literature are obtained using a wide range of instrumentation, testing and sampling/monitoring procedures. As a result, there is a need for harmonization and consistency in emissions reporting, in the representativeness of emission factors, and the inclusion of resuspension.

For brake wear emissions, the LOWBRASYS project has provided suggestions regarding the development of a suitable methodology for sampling and measuring brake wear particles as well as recommendations for the development of a representative of real-world conditions braking cycle, concluding that the developed 3h-LACT can be used for standardization and thus regulatory purposes as it fulfils the requirements for a real-world representative braking cycle (Kousoulidou, Perricone and Grigoratos, 2019[36]). More recently, an important step-forward towards a commonly accepted methodology has been made by the UNECE informal working group on the Particle Measurement Programme (UNECE, 2019[116]), which has developed a novel, publicly available WLTP-based real-world brake wear cycle[7] (Mathissen et al., 2018[117]). Similar initiatives should be taken for tyre wear and road surface (wear and resuspension) emissions. For brake wear, it is also important to conduct research on the benefits and drawbacks of different combinations of brake pads and rotors.

For road and tyre wear emissions, the influence of pavement type and structure remains largely unknown. For tyre wear, it is necessary to conduct research on the benefits and drawbacks of different combinations of road and tyre materials. Most of the available literature is based on studded tyres conditions; thus more research is needed in a standard tyres context. More research is also required to quantify the effect of low-rolling resistant tyres on tyre wear. Although durable rocks (e.g. porphyry) seem to be a logical choice in road pavement material, this material might be rare and its use not economically defensible in areas where road wear is of low priority. Road pavement characterization should accompany air quality studies dedicated to assess the impact of road wear. The impact of surface texture and state should be further investigated since a larger grain size and surface porosity appear to be associated with lower road wear emissions. The possible impact of alternative fillers (e.g. rubber and cement) and aggregates (e.g. furnace slag) should also be explored. A standardized test could conceivably assess the PM emission properties of pavement samples. Such a method could help to understand which pavement construction types and which pavement and rock aggregate properties are the most important determinants of PM emissions. This could facilitate the choice of pavements in environments where pavement wear is an important source of emissions. The Prall and the Tröger test methods could be useful methods in this regard, as suggested by Snilsberg (2008[118]), but they will require further development for the specific purpose of particle emission investigations.

For road dust resuspension, the local environment is even more important than for road wear, since both road dust loading and meteorology are important drivers of PM emissions from road dust. As current emission factors from resuspension may include wear emissions, new methods to avoid double counting should be developed. However, given the dominant role of resuspension among non-exhaust emission factors, the magnitude of double counting would probably be low relatively to the magnitude of error that is entailed by discarding resuspension. Local measurement initiatives that couple road dust loadings, mobile vehicle measurements and ambient air measurements, would significantly advance this effort. In this way, different measurement techniques can be used together to pursue a better understanding of the relationship between direct wear and road dust resuspension rates and their contributions to ambient air pollution (Denby, Kupiainen and Gustafsson, 2018[119]). A number of measurement methodologies have been used to measure road dust loadings on an ad-hoc basis (e.g. wet and dry sampling, different cut-offs). Comparing these methods and developing a harmonized methodology is a prerequisite for considering road dust resuspension in emissions inventories.

The relationship between road dust emission factors and vehicle weight also warrants further study. Although the analysis presented here does not assume a qualitative functional form for the relationship between road dust emission factors and vehicle weight, a positive relationship between the two would imply that BEVs have greater road dust emission factors than ICEVs, making policy measures targeting non-exhaust emissions even more of a priority as EV uptake spreads. Another avenue for future work would be to explore the possible impact of flatter vehicle undercarriages on road dust emissions.

Further research will also be necessary in order to better separate the contributions from road dust resuspension, brake, and tyre and road wear, given that their relative toxicity for human health and the potential need for regulations to address them are likely to be different. In this sense, valuable information can be offered by size and time-resolved PM chemical characterization and particle size distribution measurement, as well as improved source apportionment tools. Road wear studies are still lacking in countries with non-studded tyres. This is particularly the case in Central and South America, Africa and the Middle East, where both non-exhaust emissions and urban population densities – and thus damages – are likely to be high.

Further research is also needed in order to identify and quantify the impact of vehicle, road, driver and environmental features on the non-exhaust emission potential. The influence of vehicle weight, size and speed on emission factors calls for detailed investigation. More research is also needed on how driving style impacts emission factors, which may point to significant opportunities to reduce emissions, especially enabled by technological developments in DAS. The influence of vehicle maintenance (e.g. tyre pressure, brake pad replacement) should also be investigated as a determinant of non-exhaust emissions. More experimental studies on PM emissions from EVs are also warranted. Currently, comparative studies with ICEVs rely on several assumptions on vehicle weight, the relative emissions reductions made possible by regenerative braking and low rolling resistance tyres. More research on the contribution to secondary PM from ICEVs is needed in order to properly assess their emissions relative to EVs.

4.3.2. Measuring and valuing the damages caused by non-exhaust emissions

With respect to estimates of the impact of non-exhaust emissions on health, more studies using source contributions as exposure indicators are needed, and use of state-of-the-art methods will reduce uncertainty in the use of source contribution data (effect modification, residual analysis, and multipollutant modelling). Although non-exhaust emissions have been associated with a number of short- and long-term health effects that are similar or higher in magnitude to those found for exhaust emissions, more epidemiological studies are nevertheless needed in order to carry out meta-analyses for different causes of mortality and morbidity. Although the effects of long-term exposure to non-exhaust PM have been reported in cohort studies, this evidence is still inconsistent, except for copper, iron (often associated with brake wear) and zinc (often associated with tyre wear), which have been strongly linked to mortality from cardiovascular causes.

From the toxicological point of view, although there are few in vivo toxicity studies focused specifically on non-exhaust sources, emerging data indicate that non-exhaust PM can be as hazardous as tailpipe PM depending on the nature of the health effect studied (Amato et al., 2014b). This is because the oxidative stress which is often related to transition metals and/or redox active organics is one of the main biological mechanisms behind the toxicity of PM. Other important factors to be investigated are the roles played by PM size and size distribution, particle number, composition (including coating and surface modifications), shape, surface area, surface chemistry, and charge and solubility/dispersability, on health impacts. The possibility of non-linearity of these health impacts with respect to ambient PM emissions should also be investigated, as this can inform the design of more sophisticated policy measures to reduce non-exhaust emissions.[8]

Most epidemiological studies use chemical elements as indicators of exposure, but since there are no unique tracers for non-exhaust emissions, source contributions should rather be used as exposure indicators (together with their uncertainty estimates), which would allow for a better separation of non-exhaust processes as well as a direct comparison with exhaust emissions. Estimates of the benefits of reducing PM emissions from road transport should be developed for non-exhaust emissions, as the health impacts could be different from the primary and secondary PM from exhaust emissions that have already been estimated.

4.3.3. Designing effective mitigation measures to reduce emission factors and vehicle kilometres driven

More research is also needed in order to advance an understanding of the most effective measures for reducing emission factors and vehicle kilometres driven. For brake wear emissions, more research could be undertaken to optimize the mechanical relationships between brake rotor, clamp and overall design of braking systems. Continued activity in testing novel brake pad and brake rotor disc composition could also prove fruitful. An important avenue for future research on road wear and road dust resuspension concerns the role of pavement texture and mineralogy under a variety of meteorological conditions (not only in countries with snow and ice).

Finally, a number of factors should be carefully considered in the design of pricing instruments aiming to internalise the external costs entailed by non-exhaust emissions. Complementary measures or provisions could address the possible distributional effects associated with a charge for non-exhaust emissions. Consideration should also be given to how the revenues of the charge will be spent, as this can influence the social acceptability of the measure. They could be spent on additional remedial measures to mitigate non-exhaust emissions (e.g. wetting the pavement), which will depend on local conditions and costs. Given that vehicle registration fees have been shown to have a strong effect on vehicle choice, incorporating vehicle weight and possibly brake/tyre material into these fees also has potential as a complementary intervention at the point of vehicle choice. It will also be necessary to anticipate, to the extent possible, the potential for unanticipated rebound and spillover effects. When combined with a pricing disincentive addressing non-exhaust emissions, measures that improve non-exhaust emission factors may be susceptible to rebound effects (Dimitropoulos, Oueslati and Sintek, 2018[120]). Rebound effects occur if lower emissions factors and thus a lower per-kilometre cost from a non-exhaust emissions charge would induce people to travel more than they otherwise would have.

The estimated comparison between BEV and ICEVs emissions is built on different state-of-the-art methods. Future studies would indeed benefit from an improved knowledge on several aspects which represent the main limitations of this study, including more accurate data on mean weight estimates for EVs and their internal combustion counterparts, more accurate (experimental) relationships between vehicle weight/size and non-exhaust emissions, experimental measurement of emission reduction due to regenerative braking, and more accurate estimates of the contribution of different fuel engines to secondary aerosols formation (inorganic and organic).

4.4. Implications for policy

Consensus exists in the scientific literature that non-exhaust emissions are becoming the dominant source of PM from road traffic and that PM, and particularly PM2.5, have nefarious effects on human health. Despite these demonstrated negative externalities, non-exhaust emissions have been only tangentially addressed by public policies to date. Given the magnitude of the aggregate social costs they entail, and the fact that the transition to electric vehicles will not lead to significant reductions in non-exhaust emissions, policymakers should invest resources in determining how to optimally reduce them via targeted policy instruments.

To the extent that developing policies to address non-exhaust emissions will rely on a well-developed understanding of their drivers, priority should be given to the development of a standardized measurement methodology for each of the processes that generate non-exhaust emissions. Some progress has been made in this regard for brake wear, but similar initiative remains to be taken for the measurement of tyre wear, road wear and road dust resuspension. With respect to road dust emissions, even when a commonly accepted methodology has been developed, regulation based on these emissions would be difficult to apply in practice given that emissions will depend heavily on local meteorological and environmental features.

An optimally designed non-exhaust emissions charge would theoretically incentivise the reduction of non-exhaust emissions by all relevant actors (e.g. consumers and manufacturers). No precedent currently exists for such a charge, in part because non-exhaust emissions and their social costs have gone largely unnoticed, but also because of a lack of robust evidence quantifying the relationships between various vehicle characteristics and their impact on emissions. Limitations with respect to the evidence required to design such a charge, as well as the practical challenges of implementing this charge mean that other measures will also be necessary in order to address these emissions.

Given the high proportion of non-exhaust emissions generated by tyre wear, priority should be placed on measures that seek to reduce PM emissions from this source in particular, namely vehicle lightweighting and regulations on tyre composition. To the extent that lighter vehicles also emit less PM emissions from brake wear, policies that more explicitly favour vehicle lightweighting can be a particularly effective tool for addressing non-exhaust emissions.[9] Such policies could include the expansion of weight-based charges. Investing in R&D to develop lighter materials (e.g. high-strength steel and aluminium alloy) will also advance this agenda.

Insofar as population exposure is greatest in urban areas and current congestion pricing schemes are an effective means of reducing motor vehicle traffic in these areas, another policy priority for addressing non-exhaust emissions is the more widespread use of congestion pricing in city centres. These pricing mechanisms could be further optimised to target non-exhaust emissions, for example, by finding ways to differentiate electronic congestion charges by vehicle weight and distance travelled, e.g. through the use of registration data and GPS technology.

Promising avenues for technological developments that stand to reduce emission factors are regenerative braking systems and brake dust collection devices. While already used for electric and hybrid vehicles, it is also worth exploring the degree to which RBS could be easily incorporated into ICEVs given that they will continue to dominate vehicle fleets in the coming years. Preliminary indications suggest that brake dust collecting devices also have mitigation potential, but they have not yet been introduced into the market at the level of original equipment manufacturers or as aftermarket solutions.

---

[1] One solution of the former type would involve changing urban travel altogether by switching to technology that does not rely on friction for acceleration and deceleration (e.g. propulsion via

magnets, as is used by Maglev trains). This report does not explore such a fundamental shift, as it is not a realistic possibility for micro-level urban passenger travel in the near term.

[2] For more information, see www.ertico.com.

[3] Although greater distance travelled implies greater fuel use, the opposite is not necessarily true, e.g. the case of an idling car.

[4] Based on the evidence reviewed in Section 2, other features that should be taken into account include driving style, pavement type, road moisture and road dust loading. Practically speaking, however, it would be difficult to design a road charge based on these characteristics.

[5] Including brake and tyre characteristics as determinants of a vehicle's emission factor implies the development of standardised methodologies for the measurement of non-exhaust emissions from these sources. Even though non-exhaust emissions have been found to increase with vehicle weight, more research is needed to establish a robust quantitative relationship between vehicle weight and non-exhaust emissions.

[6] These benefits reflect the value of the avoided cases of premature death and illnesses avoided, quantified through a combination of willingness to pay and cost of illness estimates.

[7] Available at https://data.mendeley.com/datasets/dkp376g3m8/1.

[8] The marginal external cost of congestion increases non-linearly with traffic load: when roads are more congested, the cost of each additional car in circulation becomes greater. The extent to which the relationship between exposure to an increased concentration of PM emissions varies by ambient air quality should also be explored to investigate whether the negative health impacts of non-exhaust emissions may follow a similar pattern.

[9] Vehicle lightweighting, moreover, also reduces greenhouse gas emissions (ITF, 2017[15]).

References

ACEA (2019), *ACEA Tax Guide*, European Automobile Manufacturer's Association, Brussels, https://www.acea.be/uploads/news_documents/ACEA_Tax_Guide_2019.pdf (accessed on 14 April 2020). [8]

AIRUSE (2016), *Testing and development of air quality mitigation measures in Southern Europe (LIFE11 ENV/ES/584)*. [102]

AIRUSE (2016), *The efficacy of dust suppressants to control road dust re-suspension in northern and central Europe*. [87]

Althaus, H., M. Gauch and Empa (2010), "Comparative Life Cycle Assessment in Mobility (in Germany)", p. 162, https://www.empa.ch/documents/56122/458579/LCA-Mobilitaetsvergleich_Bericht.pdf/824aec56-3393-439e-8bc9-d1a365041e4d. [33]

Amato, F. et al. (2016), "Effects of water and CMA in mitigating industrial road dust resuspension", *Atmospheric Environment*, Vol. 131, pp. 334-340, http://dx.doi.org/10.1016/j.atmosenv.2016.02.018. [103]

Amato, F. et al. (2014), "Effects of road dust suppressants on PM levels in a mediterranean urban area", *Environmental Science and Technology*, Vol. 48/14, pp. 8069-8077, http://dx.doi.org/10.1021/es502496s. [92]

Amato, F. et al. (2009), "Evaluating urban PM10 pollution benefit induced by street cleaning activities", *Atmospheric Environment*, Vol. 43/29, pp. 4472-4480, http://dx.doi.org/10.1016/j.atmosenv.2009.06.037. [95]

American Chemistry Council (2019), *Global Automotive Declarable Substance List*, https://www.gadsl.org/ (accessed on 15 November 2019). [20]

AUDI AG (2016), *Internal investigations of braking systems for plug-in hybrid electric vehicles*, Development foundation brake. [26]

Augsburg, K. and D. Hesse (2018), *Influence of regenerative braking on the emission behavior of friction brakes*. [35]

Barlow, T. (2014), "Briefing paper on non-exhaust particulate emissions from road transport", *Transport Research Laboratory*. [31]

Barratt, B. et al. (2012), "Evaluation of the impact of dust suppressant application on ambient PM10 concentrations in London", *Environmental Research Group, Report prepared for Transport for London* November. [89]

Böhner, R., A. Hennig and C. Niemann-Delius (2011), "The use of salt solutions to reduce PM10 on paved roads in open-pit mining", *World of mining, surface & underground*, Vol. 63/5, pp. 275-279, http://dx.doi.org/999910118342. [93]

Bowei, L. (2009), *CN101292204A*. [60]

California EPA (2011), *Wheel weight alternatives assessment*, Department of Toxic Substances Control, https://dtsc.ca.gov/wp-content/uploads/sites/31/2017/05/AAWheelWeights.pdf (accessed on 15 April 2020). [75]

Campbell, P. et al. (2018), "Cost-benefit analysis for a lead wheel weight phase-out in Canada", *Science of the Total Environment*, Vol. 637-638, pp. 79-90, http://dx.doi.org/10.1016/j.scitotenv.2018.04.414. [76]

Casanova, J. and N. Fonseca (2012), "Environmental assessment of low speed policies for motor vehicle mobility in city centres", *Global Nest Journal*, Vol. 14/2, pp. 192-201, http://dx.doi.org/10.30955/gnj.000869. [83]

City of Barcelona (2019), *Plan for the Improvement of Air Quality in Barcelona (2015-2018)*, https://ajuntament.barcelona.cat/ecologiaurbana/ca/que-fem-i-per-que/ciutat-productiva-i-resilient/pla-de-qualitat-de-l-aire-de-bcn (accessed on 4 December 2019). [104]

CIVITAS (2019), *Mobility Solutions*, https://civitas.eu/mobility-solutions (accessed on 11 November 2019). [3]

Denby, B., K. Kupiainen and M. Gustafsson (2018), "Review of Road Dust Emissions", in *Non-Exhaust Emissions*, http://dx.doi.org/10.1016/b978-0-12-811770-5.00009-1. [119]

Dimitropoulos, A., W. Oueslati and C. Sintek (2018), "The rebound effect in road transport: A meta-analysis of empirical studies", *Energy Economics*, Vol. 75, pp. 163-179, http://dx.doi.org/10.1016/j.eneco.2018.07.021. [120]

Dupuis, V. (2013), *US20131611132A.* [43]

Duraiselvam, M. et al. (2014), *Laser surface nitrided Ti-6Al-4V for light weight automobile disk brake rotor application*, http://dx.doi.org/10.1016/j.wear.2013.11.025. [56]

EC (2000), *DIRECTIVE 2000/53/EC*, https://eur-lex.europa.eu/LexUriServ/LexUriServ.do?uri=CONSLEG:2000L0053:20050701:EN:PDF (accessed on 15 April 2020). [19]

ECCC (2013), *Background Study and Use Pattern for Lead Wheel Weights in Canada*, Environment and Climate Change Canada. [71]

Environment Canada (2005), *Best Practices for the Reduction of Air Emissions From Construction and Demolition Activities*. [108]

EU (2003), "Directive 2003/18/EC of the European Parliament and of the Council of 27 March 2003 amending Council Directive 83/477/EEC on the protection of workers from the risks related to exposure to asbestos at work", *Official Journal of the European Union*, Vol. L 97/48/11, pp. 48-52. [105]

European Commission (2019), *Mobility and Transport: Speed enforcement*, https://ec.europa.eu/transport/road_safety/specialist/knowledge/speed/speed_limits/speed_enforcement_en (accessed on 13 November 2019). [85]

Fann, N., K. Baker and C. Fulcher (2012), "Characterizing the PM2.5-related health benefits of emission reductions for 17 industrial, area and mobile emission sectors across the U.S.", *Environment International*, Vol. 49, pp. 141-151, http://dx.doi.org/10.1016/j.envint.2012.08.017. [114]

Goodkind, A. et al. (2019), "Fine-scale damage estimates of particulate matter air pollution reveal opportunities for location-specific mitigation of emissions", *Proceedings of the National Academy of Sciences of the United States of America*, Vol. 116/18, pp. 8775-8780, http://dx.doi.org/10.1073/pnas.1816102116. [113]

Government of Canada (2017), *Regulations to prohibit the manufacture and import of lead wheel weights - Canada.ca*, https://www.canada.ca/en/environment-climate-change/services/canadian-environmental-protection-act-registry/consultation-document-regulations-prohibit-wheel-weights.html (accessed on 15 April 2020). [72]

Gramstat, S. (2018), "Technological Measures for Brake Wear Emission Reduction: Possible Improvement in Compositions and Technological Remediation: Cost Efficiency", in *Non-Exhaust Emissions*, http://dx.doi.org/10.1016/B978-0-12-811770-5.00010-8. [69]

Greater London Authority (2006), *Best Practice Guidance: The control of dust and emissions from construction and demolition.*, https://www.london.gov.uk/file/18750/download?token=zV3ZKTpP (accessed on 4 December 2019). [110]

Grigoratos, T. (2018), "Regulation on Brake/Tire Composition", in *Non-Exhaust Emissions*, http://dx.doi.org/10.1016/b978-0-12-811770-5.00004-2. [18]

Gruden, D. (2008), *Umweltschutz in der Automobilindustrie*, Vieweg+Teubner, Wiesbaden. [77]

Guckeisen, F. (2018), *Conference communication.* [78]

Gustafsson, M. (2013), "Slitage av och partikelemissioner från betongbeläggning". [90]

Gustafsson, M., P. Jonsson and M. Ferm (2010), "Effekter av dammbindning av belagda vägar". [91]

Heise Online (2017), *Elektroautos: Streetscooter der Deutschen Post bekommen Feinstaubpartikelfilter*, https://www.heise.de/newsticker/meldung/Elektroautos-Streetscooter-der-Deutschen-Post-bekommen-Feinstaubpartikelfilter-3924498.html (accessed on 15 November 2019). [94]

Holman, C. (2014), "IAQM u GUIDANCE Construction Dust Guidance on the assessment of dust from demolition and construction", http://www.iaqm.co.uk. [106]

Holman, C., R. Harrison and X. Querol (2015), *Review of the efficacy of low emission zones to improve urban air quality in European cities*, http://dx.doi.org/10.1016/j.atmosenv.2015.04.009. [10]

Hooftman, N. et al. (2016), "Environmental analysis of petrol, diesel and electric passenger cars in a Belgian urban setting", *Energies*, Vol. 9/2, pp. 1-24, http://dx.doi.org/10.3390/en9020084. [30]

IBAS (2019), *Current Asbestos Bans*, International Ban Asbestos Secretariat, http://ibasecretariat.org/alpha_ban_list.php (accessed on 15 November 2019). [24]

ICCT (2018), *European vehicle market statistics 2018/2019*, International Council on Clean Transportation Europe, Berlin, http://eupocketbook.theicct.org (accessed on 7 March 2019). [14]

Int Panis, L. et al. (2011), "PM, NOx and CO2 emission reductions from speed management policies in Europe", *Transport Policy*, Vol. 18/1, pp. 32-37, http://dx.doi.org/10.1016/j.tranpol.2010.05.005. [84]

Integreen (2012), *The INTEGREEN project*, https://www.integreen-life.bz.it/il-piano-di-lavoro (accessed on 13 November 2019). [80]

ITF (2017), *Lightening Up: How Less Heavy Vehicles Can Help Cut CO2 Emissions Case-Specific Policy Analysis*, https://www.itf-oecd.org/sites/default/files/docs/less-heavy-vehicles-cut-co2-emissions.pdf (accessed on 13 November 2019). [15]

ITF (2016), *Shared mobility: innovation for liveable cities*. [13]

James, M., N. Murdie and B. Walker (2002), *US2002170787A*. [55]

Johansson, C. (2016), *The effectiveness of urban air quality actions in Stockholm*. [12]

Johansson, C., L. Burman and B. Forsberg (2009), "The effects of congestions tax on air quality and health", *Atmospheric Environment*, Vol. 43/31, pp. 4843-4854, http://dx.doi.org/10.1016/j.atmosenv.2008.09.015. [11]

John, A. et al. (2006), *Ntersuchung zur Abschätzung der Wirksamkeit von Nassreinigungsverfahren zur Minderung der PM10-Immissionen am Beispiel de Corneliusstraße, Düsseldorf*, Institut für Energie und Umwelttechnick e. V. [96]

Johnson, K. (2009), *WO 2009037437 A1*. [54]

Karanasiou, A. et al. (2011), "Road dust contribution to PM levels - Evaluation of the effectiveness of street washing activities by means of Positive Matrix Factorization", *Atmospheric Environment*, Vol. 45/13, pp. 2193-2201, http://dx.doi.org/10.1016/j.atmosenv.2011.01.067. [99]

Keith, H. (2009), *US20099026025A*. [45]

Keuken, M., H. Denier van der Gon and K. van der Valk (2010), "Non-exhaust emissions of PM and the efficiency of emission reduction by road sweeping and washing in the Netherlands", *Science of the Total Environment*, Vol. 408/20, pp. 4591-4599, http://dx.doi.org/10.1016/j.scitotenv.2010.06.052. [98]

Khambekar, S., H. Baumgartner and W. Pahle (2004), *US20040031652 A1*. [47]

Kienzle, A. and I. Kratschmer (2007), *US20080125306 A1*. [53]

Kim, S., E. Jung and H. Kim (2014), "Evaluation on the Effect of Air Quality Improvement Due to the Employment of Clean-Road System in Daegu", *Journal of Environmental Science International*, Vol. 23/12, pp. 2029-2034, http://dx.doi.org/10.5322/jesi.2014.23.12.2029. [101]

Konduru, N. et al. (2014), "Biokinetics and effects of barium sulfate nanoparticles", *Particle and Fibre Toxicology*, Vol. 11/1, http://dx.doi.org/10.1186/s12989-014-0055-3. [57]

Kousoulidou, M., G. Perricone and T. Grigoratos (2019), *Tackling brake emissions: The LOWBRASYS project and its contribution to improving air quality and providing policy recommendations*, http://www.lowbrasys.eu/en. [36]

Křístková, M. et al. (2004), "Influence of metals on the phenol-formaldehyde resin degradation in friction composites", *Polymer Degradation and Stability*, Vol. 84/1, pp. 49-60, http://dx.doi.org/10.1016/j.polymdegradstab.2003.09.012. [63]

Kukutschová, J. et al. (2009), "Wear mechanism in automotive brake materials, wear debris and its potential environmental impact", *Wear*, Vol. 267/5-8, pp. 807-817, http://dx.doi.org/10.1016/j.wear.2009.01.034. [65]

Kukutschová, J. et al. (2010), "Wear performance and wear debris of semimetallic automotive brake materials", *Wear*, Vol. 268/1, pp. 86-93, http://dx.doi.org/10.1016/j.wear.2009.06.039. [64]

Kupiainen, K. et al. (2011), *Street dust emissions in Finnish cities: Summary of results from 2006-2010*. [100]

Lampke, T. and I. Özer (2013), *DE102011121291 A1*. [50]

Lampke, T. and I. Özer (2012), *DE102012000487 B3*. [51]

Lembach, O. and R. Mayer (2013), *US20130087484*. [42]

Lemen, R. (2004), "Asbestos in Brakes: Exposure and Risk of Disease", *American Journal of Industrial Medicine*, Vol. 45/3, pp. 229-237, http://dx.doi.org/10.1002/ajim.10334. [22]

Ligterink, N., U. Stelwagen and J. Kuenen (2014), *Emission factors for alternative drivelines and alternative fuels*, http://dx.doi.org/10.13140/RG.2.1.2655.4483. [32]

Loza, K. et al. (2016), "Barium sulfate micro- and nanoparticles as bioinert reference material in particle toxicology", *Nanotoxicology*, Vol. 10/10, pp. 1492-1502, http://dx.doi.org/10.1080/17435390.2016.1235740. [58]

Lutz, M. (2013), "Mitigation strategies: Berlin, Germany", in *Particulate Matter: Environmental Monitoring & Mitigation*, http://dx.doi.org/10.1002/978190945315.EBO.13.489. [82]

Mathissen, M. et al. (2018), "A novel real-world braking cycle for studying brake wear particle emissions", *Wear*, Vol. 414-415, pp. 219-226, http://dx.doi.org/10.1016/j.wear.2018.07.020. [117]

Mayer, R. and O. Lembach (2012), *DE102010048075 A1*. [41]

Nopmongcol, U. et al. (2017), "Air Quality Impacts of Electrifying Vehicles and Equipment Across the United States", *Environmental Science and Technology*, Vol. 51/5, pp. 2830-2837, http://dx.doi.org/10.1021/acs.est.6b04868. [34]

Norman, M. and C. Johansson (2006), "Studies of some measures to reduce road dust emissions from paved roads in Scandinavia", *Atmospheric Environment*, Vol. 40/32, pp. 6154-6164, http://dx.doi.org/10.1016/j.atmosenv.2006.05.022. [86]

Norman, M. and C. Johansson (2006), "Studies of some measures to reduce road dust emissions from paved roads in Scandinavia", *Atmospheric Environment*, Vol. 40/32, pp. 6154-6164, http://dx.doi.org/10.1016/j.atmosenv.2006.05.022. [97]

Norman, M. et al. (2016), "Modelling road dust emission abatement measures using the NORTRIP model: Vehicle speed and studded tyre reduction", *Atmospheric Environment*, Vol. 134, pp. 96-108, http://dx.doi.org/10.1016/j.atmosenv.2016.03.035. [25]

Özer, I. (2009), *DE102009059806A1*. [49]

Özer, I. and T. Lampke (2012), *DE102011120989B3.* [46]

Parry, I. et al. (2014), *Getting energy prices right: From principle to practice*, International Monetary Fund, https://www.imf.org/en/Publications/Books/Issues/2016/12/31/Getting-Energy-Prices-Right-From-Principle-to-Practice-41345 (accessed on 11 November 2019). [112]

Patterson, W., W. Standke and K. Kocheisen (2013), *Ursachen für Unterschiede in den mechanischen Eigenschaften und der Gefügeausbildung von Gußeisen mit Lamellengraphit*, http://dx.doi.org/10.1007/978-3-663-07503-5. [39]

Piwowarsky, E. (2013), *Hochwertiges Gußeisen (Grauguß)*, http://dx.doi.org/10.1007/978-3-642-53133-0. [38]

Plachá, D. et al. (2017), "Release of volatile organic compounds by oxidative wear of automotive friction materials", *Wear*, Vol. 376-377, pp. 705-716, http://dx.doi.org/10.1016/j.wear.2016.12.016. [61]

Platform for Electromobility (2016), *Briefing: Non-Exhaust Emissions of Electric Cars*, http://dx.doi.org/10.1016/j.atmosenv.2016.03.017. [27]

Program, N. (2005), *Asbestos*, U.S. Department of Health and Human Services, Public Health Service, National Toxicology Program. [23]

Qihong, C. (2011), *CN201944152U.* [44]

Querol, X. et al. (2018), "Non-technological Measures on Road Traffic to Abate Urban Air Pollution", in *Non-Exhaust Emissions*, http://dx.doi.org/10.1016/b978-0-12-811770-5.00011-x. [9]

Regional Government of Styria Austria (2006), *Construction works manual*, http://www.feinstaub.steiermark.at. 2006. [107]

Reuter, U. (2010), "Mit CMA gegen Feinstaub? Beispiel Stuttgart", pp. 26-28. [88]

Rupprecht Consult (editor) (2012), *Guidelines For Developing and Implementing a Sustainable Urban Mobility Plan: Second Edition*, https://www.eltis.org/sites/default/files/sump-guidelines-2019_mediumres.pdf (accessed on 11 November 2019). [5]

Rychlak, S. (2010), *Patent No. DE102009001332 A1.* [79]

Rye, T. and S. Ison (2008), *The Implementation and Effectiveness of Transport Demand Management Measures*, http://dx.doi.org/10.4324/9781315556796. [6]

SAE International (ed.) (2011), *An overview of ferritic nitrocarburized (FNC) cast iron brake rotor performance and field experience..* [48]

Santamaria Razo, D. and F. Persoon (2016), "Bio-Soluble Chemical Composition for Complementary Mineral Fibres: An Enhanced Tribologic Effect and Its Influence on Disc Wear", *SAE International Journal of Materials and Manufacturing*, Vol. 10/1, http://dx.doi.org/10.4271/2016-01-1909. [68]

Shangdong Hong MA Construction Machinery Co. (2014), *High-carbon low-silicon niobium-containing cast iron brake disc and preparation method thereof.* [40]

Sichuan Province Vanadium and Titanium Brake Ltd. (2014), *High-carbon vanadium titanium grey cast iron and manufacturing method thereof, as well as vehicle brake disk and manufacturing method.* [37]

Smolen, G. (1991), *US005224572A.* [52]

Snilsberg, B. (2008), *Pavement wear and airborne dust pollution in Norway: Characterization of the physical and chemical properties of dust particules.* [118]

Stayner, L. et al. (2008), "An epidemiological study of the role of chrysotile asbestos fibre dimensions in determining respiratory disease risk in exposed workers", *Occupational and Environmental Medicine*, Vol. 65/9, pp. 613-619, http://dx.doi.org/10.1136/oem.2007.035584. [21]

SUTP (2019), *iNUA #9: Avoid-Shift-Improve (A-S-I) - SUTP*, https://www.sutp.org/publications/sustainable-urban-transport-avoid-shift-improve-a-s-i-inua-9/ (accessed on 14 April 2020). [1]

Svenningsen, L. et al. (2019), *The Use of Economic Instruments in Nordic Environmental Policy 2014–2017*, TemaNord, Nordic Council of Ministers, Copenhagen K, https://dx.doi.org/10.6027/TN2019-541. [7]

Swiss Agency for the Environment, F. (2004), *Air Pollution Control at Construction Sites.* [109]

TIA (2008), "Tire industry association best management practices to transition the tire industry away from lead wheel weights". [74]

Timmers, V. and P. Achten (2016), "Non-exhaust PM emissions from electric vehicles", *Atmospheric Environment*, Vol. 134, pp. 10-17, http://dx.doi.org/10.1016/j.atmosenv.2016.03.017. [29]

UBA (2015), *Inventory and effectiveness of measures to improve air quality*, https://www.umweltbundesamt.de/sites/default/files/medien/378/publikationen/texte_05_2015_inventory_and_effectiveness_of_measures_to_improve_air_quality.pdf (accessed on 14 April 2020). [17]

UK Department for Transport (2003), *Overloading of goods vehicles.* [115]

UN ECE (2016), *Sustainable Urban Mobility and Public Transport in UNECE Capitals*, United Nations, New York, https://dx.doi.org/10.18356/0bb693e3-en. [4]

UNECE (2019), *Particle Measurement Programme*, Transport - Vehicle Regulations, https://wiki.unece.org/pages/viewpage.action?pageId=2523173 (accessed on 15 November 2019). [116]

UNESCAP (2017), *Assessment of Urban Transport Systems*, Monograph Series on Sustainable and Inclusive Transport. [2]

UR:BAN (2013), *User-friendly assistance systems and network management*, http://urban-online.org/en/urban.html (accessed on 13 November 2019). [81]

US EPA, O. (2008), "National Lead Free Wheel Weight Initiative". [73]

USGS (2006), "Stocks and Flows of Lead-Based Wheel Weights in the United States", http://www.usgs.gov/pubprod (accessed on 4 December 2019). [70]

van Dender, K. (2019), "Taxing vehicles, fuels, and road use: Opportunities for improving transport tax practice", *OECD Taxation Working Papers*, No. 44, OECD Publishing, Paris, https://dx.doi.org/10.1787/e7f1d771-en. [111]

Van Zeebroeck, B. and G. De Ceuster (2013), *Elektrische auto zorgt voor evenveel fijn stof als conventionele auto*. [28]

WHO (2006), "Air quality guidelines - global update 2005", *WHO.* [67]

World Health Organization (2000), "Air Quality Guidelines", *Air Quality Guidelines*, Vol. 22/8, pp. 1-8, http://dx.doi.org/10.1007/BF02986808. [66]

Yun, R., P. Filip and Y. Lu (2010), "Performance and evaluation of eco-friendly brake friction materials", *Tribology International*, Vol. 43/11, pp. 2010-2019, http://dx.doi.org/10.1016/j.triboint.2010.05.001. [62]

Zhao, H. (2013), *CN103470666A*. [59]

Žnidarič, A. (2015), *Heavy-Duty Vehicle Weight Restrictions in the EU Enforcement and Compliance Technologies*, ACEA Scientific Advisory Group Report, Brussels, https://www.acea.be/uploads/publications/SAG_23_Heavy-Duty_Vehicle_Weight_Restrictions_in_the_EU.pdf (accessed on 20 May 2019). [16]

www.ingramcontent.com/pod-product-compliance
Ingram Content Group UK Ltd.
Pitfield, Milton Keynes, MK11 3LW, UK
UKHW051504290926
15471UKWH00008B/1415

9 789264 452442